P9-DTX-107

ORGANIZING BUSINESS

ORGANIZING BUSINESS

Trade Associations in America and Japan

Leonard H. Lynn
Timothy J. McKeown

American Enterprise Institute for Public Policy Research
Washington, D.C.

Leonard H. Lynn is associate professor of management policy at Case
Western Reserve University. Timothy J. McKeown is assistant professor of
political science at the University of North Carolina.

The publication of this volume was supported by a grant from the
U.S. Department of Commerce.

Distributed by arrangement with

National Book Network
4720 Boston Way
Lanham, Md. 20706

UPA, Inc.
3 Henrietta Street
London WC2E 8LU England

Library of Congress Cataloging-in-Publication Data

Lynn, Leonard H.
  Organizing business.

  (AEI studies ; 459)
  Includes index.
  1. Trade and professional associations—United States.
  2. Trade and professional associations—Japan.
  I. McKeown, Timothy J., 1951– . II. Title.
  III. Series.
  HD2425.L96 1987   061'.3   87-17468
  ISBN 0-8447-3629-5 (alk. paper)

  1 3 5 7 9 10 8 6 4 2

AEI Studies 459

Printed in the United States of America

Contents

Foreword

For much of the post–World War II period, the United States has enjoyed great economic success based largely on its ability to compete effectively in world markets. America's dominance in many world markets began to erode gradually and naturally as the European and Japanese economies recovered from the war. Most agreed that changing trade patterns and shifting market shares were healthy adjustments based on national comparative advantages operating without the strains of war's destruction. Although U.S. market shares were declining, gains made through increased global efficiency and expanding world trade would more than compensate American industry.

Trade developments since the late 1970s, however, have been far more dramatic and have raised a chorus of alarm throughout the United States. The rapid deterioration of U.S. trade and current account balances since 1981 has sparked analysts and policy makers alike to reevaluate the many factors underlying America's competitive strength. Many have focused specifically on U.S. technological capabilities, recognizing that America's competitive advantage rests largely on technological superiority. Others have concentrated on the policies and practices of our competitors, searching both for lessons from their recent successes and for evidence of unfair trade practices toward U.S. industries.

In 1983 AEI joined these research efforts by launching the Competing in a Changing World Economy Project to analyze the most significant factors determining America's ability to compete in an increasingly competitive world economy. The project has studied many issues, including industrial renewal through technology diffusion (*Automation Technology and Industrial Renewal* by Donald Hicks); technology transfer through international joint ventures (*Alliance Politics and Economics* by David Mowery); technology policies of the industrial nations (*High-Technology Policies: A Five-Nation Comparison* by Richard Nelson); and industrial policies (*The Politics of Industrial Policy* edited by Claude Barfield and William Schambra).

Leonard Lynn and Timothy McKeown's *Organizing Business: Trade Associations in America and Japan* continues in the spirit of these earlier

xi

studies. Their study provides an in-depth analysis of the role of industry trade associations in the adjustment process in Japan and the United States, emphasizing two sectors in which competition between the two nations is strongest: the iron and steel and the machine tool sectors. The authors clarify the many roles played by trade associations in Japan and the United States as the two countries pursued industrial renewal, technology development, and the fostering of international competitiveness. Their comparative analysis offers significant insight into the larger question of the importance of industrial policies to the economic successes and failures of both nations.

Economic tensions between the United States and Japan have recently reached an all-time high. Unfortunately, much of the trade rhetoric on both sides of the Atlantic rests on erroneous perceptions about the role that government plays in the U.S. and Japanese economies. Lynn and McKeown's study does much to eliminate these dangerous misperceptions. Their clear and rational assessment of one dimension of government-industry ties in the United States and Japan provides a needed dispassionate appraisal in this highly politicized debate.

CLAUDE E. BARFIELD
Director
Competing in a Changing World
Economy Project

Preface

Previous Research on Trade Associations

In the 1920s and 1930s the trade association "movement" attracted the attention both of those who saw it as a precursor to an entirely new and desirable way of organizing economic activity[1] and of those who were more skeptical of its positive value.[2] Political scientists and economists investigated the effects of associations on economic and political life.[3] The federal government also took a keen interest in trade associations during this period. Beginning in 1913 the Department of Commerce periodically performed surveys of the associations then in existence. The content of the surveys varied, but they did at least identify what associations were operating, their locations, and a few details regarding their activities. Governmental attention to trade associations culminated in the study performed by the Temporary National Economic Committee of the U.S. Congress in 1939.[4]

After World War II, however, interest by government and academics diminished, and trade associations have not been the object of much scholarly research. The Commerce Department surveys ended in 1948; economists became less concerned about the institutional structure of economic activity and more concerned with the workings of abstract markets; political scientists' concern with interest groups waned as the study of voting behavior took center stage. A text from the mid-1960s that offered a summary of existing research on associations contains no articles on and few references to trade associations.[5] The situation in Japan is somewhat different, for in that country the writing and reading of business and trade association histories is relatively popular, and there is also a relative abundance of government documents giving information on associations and their activities (most of which are not available in translation and have not yet been analyzed by non-Japanese scholars). But even in Japan, there is a paucity of analytic work on trade associations.

Today, interest in the institutional structure of economic activity seems to be increasing, perhaps as an intellectual correlate of the state of the world economy. In periods of economic growth, it is not surprising that little attention is devoted to the institutions that govern that growth, but when growth falters, it is logical for observers to consider whether institutions designed in an earlier era are still appropriate for current conditions. Sociologists and political scientists have once again turned to the study of business organizations, and we have relied on some of their research in this study. In addition, the impressive performance of the Japanese economy in recent decades has attracted widespread interest in the United States and has spawned a large literature purporting to isolate the causes of Japanese success and to suggest ways Americans can successfully copy the Japanese. With this study we hope to contribute to the substance of this debate by offering something that is not in abundant supply at the present: a comparison of how a particular set of institutions operates in the Japanese and American political and economic systems. Our comparison is primarily descriptive: little previous research has been performed on Japanese or American trade associations, and there is neither the empirical nor the theoretical base to justify a highly sophisticated analysis.

Although we have researched Japanese and American trade associations in general, we have concentrated our research on trade associations in two fields: iron and steel, and machine tools/robotics. The choice of these sectors follows from our concern with studying manufacturing sectors that are experiencing substantial international competition, that have been important in both the Japanese and the American economies for some time, and that have also had trade associations in both countries for a lengthy period. The iron and steel industry has long been dominated by a few standard production processes, while the machine tool industry, particularly in recent years, has been substantially affected by developments in electronics and computer control. The industries in the two countries have major differences between them as well. The Japanese steel industry exports a major share of its production, and even with the recent influx of imports from Korea and Taiwan controls virtually all of its home market. The U.S. steel industry has not been a serious exporter in a long time and has been battling imports for most of the past three decades. In the machine tool industry the situations in both countries were reversed for much of the postwar period. The United States was a successful exporter, while the Japanese struggled to survive in the face of more efficient and advanced foreign competitors. Recently the Japanese have become formidable competitors in the U.S. market.

Industries may adjust to economic change by economic or political means. Although some may view political adjustment as purely pathological, it is possible that policies derided by some as mere rent seeking are in fact legitimate responses to nonliberal institutional arrangements in foreign economies or to other policy concerns. This study does not attempt to resolve questions of this sort. We are interested in both the political and the economic adjustment processes, and we believe that policy makers and the public should be as well. An entirely political adjustment strategy could, of course, create and perpetuate pathologies, but we would not characterize the performance of the firms in the industries we studied in this fashion.

The Case Studies

This volume examines how business associations in the United States and Japan help coordinate economic and political activity. The study is primarily concerned with providing a better understanding of differences between Japan and the United States in the flows of information and influence between firms and trade associations, between trade associations and other business groups within their industrial sectors, and between trade associations and government. We quickly found that different sorts of data were available in the United States and Japan. Sometimes it was easy to get information in one country but not the other. Because we did not want to neglect important issues by locking ourselves into an overly rigid data collection strategy, we started with a framework of information to be sought when available. We were particularly interested in:

• Flows of personnel. How do personnel move among trade associations, other busy groups, firms, and government? What are the directions of movement? At what levels do they occur?

• Flows of information. How do trade associations, other business groups, governments, and firms exchange information? How much information is exchanged? How regular are these exchanges?

• Structure of business associations within industry sectors. What differences are there between the division of labor among organizations representing industry sectors in Japan and the United States? Who, for example, lobbies, collects statistics, sets standards, carries out collaborative research?

• Group-to-group relations. What is the nature of the relationships between the institutional actors? Under what conditions do they interact?

• Firms and trade associations. How are the interests of members aggregated in trade association activity? How are conflicts handled?

• Legal constraints. What aspects of the legal environment encourage or constrain interaction among trade associations, governments, and firms?

Methods and Data Sources

One primary source of data on U.S. trade associations was officials of trade associations, as well as those who interact with them in government and industry. Where appropriate, other authorities—academics, journalists, and retired officials—were also interviewed. In Japan we also carried out interviews, but scheduling and other difficulties made it necessary to rely more on written sources to develop our Japanese descriptions.[6] We are greatly indebted to the many business people in both countries who were kind enough to help us. Several reviewed what we had written and offered comments. Our conclusions are our own, however, and in some cases may differ from those of people who provided us with information.

We supplemented our U.S. interview data with written materials, including directories of trade associations, *Who's Who*s of business and government leaders, published materials from individual trade associations, histories of trade associations, and government publications (those on advisory commissions as well as those on trade associations). Numerous such materials exist for the United States. Fortunately, they exist in even greater profusion in Japan. Japanese organizations of all sorts produce voluminous and richly documented histories. We drew on such histories from the Japan Iron and Steel Federation, Kozai Club, Japan Machine Tool Builders Association, Japan Industrial Robotics Association, Japan Machinery Exporters Association, and the Japan Society for the Promotion of the Machinery Industry. In addition to detail on the members and officers of these associations, their organizational charters and constitutions, and the activities of their subunits, these histories often provide rich contextual histories and sometimes records of informal conversations of older officials reminiscing about one episode or another. Japanese government organizations produce detailed reports on the advisory councils and trade associations attached to them. There are also excellent Japanese commercial directories of associations and biographies of government and corporate executives. Recent studies in English by Chalmers Johnson, Ezra Vogel, Thomas Pepper et al., and Richard Samuels were also invaluable in helping us to understand the context for much of what we were interested in.[7]

Lynn, who speaks and reads Japanese, carried out the research in Japan during the summers of 1984 and 1985. McKeown performed the interviews and carried out the data collection in the United States.

Organization of the Book

Chapter 1 briefly discusses the influence of trade associations on industrial policy. In chapter 2 we turn to the history of trade associations in the United States and Japan and the development of associations in the steel and machine tool industries. We hope to give a dynamic sense of the interaction between government and the associations in these industries in the two countries over a long period of time. Chapter 2 also explores Mancur Olson's contention that prewar militarism and postwar foreign occupation explain the relative absence of debilitating special interest organizations in Japan. Some have argued that an excessive concern with enforcing antitrust laws has undercut U.S. competitiveness. Chapter 3 provides background on this issue by comparing the U.S. and Japanese antitrust environments. Chapter 4 gives a detailed description of how trade associations are structured to influence their governments in Japan and the United States, highlighting differences in how the concerns of special interest groups are aggregated and presented to the government. Government in both Japan and the United States has frequently tried to use trade associations as instruments of policy. Some recent critics of Japan have called this part of a conspiracy to "target" certain industries for Japanese domination. Chapter 5 compares government interaction with trade associations in the two countries. Chapters 6 and 7 look at trade association involvement in two areas central to the issue of international competitiveness, foreign trade and the development of new technology. Chapter 8 discusses the implications of this study.

Notes

1. Gerard Swope, in J. George Frederick, ed., *The Swope Plan, Details, Criticisms, Analysis; Plan by Gerard Swope* (New York: The Business Bourse, 1931).

2. Simon N. Whitney, *Trade Associations and Industrial Control* (New York: Central Book Company, 1934).

3. Arthur R. Burns, *The Decline of Competition* (New York: McGraw-Hill, 1936); Oliver Garceau, *The Political Life of the American Medical Association* (Hamden, Conn.: Archon Books, 1961) (originally published 1941).

4. Temporary National Economic Committee, *Trade Association Survey*, Monograph 18 (Washington, D.C.: U.S. Government Printing Office, 1940).

5. William A. Glaser and David L. Sills, eds., *The Government of Associations: Selections from the Behavioral Sciences* (Totowa, N.J.: Bedminster Press, 1966).

6. It was possible to do much of the analysis of published sources on Japanese trade associations before going to Japan. Since our time in Japan was severely limited, we attempted to use interviews there primarily to fill in gaps in our understanding.

7. Chalmers Johnson, *MITI and the Japanese Miracle* (Stanford, Calif.: Stanford University Press, 1982); Ezra Vogel, *Comeback: Case by Case—Building the Resurgence of American Business* (New York: Simon and Schuster, 1985); Thomas Pepper, Merit Janow, and Jimmy Wheeler, *The Competition* (New York: Praeger, 1985); Richard J. Samuels, *The Business of the Japanese State* (Ithaca, N.Y.: Cornell University Press, forthcoming).

ORGANIZING BUSINESS

1
Trade Associations and Industrial Policy

In recent years U.S. industry has seemed increasingly uncompetitive in global competition. Exports and imports account for a far bigger share of the U.S. gross national product (GNP) than ever before, but U.S. products are having difficulty finding foreign markets. The trade deficit has reached $170 billion per year, and a recent study by the Institute for International Economics finds that a continuation of present trends would lead to a U.S. debt of $1 trillion by the end of 1990.[1] Traditional U.S. leads in technology and labor productivity have largely disappeared.

One explanation of the U.S. decline in competitiveness appears in a variety of sources, but is perhaps best put in theoretical terms by Mancur Olson in his The Rise and Decline of Nations.[2] Olson argues that special-interest organizations representing relatively small parts of a society can reduce the society's economic efficiency and aggregate income. Such organizations can benefit their members most by seeking a larger share of the society's wealth (for example, through special tax breaks, tariff protection, or other favorable government policies that confer "rents" to favored groups), often at a cost to the overall economic efficiency of the society. Conversely, "encompassing" organizations, which represent large cross sections of a given society, can gain little by transferring wealth from one part of society to another (assuming both parts are encompassed in the organization) and can best benefit their members by working to increase the overall wealth of the society. Olson argues that the proliferation of special interest organizations and coalitions slows the pace of technological innovation in a society, which in turn explains why U.S. economic growth has been slower than that of such international competitors as Japan, West Germany, Korea, and other nations. These nations, he argues, had their systems of special interest organizations dismantled by war and foreign occupation, shattering old coalitions of rent-seeking organizations and creating new possibilities for economic growth.

Olson expressed these ideas abstractly, but others have said similar things, particularly in comparing the United States with its major economic competitor, Japan. In his influential books Ezra Vogel describes with admiration how industry associations in Japan facilitate cooperation between business and government. By playing this role, Vogel says, trade associations form part of a fair system for coordinating the expansion or contraction of industries, broaden the range of interest representation, and generally support democratic values. The United States, Vogel suggests, could use more such cooperation and coordination.[3] This theme is also taken up by William Ouchi in *The M-Form Society* and in a recent advisory report to the U.S. government.[4] It has appeared, as well, in reports to the U.S. Congress and in several volumes outlining industrial policies for the United States.[5] One tangible effect of these arguments occurred in 1984, when after considerable discussion of the alleged advantages the Japanese derive from their large-scale collaborative research projects, U.S. laws were modified to facilitate the formation of joint research organizations.

New patterns of international trade and new interactions between technology and the economy *may* make it desirable for the United States to implement new industrial policies. But current discussions of the Japanese experience encourage us to borrow from Japan when we still know little about key aspects of the Japanese system. General accounts of the relationship between trade associations and government in Japan have been included in works with a broader focus, and there are brief discussions of specific associations and episodes of their interaction with government, but little has been written regarding what safeguards (if any) prevent the abuses that U.S. antitrust policy has been designed to curb.[6] It is bad enough that there are pressures to borrow ideas from a poorly understood foreign model, but the nature of interaction between trade associations and government in the United States is not at all well understood. If we are to learn from the Japanese (or at least learn how to cope with their practices), we need to reach a far better understanding of our system as well as of theirs.

The Importance of Trade Associations

Trade associations are relevant to economic policy making and hence to economic performance for a variety of reasons. First, they provide an important communications link between government and business. Particularly for industries that do not contain extremely large firms, the trade association plays an important role in day-to-day contact with legislative and executive branch officials. Government policies that require some form of public–private cooperation in order to succeed should be designed with some awareness of the role of trade associations as the mediator between government and individual firms. Second, the potential of associations for collective action—in both an economic and a political sense—is substantial. From the standpoint of public policy, some forms of collective action may be viewed with approval, others as problematic or simply improper. Aside from narrow legal questions regarding the conduct of these organizations, the social consequences of rent-seeking behavior merit serious consideration.

Trade associations also perform other activities relevant to a nation's economic performance that are not aimed primarily at influencing government policy, but rather at assisting members' firms by performing tasks they find uneconomical to perform themselves. The most common are:

1. Product promotion: promoting sales of the industry's products—most commonly, advertising or using other communications tools to increase customer awareness, or holding trade shows
2. Labor relations: monitoring labor agreements in the industry; providing consulting and technical services relating to collective bargaining; conducting wage and benefit surveys
3. Standard setting: working with private or public agencies to develop product or process standards for the industry; developing an industry position and then ensuring that the position is enacted
4. Data collection: compiling statistics from member firms or from other sources (such as government agencies) on industry production, sales, capacity utilization, and imports and exports, and providing members and others with this information
5. Research and development: performing or funding R&D; disseminating technical information to members and, when deemed appropriate, to customers or others
6. Economic services to firms: offering group buying plans, group insurance, member discounts on various products, special member prices for consulting or technical services, credit bureaus, and collection services
7. Educational services: preparing seminars, audio-visual materials, printed matter pertaining to just about any subject which may be germane to successful operations in the industry in question
8. Conventions and general membership meetings
9. Public relations (often closely related to government relations or to product promotion)

3

Not all trade associations perform all these activities, but most associations perform at least some of them. In special circumstances an association can operate as a quasi-governmental entity imposing authoritative decisions upon its membership and holding some officially recognized role in a governmental decision process. Under wartime conditions, associations in the United States and Japan have played such a role; to some degree and in some circumstances, government–association relations in Japan even in peacetime have this cast.

Two general factors decisively shape the activities and behavior of any association: the legal-institutional environment for association activities and the activities of other associations. Since industries in different countries may be served by different associations for different purposes, any cross-national comparison of association activities must take into account the different functional niches occupied by comparable associations. In the machine tool industry in Japan, for example, there are separate associations for metal-cutting and metal-forming machine tools, but not any longer in the United States; there is a trade association in Japan for the machinery sector in general, but not in the United States; peak associations (large "encompassing" associations representing the interests of a large variety of firms) in Japan are probably stronger than in the United States, and some government assistance to associations is provided in Japan, whereas this is not true in the United States as far as we can tell. Similarly, associations in different countries are legally authorized to do different things. There is no obvious American analogue to the Japanese institution of the depression cartel, for example.

Another factor complicating cross-national comparisons of associations is that the member firms may be in rather different economic circumstances. Firms that are exporters have interests in acquiring information about overseas markets, which firms that are import-competitive seldom have. Firms operating under severely depressed financial circumstances will have little rational incentive to support long-run research if they may not survive long enough to benefit from such efforts.

For these reasons, we are cautious about evaluating a given practice as more desirable than the comparable practice in the other nation.

Notes

1. Norman Jonas, "A Strategy for Revitalizing Industry," *Business Week*, March 3, 1986, pp. 84–85.

2. Mancur Olson, *The Rise and Decline of Nations: Economic Growth, Stagflation and Social Rigidities* (New Haven, Conn.: Yale University Press, 1982).

3. Ezra Vogel, *Japan as No. 1: Lessons for America* (Cambridge, Mass.: Harvard University Press, 1979) and Ezra Vogel, *Comeback: Case by Case—Building the Resurgence of American Business* (New York: Simon and Schuster, 1985).

4. William G. Ouchi, *The M-Form Society* (Reading, Mass.: Addison-Wesley Publishing Company, 1984) and President's Commission on Industrial Competitiveness, *Global Competition: The New Reality, Volume II*, Appendix E: "The Microeconomic Policy Dialogue: Analysis and Recommendations," William G. Ouchi with assistance of Booz, Allen & Hamilton, James Robins, 1985.

5. See, for example, Robert Reich, *The Next American Frontier* (New York: Times Books, 1983).

6. Chalmers Johnson, *Japan's Public Policy Companies* (Washington, D.C.: American Enterprise Institute, 1978); Chalmers Johnson, *MITI and the Japanese Miracle* (Stanford, Calif.: Stanford University Press, 1982); Leonard H. Lynn, *How Japan Innovates* (Boulder, Colo.: Westview Press, 1982); Richard J. Samuels, "The Industrial Destructuring of the Japanese Aluminum Industry," *Pacific Affairs*, vol. 56 (Fall 1983), pp. 495–509.

2
The Development of
Trade Associations in the
United States and Japan

Trade and professional associations have served broad and roughly comparable purposes in the United States and Japan—attempting to control the conditions of competition, generating and exchanging information, drawing up standards, mobilizing political strength on behalf of their industries, and acting as a conduit for government coordination. The precise activities and organizational forms in the two states have differed, however, reflecting both the different economic circumstances and institutional structures of the state and the different philosophies of business–state relations.

Trade associations may be defined as nonprofit membership organizations whose members are primarily business firms rather than individuals and which perform a variety of activities for their member firms. Some business organizations fit this definition only partially, primarily because they are created to serve highly specific, limited purposes. In the United States, Webb-Pomerene associations, a form of export cartel, and newly authorized export trading companies exist to facilitate exports and export-related services for American producers. Export and import cartels play similar roles in Japan. Research associations or research consortia limit their activity to a specific research agenda; joint ventures in research and development with broad participation may also begin to acquire the characteristics of a formal research association, except that there is no presumption that the association will exist beyond the life of a specific project. Professional societies enrolling technical or professional employees of a given industry may take on many activities that could be performed by a trade association, but for the purposes of this study they are treated as separate entities. In Japan certain nonprofit membership entities have been created and subsidized by the government to help funnel government aid to industry (sometimes through trade associations) and also to provide links between trade associations in the same

6

and different sectors. For these reasons, we will give them some attention.

Trade Associations in the United States: Historical Overview

Although the proliferation of trade associations is a twentieth century phenomenon, a few trade associations in the United States have existed for a relatively long time. Local chambers of commerce appeared in the 1700s, and some American trade associations can trace their history as far back as the mid-nineteenth century. Of course, it was only in the twentieth century that trade associations became common in most branches of American industry; there were already over 1,200 associations in existence by the 1920s.

Two of the oldest and most important national associations, the U.S. Chamber of Commerce and the National Association of Manufacturers, illustrate two forces that have had a substantial influence on the formation and activities of U.S. trade associations: the desire of government officials to strengthen the organization of some group of economic agents, and changes in the international trading environment that have given domestic competitors a common interest that counterbalances their usually conflicting interests. The role of federal officials in the formation of the Chamber of Commerce is discussed in chapter 5; and as is briefly noted in chapter 4, politicians played important roles in the formation of the Business Council, the Committee for Economic Development, and the Business Roundtable. Recent studies of the formation and dissolution of U.S. trade associations in this century provide systematic support for what scholars have long surmised: the creation of the National Recovery Administration stimulated more trade association births in the United States than any other single event in this century, and its demise similarly triggered more association dissolutions than any other single event.[1]

A prospective change in tariff policy as well as international trading conditions were very much on the minds of the founders of the National Association of Manufacturers. NAM was founded by a group of Ohio machine tool builders concerned about abandonment of reciprocity provisions by Congress in the early 1890s. Machine tool builders were often successful exporters, and they were fearful that American abandonment of reciprocity in favor of pure protection would incite retaliation that would close them out of foreign markets. In general, large firms had the resources to manage the transportation, marketing, and actual sale of their exported goods without relying on external assistance, as well as the wealth and size to command political influence in their own right; but small firms, which have historically composed a large proportion of industries, such as machine tools, could not accomplish these objectives without external assistance. They thus sought to create associations such as NAM and also worked for government programs to assist exporting efforts.

It would be a mistake to view the interest in exports as a majority concern in American industry of the day: in an 1890s survey of 2,000 U.S. manufacturers by the U.S. Industrial Commission, 72 percent of the responding firms indicated they had no export markets.[2] The National Association of Manufacturers was at that time the best organized and largest association devoted to trade expansion, and in 1900 it had only about 1,000 members. (At that time there were about 80,000 manufacturing corporations in the United States.) Andrew Carnegie's attitude that exports were a regrettable necessity in times of domestic economic distress may have been widely shared in his industry in his time: the *Bulletin of the American Iron and Steel Association* frequently attacked the idea of foreign trade expansion, arguing that overseas markets were too costly in terms of what would have to be given up by reducing tariffs and opening the domestic markets to more imports.[3] Concern about imports probably has been a more historically significant source of American trade association activity than a desire to increase exports.

Business people first began banding together in ad hoc coalitions to lobby Congress on tariffs in the early 1800s.[4] Tariff policy is an important exception to the view that nineteenth century American government was noninterventionist. Since obtaining the benefits (or suffering the losses) of protection was a realistic possibility, and since legislative action generally required assembling coalitions rather than making unilateral bids, it is not surprising that trade associations were interested in tariffs, nor is it surprising that those interested in tariffs were also interested in forming trade associations.

Trade associations' interest in trade policy has fluctuated substantially. In the depression of the early and mid-1890s business interest in export expansion and in protection was intense, but both seem to have faded as a cyclical upturn occurred.[5] E. E. Schattschneider's famous study of the Hawley-Smoot Tariff legislative process, which occurred at the onset of the Great Depression, reveals very substantial trade association activity, but Bauer, Pool, and Dexter's study of trade politics in the more prosperous mid-1950s shows trade associations to be neither very interested in nor very well endowed with resources to contend on this issue.[6] These surges of interest in protection are likely triggered by the existence of idle resources in business downturns and by the presence of many economic assets that cannot be readily converted to alternative uses.[7]

8

Trade Associations in the U.S. Steel and Machine Tool Industries

Iron and Steel. The most important trade association in the American iron and steel industry has long been the American Iron and Steel Institute (AISI). The institute's predecessor associations were founded before the Civil War; the institute itself was founded in 1908 and had its first general meeting in New York City in October 1910.[8] Its president until his death in 1927 was Elbert Gary of U.S. Steel. He was also chairman of each standing committee of the organization. The second president, Charles Schwab of Bethlehem Steel, also held the chairs of the standing committees, but for only one year. No single individual could duplicate Gary's personal importance and influence within the industry, and the chairs of the standing committees were soon distributed among other members, although the president retained the status of ex officio member of each of the standing committees.

Standing committees of the institute in the Gary years were initially created for improvement in production methods, foreign relations, and membership; committees on (employee) welfare, on the twelve-hour day, and (in 1935 and thereafter) on labor relations existed sporadically during this period. Just before Gary's death, the first standing committee not chaired by Gary (on statistics) was created. After his death, the rate of turnover among AISI officers increased, and some of the special committees were given the status of standing committees. The passage of the National Recovery Act (NRA) led to a temporary proliferation of committees and subcommittees and to an increase in staff size from sixty-two to eighty to deal with the institute's responsibilities for administering the steel codes for the NRA. On the eve of American involvement in World War II the institute had fifteen standing committees.[9]

In its early days the AISI was as concerned as its latter-day Japanese counterparts about the effects of "ruinous" competition. In the pre–World War I era the institute also had a noticeable international orientation, inviting the top executives of the major European steel firms to the first AISI meeting in New York to discuss the need to moderate excessive and international competition. By the 1920s, the international orientation in the meetings had largely evaporated, probably because the more depressed international economy and higher tariff levels domestically and abroad made the opportunities for a substantial improvement in steel exports appear quite meager. The paucity of formal structure and the general stability of the officers of the institute during the Gary years, the importance of U.S. Steel to the steel industry, and the importance of the steel industry to the

American economy, as well as Gary's and U.S. Steel's close ties to important financial interests, all suggest that Gary and his stalwarts enjoyed the kind of influence inside and outside the institute that, as we shall see, top executives of Nippon Steel enjoyed into the 1980s within their industry and their domestic political-economic system.

Machine Tools. The National Machine Tool Builders Association was formed in the spring of 1902 by 167 lathe builders. Its earliest effort was to raise prices for machine tools by means of an industry agreement. In its first decades the association was concerned with standardization and tariff reciprocity (the industry's strong export position led to both interests); cost accounting and sharing of statistical information (to help owners identify prices that were too low to recover costs and to discourage overexpansion of capacity); and apprenticeships (a perceived shortage of machinists apparently existed as long ago as 1907).[10]

The structure of the industry gave rise to concerns at a fairly early date about the possibilities for collective action. The American Society of Mechanical Engineers suggested in 1929 that the relatively small size of machine tool building firms implied a need for more collectively supported research. During the early 1930s officials in the Bureau of Foreign and Domestic Commerce encouraged formation of an association for all machinery builders. They estimated at the time that only about 10 percent of all U.S. machinery builders were organized; the German industry, by comparison, at one time in the 1920s had 90 percent of its firms within a single machine tool trade association.[11] The same bureau encouraged the industry to undertake more standardization activities. As federal government industrialization planners saw the possibilities of U.S. involvement in a major war, they became interested in standardization as a means of facilitating rapid industrial mobilization.[12]

These efforts to encourage more joint activities were not very successful. Metal-cutting and metal-forming companies did not unite in the same trade association until 1947. There was even substantial resistance by machine tool firms to providing trade associations with information for the compilation of industry-wide statistical surveys.[13]

Trade Associations in Japan: Historical Overview

Japanese businesses, like those in the West, have organized into guilds, exchanges, leagues, and chambers of commerce for several hundred years. Also like their Western counterparts, they provided protection against competition, controlled prices and the quality of goods, jointly acted against dishonest suppliers, provided credit, operated common warehousing and shipping facilities, set wages, and served as an important social group. The Japanese business organizations, however, were more closely tied to government than was typically the case in Europe or the United States.[14]

Given this tradition, it is not surprising that the leaders seeking to modernize Japan during the Meiji Restoration (after 1868) encouraged the formation of new business organizations. In 1876 an association of bankers from national banks was organized, and in 1880 the earliest modern Japanese trade association in industry, the Japan Paper Manufacturing Federation, was established.[15] The federation carried out many of the functions of trade associations in the West, facilitating the sharing of technical information and controlling prices, for example, and seeking to eliminate the common practice of firms' raiding competitors for employees. These activities had their intrinsic value to members, but were primarily justified as measures to enable members to compete with Western imports. Although American trade associations also frequently had a major interest in international trade (lobbying for tariff protection, for example), those in Japan have had a broader and more consistent interest in this area. This is not suprising given the greater exposure and vulnerability of the Japanese to more advanced foreign competition.[16]

A few other trade associations were also established during the remainder of the nineteenth century and in the early twentieth century. The powerful Japan Cotton Spinners Association was established in 1882, and others were set up in the linen yarn, home-produced petroleum, and regional coal mining industries. In addition to issues related to trade, some of the associations were strongly concerned about labor. A continuing issue was the pirating of employees, but some of the associations were also involved in lobbying to defeat reformist efforts to introduce laws that would protect workers. The cotton spinners, for example, were instrumental in defeating the first major piece of labor legislation to come before the Japanese Diet in 1910.[17]

During the first decades of the twentieth century Japanese big business began organizing cross-sectoral associations to influence tax, trade, and other government policies. The Japan Industrial Club (Nippon Kogyo Kurabu) was established in 1917 with some 185 large companies as members. This organization was dominated by the *zaibatsu* firms and was headed by Mitsui's Dan Takuma.[18] In 1922 a new organization, the Japan Economic Federation (Nippon Keizai

Renmei), was established to take over most of the direct political activities of the Industrial Club, with the club remaining primarily as a social organization. Dan was also head of the federation.

In the 1920s Japan established export associations similar to Webb-Pomerene associations and manufacturers' associations resembling those set up during the 1930s in the United States under the National Recovery Act. Some of these organizations inspected goods that were to be exported to enforce quality standards. In some cases organizations of manufacturers collectively responded to foreign complaints about Japanese imports. In 1933, for example, the British proposed to restrict the import of electric lamps from Japan. Like Japanese steelmakers responding to U.S. demands for "voluntary" quotas half a century later, the electric lamp makers organized associations to deal with this threat. Initially, they organized the Federation of Electric Lamp Manufacturers Associations to raise prices.in the hope of satisfying the British. When that measure failed, they organized an Electric Lamp Exporters Association for England to administer and enforce a limitation on the volume of their exports. Other quota-setting associations of exporters were established by producers of pencils, cotton-piece goods, velveteen, matches, and other products being sold in the United States, Latin America, and other parts of the world.[19]

Labor and trade issues continued to occupy the business associations in the 1930s. In 1931 they were successful in defeating a law that would have given legal rights to unions. In the wake of this success, business leaders organized the Zenkoku Sangyo Dantai Rengokai (National Federation of Industrial Organizations), which took over the labor-related activities that had been handled by the Japan Economic Federation, leaving the federation to concentrate on trade and other issues.[20]

During World War II many of the manufacturers' associations were transformed into official "control associations" to allocate supplies of raw materials, labor, capital, and products. Big business and the military struggled for authority over the control associations, but in most industries big business appears to have won out. Existing associations generally transformed themselves into control associations, collecting new official powers in the process. The large firms that had dominated the trade associations thus obtained the power to force smaller enterprises to fall in with plans to "rationalize" industries to the advantage of the large firms.[21] By the end of World War II there were more than 1,500 control associations at the national level in Japan; three special cross-industry associations were also established from existing organizations to facilitate the control of the Japanese economy during the war. These were the Council for Vital Industries (Juyo Sangyo Kyogikai), which was established in 1941; the Economic Association for Commerce and Industry (Shoko Keizai-kai), which was established in 1943; and the Association of Industries for National Strength (Sangyo Hokokukai), which was established in 1943.

The U.S. Occupation authorities planned to eliminate the control associations, but it was not until 1947 that the administrative machinery was set up to do so, and some control associations were not dissolved until 1949. In the meantime, some of the control associations had reorganized as trade associations. We will see later how this process took place in the steel industry. New peak associations were also organized during the Occupation years to replace disbanded wartime organizations.[22] The most prominent of these, Keidanren, was formed in 1946 to replace the Council for Vital Industries.[23] Keidanren, an organization of major firms and of trade associations, is dominated by a carefully balanced group of senior executives from various industries. A second major peak association, Nikkeiren, was established in 1948 to replace the Association of Industries for National Strength as an association of employers.[24] Nikkeiren does not have corporate members, but is run by the top managers of major firms. The third major peak association, the Japan Chamber of Commerce and Industry (Nippon Shoko Kaigisho), has a history that goes back to 1892. In its wartime manifestation it was the Economic Association for Commerce and Industry. The chamber was given permission to reestablish itself by the Occupation authorities in 1949. Its major function is to represent small and medium-sized businesses, yet its chairmen have included figures from big business such as Nagano Shigeo,[25] who was chairman of Nippon Steel. Councillors for the chamber include leaders or former leaders from Keidanren and Nikkeiren.

The fourth major postwar peak association, Keizai Doyukai,[26] was organized in 1946 as a discussion forum for younger executives, and its members are individuals rather than corporations. American Occupation officials believed that Japanese business needed an organization similar to the Committee for Economic Development (CED) in the United States to reduce their fixation on profits, increase their concern with broader policy issues, and lessen their subservience to the state. Many of the founders of Keizai Doyukai were (or later became) very prominent in Japanese industry. Some of those of special interest here are the ubiquitous Nagano Shigeo (later chairman of Nippon Steel and a leader of the Japan Iron and Steel Federation and

13

Japan Chamber of Commerce) and Fujii Heigo (later an executive vice-president of Nippon Steel and a member of the upper house of the Diet).

In 1966 another peak association, the Council for the Study of Industrial Problems (Sangyo Mondai Kenkyukai), was established by a group of industrial leaders. This "second cabinet," as one press commentator termed it, met monthly to discuss economic policy. Nagano, once again, was one of the powers in this organization, as were other of the steel industry leaders whom we will discuss later. The council helped promote the merger of Yawata and Fuji Steel in 1970 to establish Nippon Steel and was frequently involved in trade issues. Most of its activities ceased after the death in 1977 of Kikawada Kazutaka, its major leader.

Since the early 1950s Japanese law has allowed firms to form cartel-like associations for certain specific purposes. Several groups have been organized among exporters, for example, and among users of imported raw materials such as scrap. Japanese law also allows the formation of "depression cartels" to restrict production during economic turndowns. Generally these cartels are organized under the auspices of the trade associations. In other instances the government has encouraged the formation of associations to develop or use new technologies. There are now approximately 3,000 national trade associations in Japan. We discuss the various trade associations sanctioned under the Japanese antitrust laws in chapter 3.

In Japan, as in the United States, parts of the government have tried very hard to ride herd on the associations. The Japanese Fair Trade Commission was formed under pressure from U.S. Occupation authorities shortly after World War II. Although initially the organization had little influence, in the late 1960s this new organ of government began to come into its own. The next chapter discusses the Japanese Fair Trade Commission's major success in 1973 when it was able to gain indictments against the Petroleum Association of Japan for operating an illegal price cartel.

The development of trade associations in the Japanese steel and machine tool industries illustrates the general trends and patterns mentioned above and provides some interesting contrasts. The steel industry was made up of large firms with close ties to the government. Indeed the largest firm during the prewar period was directly controlled by the government. To a significant extent, the steel industry continued to have unusual influence over the government in Japan after World War II. The machine tool industry was made up of numerous small firms. During periods of crisis, most notably in the 1930s, this industry attracted the strong interest of government. It did not, however, have nearly the level of strength in dealing with the government that the steel industry did.

Trade Associations in the Japanese Steel Industry

Most of the important associations in the steel industry before World War II were created under strong government encouragement as instruments of public policy. This characterization takes on some current significance when we realize that although Japan's defeat in World War II certainly caused disjunctures in the organization of trade associations and in their relationships with the government, these disjunctures were by no means complete. Indeed there was, and is, remarkable continuity among the people and organizations involved.

Before the Cartels. The basic contours of the modern Japanese steel industry were drawn in the first fifteen years of this century. The Yawata Works, an integrated steelworks administered by the Ministry of Agriculture and Commerce, began producing steel in 1901. Yawata was the first fully integrated modern iron and steel works in Japan. It was also the major predecessor of Nippon Steel Corporation, which is now the world's largest steelmaker. The other major firms that still dominate the Japanese steel industry, Nippon Kokan, Sumitomo, Kawasaki, and Kobe, as well as numerous other private firms, were also established in the years before World War I.[27] The Ministry of Agriculture and Commerce underwent numerous transformations over the years, with part of it becoming the Ministry of Commerce and Industry in 1925. The latter became the Ministry of Munitions during World War II, the Ministry of Commerce and Industry again in 1945, and the Ministry of International Trade and Industry in 1949. The link between Yawata (and its descendants) and the Ministry of Agriculture and Commerce (and its descendants) has been at the center of government–business relations in the steel industry throughout this century.

Before World War I the Japanese steel industry as a whole was weak. Foreign firms supplied over half the iron and some two-thirds of the steel used in Japan. And within the Japanese industry Yawata produced some two-thirds of the pig iron and four-fifths of the steel. World War I was a watershed for the private iron- and steelmakers. During the war the Western countries completely suspended steel exports to Japan, causing serious shortages and a strong belief on the part of business and government leaders that Japan should build up an independent steel industry. Government provided assistance to the private sector to build up capacity, and Japanese steel production nearly doubled during the war years. The number of privately owned plants with a capacity of over 5,000 tons per year increased from seven to forty-two, and the share of steel production accounted for by private firms rose from 18 percent in 1914 to 43 percent in 1918.[28]

When the war ended, Japanese iron- and steelmakers were faced with both a collapse in the demand for steel from the military and a resumption of import competition. The largest producer, state-owned Yawata, was not required by the government to make a profit and had considerable freedom to lower prices to avoid cuts in production. Yawata aggressively moved its products from its former military markets to civilian markets. The price of pig iron dropped from a peak of 406 yen per ton in 1918 to 164 yen per ton a year later and to less than 70 yen per ton in the early 1920s. There was a comparable collapse in the price for steel. Profits disappeared. Many firms failed. The number of plants producing pig iron dropped from twenty in 1920 to nine in 1923. The private producers attempted to organize trade associations to protect the industry, but these efforts met with little success. Most of the private iron- and steelmakers came under the control of the zaibatsu. By the mid-1920s the only producers of pig iron remaining in Japan and the territories it controlled in mainland Asia were the firms controlled by the Mitsui, Mitsubishi, and Okura zaibatsu, the state-owned Yawata works, and the plants of the state-owned South Manchurian Railroad. The steel producers included a few independent firms as well as those controlled by the Mitsui, Mitsubishi, Asano, Sumitomo, Kawasaki, and Suzuki zaibatsu.[29]

Despite their difficulties, the private iron and steel firms found it difficult to organize to seek relief. The state-controlled Yawata Works, giant of the industry, saw little reason to cooperate with the private firms. The zaibatsu ironmakers (and the politicians they controlled) favored import protection and subsidies for iron production. They were opposed not only by steelmakers who feared that this would raise the cost of pig iron, but also by major industries that used steel. While the steelmakers opposed tariffs on pig iron, they wanted tariff protection against steel imports. Some militarists and others opposed subsidies and tariffs as schemes to enrich the zaibatsu at the expense of others in Japan. The steelmakers did manage to win a tariff increase in 1921, but the pig iron producers gained no such relief.[30]

The First Cartel Period: 1925–1930. The initiatives that finally allowed (indeed pushed) the iron- and steelmakers to organize strong trade associations came from the government, which was greatly concerned about the large influx of imported iron and steel. In 1924 the minister of commerce and industry, Takahashi Koreikiyo, established an Iron and Steel Study Group with himself as chairman.[31] Takahashi did not achieve his ambition of consolidating the public and private steel firms, but his successor, Kataoka Naoharu, was able to institute a set of policies that stressed coordination between the public and private firms. In 1925 Kataoka encouraged firms to establish a self-regulating body, believing they should better coordinate their actions with Yawata. The minister also provided Yawata with a strong incentive to cooperate with the private firms by instituting an accounting system that made it necessary for Yawata to take its costs of production into account when setting prices. As a result Yawata and nineteen private firms organized the Iron and Steel Council (Tekko Kyogikai) in December 1925.[32] This organization was a more or less direct ancestor of today's most important trade associations in the steel industry, the Japan Iron and Steel Federation and the Kozai Club.[33] The council investigated foreign steel industries and unified standards; it also organized the firms in efforts to influence government policy, calling for increases in tariffs and reductions in railway freight rates, and was instrumental in the organization of several cartels in the following years.[34]

The first of the cartels parented by the council was the Pig Iron Cooperative Association (Sentetsu Kyodo Kumiai), which was organized in 1926 as a joint sales and price-setting organization. Although the government did not impose new tariffs to protect the pig iron producers, it granted per ton subsidies for the production of iron, which enabled the firms to earn profits in some years during the late 1920s when they would otherwise have had losses. The domestic iron producers, however, were not competitive with the firms emerging in Manchuria. In an effort to strengthen the cartel in 1932, it was reorganized as the Pig Iron Joint Sales Company. This effort to save the cartel failed in the wake of increased demand for steel and increased competition from outsider firms.[35]

The steelmakers watched the organization of a cartel among the ironmakers with some concern, since a strong pig iron cartel could result in higher pig iron prices for the steelmakers. They wanted to form their own cartels, but because it included firms involved in several different product areas this segment of the industry was difficult to cartelize. Although most of the steel cartels were not organnized until the early 1930s, some collective action did occur in the late 1920s. In 1926 an agreement was reached on steel bar production, the steel product area that had caused the most contention in the industry. The Bar Agreement Association (Joko Bunya Kyoteikai) included Yawata and ten private firms which accounted for 93 percent of the market. In 1927 Yawata also joined three private firms in the Kanto

17

Steel Materials Sales Association (Kanto Kozai Hanbai Kumiai) to coordinate the production and sale of round bar. This agreement lasted until 1937.

The private firms attempted to organize several other associations during the late 1920s, but given the depressed economic conditions after the financial panic of 1927 and severe import competition they were unable to achieve stability. During this period Yawata's managers were developing a growing interest in using cartels to stabilize the market for steel. In 1929 a manager from Yawata's sales division sent reports back to Yawata from Germany on how firms in the German iron and steel industry had organized to avoid "excessive" competition. These reports further heightened the interest of several Yawata managers in cartelization as a solution to the problems of the Japanese steel industry.[36]

As a result, steel producers established a group of cooperative sales associations that included both the government and private producers. Cooperative sales associations were organized for black plate (1930), wire rod (1930), plate (1931), medium plate (1930), small angles (1931), and medium angles (1931). All of these organizations included Yawata. A key figure at the operational level in this cartelization was Inayama Yoshihiro, a major figure in steel industry inter-firm and business–government relations until the 1980s.[37] Although the cooperative sales associations sought to regulate prices and market share, some outsider firms never joined them and none of them survived very long. The Medium Plate Cooperative Sales Association was dissolved only seven months after it was organized; and the Medium Angles Steel Cooperative Sales Association was dissolved three months after it was organized. After the Japanese army took over Manchuria in 1931 demand for steel increased. The Ministry of Commerce and Industry warned repeatedly that steel prices were too high. Ironically, MCI's solution to the problem of high prices was similar to the earlier solution to the problem of low prices: Encourage steelmakers to organize. This would allow the ministry to pressure the industry as a whole to keep prices down. One tool at the ministry's disposal in encouraging the firms to organize was the Important Industries Control Law (Juyo Sangyo Tosei Ho) of 1931. This law, which Chalmers Johnson describes as originating today's system of administrative guidance, allowed two-thirds of the firms in an industry to apply to the ministry for permission to establish a cartel that would be binding for all firms.[38]

The Consolidation of the Industry. In 1930 as part of its effort to make the Japanese iron and steel industry more internationally competitive, the Temporary Industrial Rationalization Bureau, which was attached to the Ministry of Commerce and Industry, recommended that Yawata and all the other iron and steel producers be amalgamated into a single iron and steel company. Yawata officials had previously opposed this idea, but given the depressed economic situation began to favor it as a means of strengthening the industry. The private firms, including those controlled by the *zaibatsu*, also favored the plan because of the depression. In 1932 Takahashi Korekiyo, who had supported a consolidation of the steel industry since his service as minister of commerce and industry in the 1920s, became minister of finance, and Nakajima Kumakichi, another advocate of industrial rationalization, became minister of commerce and industry. In March 1933 the Diet passed the Nippon Steel Law, and in 1934 the government-private Nippon Iron and Steel Company was formed.[39]

The new semigovernmental trust had 79 percent of its capital paid in by the government, with most of the rest credited to the Mitsui, Mitsubishi, Yasukawa/Matsumoto, and Shibusawa interests. Eleven of its twenty top executives were from the government.[40] This majority of government officials did not necessarily make the new company a compliant follower of Ministry of Commerce and Industry policy, however. Many of the Nippon Iron and Steel executives were transferred from various branches of the government that were often in conflict with the Ministry of Commerce and Industry—for example, the Ministry of Finance, the Ministry of the Army, the Ministry of the Navy, and the Ministry of Railways.[41] At the time of the merger, Ministry of Commerce and Industry officials were given the option of leaving Nippon Steel to return to the ministry, and many did so. Further, some of the key management positions were assumed by executives from the old *zaibatsu* companies.[42] Some of the executives from outside the Ministry of Commerce and Industry made their power felt in 1940 by establishing Hirao Hachisaburo as chief executive officer of Nippon Steel. Two plotters in this Nippon Steel coup d'état, Nagano Shigeo and Fujii Heijo, were later important figures in the steel industry and in trade associations in the industry. Shortly after the "coup," Nagano became manager of the purchasing department, the youngest division manager at Nippon Steel. A year later Hirao became chairman of the Iron and Steel Control Association and took Nagano with him as a director.[43]

Nor was the trust as comprehensive as its planners had hoped. By 1934 economic conditions had improved, and several major firms that were to have become part of the new trust under the original plans for Nippon Steel refused to join.[44] Although Nippon Steel did account for some 96 percent of Japan's ironmaking capacity, it accounted for only some 51 percent of its steel production. The outsiders included all of the four major rivals to today's Nippon Steel. At this time the government's policy of supporting the cartels shifted to one of attempting to destroy them, with a view to forcing their members to join the Nippon Steel trust. The firms that had joined Nippon Steel withdrew from the cartels. The government applied additional pressure by delaying or refusing permission for private firms to build new facilities.[45]

This changed in 1936. After the so-called February 26, 1936, Incident, in which young army officers attempted to assassinate several high officials of the Japanese government (successfully, in the case of Takahashi Korekiyo), a new government was formed that began to move Japan toward a wartime footing. In the last half of 1936, because of a severe shortage of steel and rapidly rising prices, the military and the new government had less interest in expanding Nippon Steel's control over the steel industry than in expanding iron and steel production, and they drew up a five-year plan for the iron and steel industry.

The Second Cartel Period: 1937–1939. As the political situation in the Far East deteriorated, the efforts to mobilize the steel industry intensified. The war with China began with the Marco Polo Bridge Incident in July 1937. A month later the Iron and Steel Enterprise Law (Seitetsu Jigyo Ho) was enacted, establishing controls over the distribution and consumption of steel and implementing import controls. The law prohibited, for example, the use of steel for such noncritical uses as the construction of theaters, restaurants, and department stores. The distribution of iron and steel was more generally brought under control through a rationing system. August 1937 also saw the establishment of a new trade association, the Japan Iron and Steel Sales Federation (Nippon Kozai Hanbai Rengokai). The principal actors in the organization of this new federation were Inayama Yoshihiro (again) from Yawata and Watanabe Masao from Nippon Kokan.[46] The federation served as an umbrella organization for new joint sales associations for seven major product areas. It seemed better designed to serve the interests of the government than those of its private members. As Inayama put it: "This cartel was not for price maintenance, it was intended to restrain the outsiders and to control the rapid price increases occurring after the Manchurian incident."[47] While seeking to bring the industry under tighter control, the law also offered steelmakers tax relief to encourage their expansion.

The government controls intensified. In February 1938 the Iron and Steel Control Council was established within the Ministry of

Commerce and Industry. The council drew up plans and issued directives to self-governing bodies in industry regarding the volume of production of each category of steel product, the volume of imports by category, and exports. Its members included both members of government and representatives of the iron and steel industry. In March 1938 the federation was reorganized into the Japan Iron and Steel Materials Federation (Nippon Kozai Rengokai), which controlled some 90 percent of steel sales in Japan. The federation, the joint sales organizations, and other organizations were responsible for carrying out the plans drawn up by the Iron and Steel Control Council. In April 1938 the Iron and Steel Conference was reorganized as the Iron and Steel Federation (Tekko Renmei). In June 1938 regulations for the control of iron and steel supply and demand were issued. One objective was to improve coordination of iron and steel production in Manchuria with that in Japan. In July 1938 a new company, Japan-Manchuria Iron and Steel Sales, Inc. (Nichi-man Tekko Hanbai Kabushiki Kaisha) was formed from the Pig Iron Cooperative Sales Association and the Semifinished Products Cooperative Sales Association.[48]

In 1939 control over the industry was further consolidated. The various cooperative sales associations that had been organized in the previous two or three years were dissolved, and three new sales organizations were established under the direction of the minister of commerce and industry. Four of the joint sales associations were formed into the Japan Iron and Steel Materials Sales Company (Nippon Kozai Hanbai Kabushiki Kaisha). Three associations were united in the second Iron and Steel Materials Sales Company (Daini Kozai Hanbai Kabushiki Kaisha), which Inayama played a key role in establishing.[49] And two associations were united into the Japan Pipe and Tube Sales Co. (Nippon Kokan Hanbai Kabushiki Kaisha).

The Period of State Control: 1941–1945. As the political situation continued to worsen, the Japanese saw a need for more coordination and control over the steel industry. In October 1940 the United States banned scrap exports to Japan, further compounding the long-term scrap shortage of the industry. In December 1940 the Japanese government announced its New Economic Order, which was to shift the emphasis from profits of private firms to service to the state. The trade associations were to be reorganized to carry out various government policies related to this overall goal. In 1941 the Iron and Steel Control Association was established to unify control over raw materials and production. The head of the control association was Hirao Hachisaburo, president of Nippon Steel Corporation. Another director of the association was Nippon Steel's youngest division manager, Nagano Shigeo, one of the dominant figures in the postwar history of the Japanese steel industry.[50] Also sent to the control association were Yukawa Masao, a prominent postwar executive of Yawata Steel, and Inayama Yoshihiro.

In 1941 the Important Industries Associations Order was promulgated, giving a new legal basis for broader activities by the control associations. In an attempt to rationalize the purchase and distribution of raw materials, the association bought out the Japan-Manchuria Iron and Steel Sales, Inc. and the Japan Iron and Steel Materials Federation, merged the two companies, and took over the three steel products sales companies. The association was formally reorganized under the Important Industries Association Ordinance in late 1941, and further strengthened under still another new law in 1942.[51] Other control organizations were spun off from the control association: the Iron and Steel Raw Materials Control Corporation (of which Nagano Shigeo was president for a time) and the Iron and Steel Sales Corporation.[52]

Powerful leaders. Although the chairman and several important officials of the control association were from Nippon Steel, several officials representing *zaibatsu* interests in Japanese-controlled mainland Asia were also powerful in determining policies. As the coordination of mainland steel operations with those in Japan became impossible near the end of the war (shipping was thoroughly disrupted by U.S. submarines and aircraft), these officials lost power and in mid-1945 they resigned, leaving as directors Nagano Shigeo, Inayama Yoshihiro, Yukawa Masao, and Fujii Heigo (the executive director).[53]

All of these men were important leaders of the postwar Japanese steel industry. Nagano became the managing director of Nippon Steel in charge of business affairs in 1946; his deputy was Inayama Yoshihiro. When Nippon Steel was split up by Occupation authorities, Nagano became president of one of the two major resulting steel companies, Fuji Steel. With Inayama, he engineered the merger of Fuji Steel and Yawata in the late 1960s to form today's Nippon Steel. Nagano then served as first chairman of Nippon Steel from 1970–1973. Inayama became president of Yawata Steel in 1962, a position he held until the formation of Nippon Steel. He was the first president of the newly formed Nippon Steel from 1970–1973 and then chairman from 1973–1981. Yukawa Masao became general manager of technology at Nippon Steel at the end of the war. He was a managing director of Yawata after 1950 and then a vice-president of Yawata Steel.

Fujii Heigo became managing director of the Japan Iron and Steel Association after the war. He was a managing director at Yawata from 1950, became a Yawata vice-president in 1962, and a vice-president of Nippon Steel in 1970. After retiring from active management in 1973 he remained a senior adviser to Nippon Steel until his death in 1980.

These men were also important in Japan outside the steel industry. Nagano was one of the most powerful economic leaders until his death in 1984 at the age of 83. He was one of the founders of the Keizai Doyukai in April 1946, and an executive secretary of that organization in the 1950s. He was a deputy director of the Economic Planning Agency in 1947–1948 (an old school friend, Wada Hiroo, was director), president of the Japanese Chamber of Commerce (1969–1984), and president of the Tokyo Chamber of Commerce. He was popularly known as one of the four emperors of the Japanese business community. His brother was a Diet member and cabinet minister. As a young man, Nagano married a daughter of the vice-chairman of the Tokyo Chamber of Commerce. In a not entirely fanciful 1973 description of the board of directors of "Japan, Incorporated," a Japanese scholar identified Nagano as being chairman of the board.[54] Inayama was long president of the Kozai Club and the Japan Iron and Steel Federation (1965–1979), chairman of Keidanren, Japan's most important trade association (1980–1986), and a leader of the most important of Prime Minister Sato's support organizations. Fujii Heigo went from being executive director of the control association at the end of the war to being executive director of the postwar trade association that replaced it.[55] He was also an official in the Keizai Doyukai and in 1974 was elected to the upper house of the Diet.

While in the control association and related bodies, these men and others of lesser influence worked closely with officials of the Ministry of Munitions, people who in some cases became powerful in the postwar Ministry of International Trade and Industry or in the steel industry itself. Examples include Ojima Arakazu, Hirai Tomisaburo, and Sahashi Shigeru.[56]

Ojima was vice-minister of the Ministry of Munitions in 1941. At the end of the war he was vice-president of Nippon Steel. Later he became president of Yawata Steel and chairman of the Japan Iron and Steel Federation. Hirai, who had begun his Ministry of Commerce and Industry career at the Yawata Works, had thereafter returned to work in the ministry proper and, according to some accounts, was a key figure in dissolving the Ministry of Munitions at the end of World War II (so it could be reorganized by the Japanese rather than by the Occupation authorities). He served as vice-minister of MITI from 1953–1955, then joined Yawata Steel, and from 1973–1976 was president of Nippon Steel. Sahashi, who was in the Munitions Ministry Iron and Steel Bureau during the war, was a key official in MITI, capping his career as vice-minister from 1964–1966. Sahashi was long known as Mr. MITI in Japan. As a MITI official, Sahashi worked closely with Inayama to design and carry out various industrial policies related to steel. Chalmers Johnson notes that while Sahashi Shigeru was vice-minister, leaders of Sumitomo Metals charged that MITI had become a branch office of Yawata Steel.[57] Johnson credits him with institutionalizing the postwar system of "administrative guidance."

Nor were the people mentioned here the only ones involved in Japan's wartime steel industry control apparatus who were prominent in the postwar industry. Inayama's deputy during the war was his school friend Tomiyama Eitaro, senior executive at Nippon Kokan from the late 1940s until the 1960s. Hasegawa Kiyoshi, the long-time executive director of the Kozai Club was also in the second Steel Materials Sales Corporation in 1939, and later in the Iron and Steel Control Association. He began working for the Kozai Club when it was founded in 1947, becoming a director in 1968 and executive director in 1980, a position he still holds. Hasegawa is also executive director of the Japan Iron and Steel Exporters Association, as well as a high official in other organizations.

The Occupation Period: 1945–1952. The large number of wartime officials who continued to play major roles in the postwar Japanese steel industry may surprise readers who believe the Occupation authorities eliminated all of those who held positions of power during the war. We turn now to the broader issue of how the defeat in World War II disrupted the individuals and interests that had run the Japanese economy. In brief, we conclude that although the Allied Occupation certainly brought important reforms to Japan, it is an exaggeration to suggest, as Mancur Olson does, that these reforms ensured that "institutional life would start almost anew."[58]

A major intention of the Occupation reforms was to remove the influences that were thought to have caused Japan to become militaristic. Companies designated as having excessive control over their markets were to be broken up. The power of the wartime military and of police officials was to be destroyed. Individuals who had been involved in military-related industries were to be purged. Frequently, however, these ambitions diminished as policies were executed. Under the 1947 Elimination of Excessive Concentration of Economic Power Law, for example, 325 companies were identified as having had excessive economic power and were designated to be broken up. In fact, only eighteen companies, including Nippon Steel, were ever broken up, and many, including Nippon Steel, had reconsolidated by the end of the 1960s.[59]

The postwar purges effectively removed military and police officials from power and eliminated the influence of the families who had owned the *zaibatsu*. They did little, however, to remove the wartime economic bureaucrats and the operating managers of key industries. The Supreme Commander of the Allied Powers (SCAP) purged hundreds of economic leaders and imposed an antimonopoly law. But the purge was administered by the Japanese bureaucracy, which itself was little changed by the Occupation authorities. Johnson says the Supreme Commander of the Allied Powers "had decided on an indirect occupation, which left the Japanese government intact even if taking orders from SCAP. . . ."[60] The officials in the Japanese government delayed implementation of the purge and ended it as quickly as they were able to do so. Thus instead of lasting ten years, as the occupying powers had intended, the purge was fully in effect only in 1948–1949, with some restricted effects in 1946–47 and 1950–1951. There were violations and evasions, and the Japanese government was sympathetic to appeals. By the time an executive was to be purged, he had most likely already resigned and appointed a protégé in his place. Some purged economic leaders wielded considerable influence behind the scenes. The purge did not extend to people just below the top who had considerable experience in setting policies for their organizations, and thus the break in continuity of influence intended by the Occupation did not occur, nor was the break in the patterns of government-business interaction as complete as intended. An authority commenting on the effects of the economic purge shortly after its conclusion said: "When the return of the old business leaders to full and free participation in Japan's economic life gained momentum in 1951, it took place under the aegis of a government that had withstood in its own field and maintained continuous and close contact with the business group throughout the occupation period."[61]

In the steel industry, many of the wartime and prewar leaders continued their strong influence. Watanabe Gisuke, for example, was chairman of the control association and president of Nippon Steel. As head of both a control association and a "national policy" company he was doubly subject to being purged; he continued as head of these organizations for several months after the Japanese surrender and then in March 1946 resigned to avoid being purged. He was replaced by Miki Takashi, the head of the Yawata Iron and Steel Works. In 1950 Nippon Steel broke into two major private companies. Miki became head of the larger of the two, a new Yawata Steel. When Miki was killed in an airplane crash in 1952, Watanabe Gisuke came back to replace him both at Yawata and as head of the Japan Iron and Steel Federation. The second-ranking executive at Nippon Steel in 1946 was Ojima Arakazu, a former vice-minister of munitions. Ojima was also designated to be purged and also resigned, but later was able to return to Yawata Steel. When Watanabe died in 1956, he was replaced by Ojima, who served as president of Yawata and chairman of the Japan Iron and Steel Federation until 1962.[62]

Another of the hundreds of executives purged under the Occupation was Asada Shopei, the president of Kobe Steel. Asada, who worked with Ojima to convert the wartime Iron and Steel Control Association into a voluntary association that would be acceptable to the Occupation, resigned as president of Kobe in 1946. He returned as president from 1952 to 1958, served as chairman of Kobe Steel until 1965, and was a special counselor to the company from 1965 to 1970.

Executives at slightly lower levels were not purged, though many were instrumental in running the Japanese wartime economy. None of the four directors of the Iron and Steel Control Association, for example, was purged, and all of them became important postwar leaders of the Japanese steel industry. Although several top managers did leave Nippon Kokan and Sumitomo Metals, the senior manager in charge of the steelmaking division of Kawasaki Heavy Industries, Nishiyama Yataro, was not purged. When the steelmaking division of Kawasaki became independent, Nishiyama continued as its head, a job he held until his death in 1966.[63]

The evolution of postwar associations. Nor did the wartime system of economic controls disappear immediately on the surrender of Japan. Although the Ministry of Munitions changed its name back to the Ministry of Commerce and Industry, the change was little more than cosmetic, and the control associations continued to function for some time after the war.[64] Occupation officials used the associations to help control the economy; indeed, it was not until 1949 that the last of the control associations disappeared.[65]

The iron and steel control association was dissolved by order of the minister of commerce and industry in 1946, but some time before this, the steelmakers had organized a new civilian body, the Japan Iron and Steel Council (Nippon Tekko Kyogikai), to take over some of the old functions of the control association. The new organization had a different charter, with more rights for the smaller members, but was led by the same chairman and executive director who had run the control association, Watanabe Gisuke and Fujii Heigo.[66] The council cooperated with the government in regulating the supply and demand for steel, but under an amendment to the Temporary Materials Supply and Demand Control Law (Rinji Busshi Jukyu Chosei Ho), promulgated on April 15, 1947, the major activities of the council were no longer legal, and it was dissolved in the following month and replaced by another new trade association, the Japanese Iron and Steel Association (Nippon Tekko Rengokai). In December 1947 it too was dissolved and replaced by the Japan Iron and Steel Society (Nippon Tekkokai). The chairman of the society was Miki Takashi, the president of Nippon Steel who had replaced the purged Watanabe Gisuke. In November 1948 the society merged with the Japan Iron and Steel Industry Managers Association (Nippon Tekkogyo Keieisha Renmei) to form the Japan Iron and Steel Federation. Miki became the first president. This organization remains the central trade association in the Japanese iron and steel industry.[67]

The prewar and wartime control apparatus had included "designated" traders of iron and steel who were given exclusive rights to sell certain iron or steel products by the cartels and associations. During the war the coordination of this system had been entrusted to the sales and control companies and finally to the iron and steel control association. This function had been spun off during the transformation of the control association into a civilian trade association conforming to the postwar antitrust laws. Self-regulation of the distribution system did not end, however. In 1947 the wartime Iron and Steel Sales Corporation was revived. This organization also ran into legal difficulties, and its functions were taken over by the Industrial Reconstruction Corporation in July. Soon a new association of designated iron and steel traders was established and then joined with the Japanese Iron and Steel Association to form the Iron and Steel Materials Conference (Kozai Konwakai) to regulate the supply and demand for steel. At the end of 1947 this organization also was dissolved and replaced by today's Kozai Club.[68]

The Kozai Club includes both the major steelmakers and the major traders of steel. From its establishment until 1979 its chairman was Inayama Yoshihiro of Nippon Steel. Its executive director in recent years has been Hasegawa Kiyoshi, another control association veteran. The initial role of the Kozai Club was to cooperate with the government in regulating the supply and demand for steel by bringing together the steelmakers and trading firms. This quasi-official role was dropped in the wake of legal changes, but aside from carrying out more conventional trade association activities such as making market studies, forecasting demand, collecting data and statistics, and organizing committees to promote demand for steel, the Kozai Club continued to work closely with the government into the 1950s. It served as a point of contact between government and industry in allocating the supply of steel, setting prices, and allocating government subsidies.[69]

In 1955 the three leading blast furnace steelmakers established a sales-quotation system under which all steelmakers were to "accept orders at the quoted prices instead of determining, case by case, special contract and delivery prices." The leading steelmakers were unable to maintain this system during periods of extreme price instability and sought the help of MITI. In 1958 Inayama (then head of the Kozai Club) and Sahashi Shigeru (a MITI official who had worked with Inayama during the war) developed the public sales system (kokai hanbai seido).[70] Johnson describes this as "an ingenious system of price rigging" and says MITI forced the Japanese Fair Trade Commission to accept it. The Kozai Club was entrusted with responsibility for administering this system.[71]

Trade Associations in the Japanese Machine Tool Industry

It is more difficult to trace the origins of the machine tool than of the steel industry because the distinction between machine tools and other types of equipment is not completely clear and also because this industry contains smaller, sometimes transient firms. Japanese sources trace the origins of the industry to around 1890 when several of Japan's leading machine tool-building firms were established— Ikegai Corporation, Niigata Engineering, and Okuma Machinery Works.[72]

The domestic machine tool industry remained weak through the first decades of the twentieth century, and Japan continued to depend heavily on imported machine tools. During World War I foreign supplies of machine tools, like foreign supplies of steel, disappeared. The value of imported machine tools had averaged just under 3 million yen per year in the three years before the war. In 1915 it dropped to less than one-third of that, providing an opportunity for the expansion of the domestic industry. Between 1915 and 1918 domestic shipments increased twelve-fold—from less than 1½ million yen to 18 million yen. By the end of the war there were about 100 firms in the industry.

Through the 1920s the Japanese produced an increasingly broad variety of machine tools, but the market was severely depressed and by 1931 fewer than ten firms survived. In its efforts to build Japan's military strength in the 1930s, the government became concerned about the technical and economic weakness of the industry. Few firms could produce such equipment as gear cutters. Measures were taken to strengthen the industry as rapidly as possible. In 1938 the Machine Tool Production Activity Law (Kosaku Kikai Seizo Jigyoho) was implemented. Under this law, firms meeting certain conditions were designated as authorized companies *(kyoka kaisha)* and given priority by the government. Benefits under the law included exemption from taxes, protection against imports, and government subsidies. The authorized firms formed the Japan Machine Tool Production Industry Association (Nippon Kosaku Kikai Seizo Kogyo Kumiai), which became the control association during the war. The other machine tool builders formed another association, the National Association of Machine Tool Builders Associations (Zenkoku Kosaku Kikai Kogyo Kumiai). This association had some 403 members by 1940. In 1939 the six "designated" firms accounted for 27.3 percent of machine tool sales. By 1941 there were twenty-one designated firms accounting for 47 percent of sales.[73] Most of these twenty-one firms are now leading members of the Japan Machine Tool Builders Association. Johnson cites the Machine Tool Production Activity Law, among others, as "part of the prewar heritage most directly relevant to postwar industrial policy."[74] In 1940 the United States, which in 1939 had accounted for more than 80 percent of Japan's machine tool imports, banned the shipment of machine tools to Japan, further encouraging Japanese efforts to control the production and distribution of machine tools. In 1942, under the Important Industries Association Ordinance (Juyo Sangyo Dantai Ho), the Precision Machinery Control Association (Seimitsu Kikai Toseikai) was established to control the production and distribution of industrial machinery and to allocate raw materials. In 1943 this organization became an auxiliary organ of the Ministry of Commerce. It had some 381 members.

As a result of these measures the Japanese machine tool industry enjoyed phenomenal growth. In 1931 the entire industry included only an estimated 1,920 employees producing less than 4 million yen worth of tools. By 1944 the industries included more than 100,000 employees producing over 700 million yen worth of tools.[75]

Postwar Developments. During the first years after the war the Japanese machine tool builders, like the steelmakers, found it difficult to function at all. Steel, however, was considered an essential product for Japan's recovery, and the government gave the steel industry special attention. As the Japanese economy recovered, there was a tremendous domestic market for steel, but the small firms producing machine tools were faced with a different situation. There was no shortage of machine tools; indeed many of the machine tools that had been used in military production were suddenly released to the

29

civilian market, resulting in a glut of some 600,000 used machine tools just after the war.[76]

The small firms making up the machine tool industry made some efforts to organize, but as in the steel industry changing laws governing interfirm cooperation made organization difficult. In 1946 members of the industry set up the Japan Machinery Association (Nippon Kikai Kyokai). This association was disbanded in 1948 as a "closed institution" *(heisa kikan)*. Firms producing hydraulic presses and other metal-forming equipment established the Japan Metal Forming Machine Builders Association (Nippon Tan'atsu Kikai Kogyokai) in 1947, and in 1948 the Japan Machinery Federation (Nippon Kikai Kogyo Rengokai) was established. Both associations, as we shall see, continue to be important.

In 1948 an association primarily for producers of metal-cutting machine tools, the Machine Tool Association (Kosaku Kikai Kyokai), was established and then dissolved a year later. In 1949 the Eastern Japan Machine Tool Association (Higashi Nippon Kosaku Kikai Kyokai) was established, forming the core of the leading trade association in the industry today, the Japan Machine Tool Builders Association (JMTBA), which was established in 1951 with forty members. Its first chairman was Sano Shigeru, the chief executive of Hitachi Seiki, who had formerly been chairman of the Eastern Japan Machine Tool Association.

Other associations in the machine tool industry have focused on sales. The All Japan Federation of Machine Tool Merchants (Zen Nippon Kikai Kogu Shorengokai), established in 1948, was such an organization. In 1952 an exporters' association, the Japan Machinery Exporters Association (JMEA) (Nippon Kikai Yushutsu Kumiai), was set up almost immediately after the Export Transactions Law gave a legal basis for the formation of such organizations. According to the association's official history, it was established through the cooperation of the Japan Machinery Association and the Machinery Exporters Conference (Kikai Yushutsu Konwakai), an organization of some eighty trading companies dealing in machinery.[77] Still another association, an incorporated foundation called the Machinery Promotion Association (Kikai Shinkokai), was established in 1964. We discuss the current activities of these and other associations in chapter 4.

Some Observations about Trade Associations in the United States and Japan

In comparing the development of trade associations in Japan and the United States one sees a complex mix of similarities and differences.

In both countries the activities of an industry historically dominated by large firms (the steel industry) differ markedly from those of an industry consisting of smaller firms (the machine tool industry). One possible explanation is that although activities such as trade protection may be appealing at certain periods to associations in both types of industry, industries dominated by smaller firms seem more likely to pursue other activities such as the joint promotion of exports or joint research. Large firms have the resources to carry out these activities on their own; small firms may not.

Some of the differences between trade associations in the United States and Japan have been temporary and based on special circumstances. Throughout the nineteenth century, there was a strong (if somewhat episodic) concern on the part of U.S. trade associations with tariff policy. Japanese business could do little in this area because a series of treaties limited the ability of the Japanese government to set tariffs until the eve of World War I. In the 1920s the Japanese steel industry showed a strong interest in tariff policy, and in the postwar period Japanese industry was protected both by tariffs and by a wide range of nontariff barriers. The postwar Japanese steel industry has been more internationalist than its American counterpart, but the American Iron and Steel Institute exhibited some international orientation earlier in this century, when it, like the latter-day Japanese industry, was an exporter, rather than import-competitive.

The industries emphasized in this study have occupied special positions in Japan and the United States—positions that have not always been comparable in the two countries. Although the steel industry has been important in both countries, in the years since World War II the Japanese industry has had extraordinary influence through the connections of such leaders as Inayama and Nagano. This was far less true in the United States, although Elbert Gary and some of the other early leaders may have been similarly well connected in the first decades of this century. The U.S. steel industry has sharply declined in influence, and there are signs that the Japanese industry is undergoing a decline as well. In both cases, the rise of new industries and the loss of international comparative advantage have worked against the industry's political influence.

While the U.S. government has made use of trade associations at various points in the advancement of certain policies, government and business in Japan have formed much closer links and are more inclined to use trade associations as part of this link. In the United States cooperation between government and trade associations has tended to occur only during periods of perceived emergency; in the 1930s, for example, officials of the U.S. Bureau of Foreign and Domestic Commerce encouraged the formation of an association for the U.S. machinery industries to cope with German competition. But this and other such efforts seem trivial compared with those conducted by Japanese Ministry of Commerce and Industry officials during the same period. In some respects the Japanese have for the past 120 years regarded themselves as being in a chronic state of emergency vis-à-vis foreign competition. As a result, private and public interests have more frequently and consistently felt the need to work together than has been the case in the United States.[78] In this respect, the Japanese may not be particularly unusual: some scholars have suggested that there is a general relationship between national perceptions of domestic weakness in the face of foreign competition and this pattern of business-government interaction.[79]

In the Japanese steel industry, the boundaries between government and trade associations were substantially less clear than in the United States, at least until the early 1950s. The leading firm in the Japanese steel industry had executives who had begun their careers as government employees. Such men as Watanabe, Inayama, and Hirai entered Yawata via the civil service. Hirai returned to the Ministry of Commerce and Industry for much of the rest of his career, Inayama chose to stay with Yawata (and Nippon Steel). Ojima was a vice-minister of the Ministry of Munitions and later a vice-president of Nippon Steel. These men, in succession, were presidents of the old Nippon Steel, Yawata, and the new Nippon Steel until the late 1970s. As such they were also the heads of the Japan Iron and Steel Federation and of various lesser trade associations. By contrast, the leaders of the American steel industry generally have had no career experience in the federal government.

The continuity in leadership of the Japanese peak associations and the associations in the steel industry is striking. To be sure, these organizations have changed drastically in their structure and may even have been "democratized" in some respects; in large part, though the organizations such as Keidanren and the Japan Iron and Steel Federation, which officially trace their histories back only to the immediate postwar period, are substantially extensions of organizations that existed during and before the war. Often the wartime organizations reorganized under the same leadership to become "new" organizations.[80] Further, some of the Occupation reforms seem to have increased the number of distributive coalitions. The percentage of workers in labor unions, for example, increased from virtually zero in 1947 to 60 percent in 1948, very high by international standards.[81] This casts doubt on Mancur Olson's assertion that much of the explanation of the Japanese postwar "economic miracle" lies in the dissolution of distribution coalitions by Occupation authorities.[82]

Notes

1. Howard Aldrich and Udo Staber, "How American Business Organized Itself in the 20th Century" (Paper presented to the American Sociological Association meeting, 1986).

2. The commission sent 2,000 inquiries but received only 416 replies.

3. William H. Becker, *The Dynamics of Business-Government Relations: Industry & Exports, 1893–1921* (Chicago: University of Chicago Press, 1982), pp. 41–52.

4. Jonathan J. Pincus, *Pressure Groups and Politics in Antebellum Tariffs* (New York: Columbia University Press, 1977).

5. Becker, *Dynamics of Business-Government Relations*, pp. 42–51.

6. E. E. Schattschneider, *Politics, Pressures and the Tariff* (New York: Prentice-Hall, 1935); Raymond A. Bauer, Ithiel de Sola Pool, and Lewis Anthony Dexter, *American Businessmen and International Trade* (New York: Atherton, 1963).

7. James Cassing, Timothy McKeown, and Jack Ochs, "The Political Economy of the Tariff Cycle," *American Political Science Review,* vol. 80, no. 3 (1986), pp. 843–62.

8. This section draws heavily on the American Iron and Steel Institute *Yearbook* for the years 1910–1940.

9. They were the executive committee, the general technical committee, and the committees on arrangements, finances, foreign relations, membership, statistics, tariffs, industrial relations, building codes, manufacturing problems, productive capacities, publicity, stream pollution, and traffic.

10. The discussion in this section is based on Harless D. Wagoner, *The U.S. Machine Tool Industry from 1900 to 1950* (Cambridge, Mass.: MIT Press, 1968).

11. Gerald Feldman and Ulrich Nocken, "Trade Associations and Economic Power: Interest Group Development in the German Iron and Steel and Machine Building Industries, 1900–1933," *Business History Review* (1974), pp. 413–45.

12. Wagoner, *U.S. Machine Tool Industry*, pp. 146–47.

13. Ibid., p. 159. It is noteworthy that the Robotics Industry Association has recently experienced similar difficulties in persuading all member companies to contribute information for their statistical surveys of industry conditions.

14. Johannes Hirschmeier and Tsunehiko Yui, *The Development of Japanese Business: 1600–1973* (Cambridge, Mass.: Harvard University Press, 1975), p. 36.

15. This account draws on Eleanor Hadley, *Antitrust in Japan* (Princeton, N.J.: Princeton University Press, 1970); T. A. Bisson, *Japan's War Economy* (New York: Institute of Pacific Relations, 1945); Jerome B. Cohen, *Japan's Economy in War and Reconstruction* (Minneapolis: University of Minnesota Press, 1949); and E. B. Schumpeter, ed., *The Industrialization of Japan and Manchukuo, 1930–1940* (New York: Macmillan, 1940).

16. Indeed, under agreements signed in 1858 and 1866 the Japanese did not have the power to set tariffs with the Western powers. Even after recovering tariff autonomy in the 1890s, the Japanese were limited in their ability to set tariff rates until a general tariff revision took place in 1911.

17. For an excellent description of how business organized to counter labor in the decades before World War II, see Andrew Gordon, "The Business Lobby and Bureaucrats on Labor, 1911–1941" (Paper prepared for Japanese Business History Workshop, University of British Columbia, February 1982).

18. The *zaibatsu* were the great business combines, such as Mitsui, Mitsubishi, Sumitomo, and Yasuda, that dominated the Japanese economy until the end of World War II. Their postwar successors (often with the same names) are much less centrally controlled.

19. William T. Lockwood, *The Economic Development of Japan* (Princeton, N.J.: Princeton University Press, 1954) and Tokyo Association for Liberty of Trading, *The Trade Agreements between Japan and Some Other Countries* (Tokyo: Tokyo Association for Liberty of Trading, 1937).

20. A similar division of labor characterizes the postwar Nikkeiren (Federation of Japanese Employers) and Keidanren (Federation of Economic Organizations).

21. T. A. Bisson, "The Zaibatsu's Wartime Role," *Pacific Affairs*, vol. 18 (December 1945), pp. 355–64.

22. Much of this account draws on Yujiro Shinoda, "Economic Organizations and Business Leaders in Postwar Japan," *Sophia University Socio-Economic Institute Bulletin*, vol. 43 (1973), pp. 2–22; and Yujiro Shinoda, "Japan's Management Associations," *Sophia University Socio-Economic Institute Bulletin*, vol. 15 (1967), pp. 1–27. It should be noted that whereas the prewar peak associations were largely dominated by the *zaibatsu*, the postwar organizations have had much broader representation.

23. Keidanren is the shortened form of Keizai Dantai Rengokai, the Federation of Economic Organizations.

24. Nikkeiren is the shortened name of Nippon Keieisha Dantai Renmei, the Federation of Japanese Employers.

25. Japanese names are given in the Japanese order, that is, with surnames first.

26. This translates as "Committee for Economic Development," borrowed from the American organization of the same name. See Alfred C. Neal, *Business Power and Public Policy* (New York: Praeger, 1981), pp. 1–2.

27. Several Japanese sources cover this history. See, for example, Kawasaki Tsutomu, *Nippon Tekkogyo no Hatten to Tokushitsu* (Tokyo: Kogyo Tosho Shuppan, 1962).

28. Ibid., p. 257.

29. Iida Ken'ichi, Ohashi Shuji, and Kuroiwa Toshiro, *Tekko: Gendai Nihon Sangyo Hattatsushi V* (Tokyo: Gendai Nihon Sangyo Hattatushi Kenkyukai), pp. 201–03.

30. Ibid., pp. 265–66.

31. Takahashi, who has been called the Keynes of Japan, is best known for his role in guiding Japanese economic policy in the 1930s.

32. Iida et al., *Tekko*, pp. 265–70.

33. The line of descent is described below, but in his memoirs Inayama Yoshihiro includes a genealogy that also makes this point. See Inayama Yoshihiro, *Watakushi no Tekko Showa Shi* (Tokyo, Toyo Keizai Shinposha, 1986), pp. 228–29.

34

34. Iida et al., pp. 265–70.

35. Ibid., pp. 270–79.

36. Inayama, *Watakushi no Tekko Showa Shi*, pp. 280–302.

37. In his memoirs Inayama describes how he organized the Small Angle Cooperative Sales Association over lunch with a Mitsui executive (at the time, Mitsui's Kamaishi Kosan Works was the only private producer of small angles). Inayama also represented Yawata in organizing and operating the Japan Plate Cooperative Sales Association. Ibid., p. 36.

38. Johnson, *MITI and the Japanese Miracle*, p. 110. Administrative guidance is described in detail in chapter 5.

39. M. Udagawa and S. Nakamura, "Japanese Business and Government in the Inter-war Period," in Keiichiro Nakagawa, ed., *Government and Business* (Tokyo: University of Tokyo Press, 1980), pp. 83–101.

40. Tamaki Hajime, *Nihon Zaibatsu-shi* (Tokyo: Shakai Shiso, 1976), p. 45.

41. Nagano Shigeo, "Nagano Shigeo," pp. 7–94 in *Watakushi no Rirekisho— Keizaijin*, vol. 12 (Tokyo: Nihon Keizai Shinbun, 1980).

42. Inayama, *Watakushi no Tekko Showa Shi*, p. 53.

43. Nagano, "Nagano Shigeo," p. 53. The coup itself is described in Inayama, *Watakushi no Tekko Showa Shi*, p. 61.

44. Indeed, many of these firms had not been as heavily affected by the depression in the early 1930s and had recovered rather quickly.

45. Udagawa and Nakamura, "Japanese Business and Government," pp. 90–91.

46. Watanabe, then a managing director, was later a vice-president and in 1946–1947 president of Nippon Kokan.

47. Inayama, *Watakushi no Tekko Showa Shi*, p. 41.

48. Kanae Hatano, "From Semi-wartime to Wartime Control of the Iron and Steel Industry," in Secretariat, Institute of Pacific Relations, ed., *Industrial Japan: Aspects of Recent Economic Changes as Viewed by Japanese Writers* (New York: Institute for Pacific Relations, 1941), pp. 114–31.

49. Inayama, *Watakushi no Rirekisho* (Tokyo: Toyo Keizai Shinposha, 1986), p. 257.

50. Nagano, "Nagano Shigeo," p. 54.

51. Iida et al., *Tekko*, pp. 266–71, 349–50.

52. Nagano also became a director of a special public corporation *(eidan)* created to control general trading. See Nagano, "Nagano Shigeo," p. 54.

53. For a description of these events see Inayama, *Watakushi no Tekko Showa Shi*, pp. 67–68.

54. Yujiro Shinoda, "Economic Organization and Business Leaders in Postwar Japan," *Sophia University Socio-economic Institute Bulletin*, vol. 43 (1973), pp. 2–22. The term Japan, Incorporated was introduced almost two decades ago to suggest a well integrated system in which the Japanese economy was run by relatively small groups of bureaucrats and business leaders. James Abegglen, ed., *Business Strategies for Japan* (Tokyo: Sophia University Press, 1970), p. 72.

55. Nippon Tekko Renmei, *Sengo Tekko-shi* (Tokyo: Nippon Tekko Renmei, 1959), appendix p. 2.

56. The wartime links between these men are pointed out by Chalmers

Johnson, *MITI and the Japanese Miracle*, pp. 245–46.

57. Johnson, *MITI and the Japanese Miracle*, pp. 246 and 272.

58. See, for example, Mancur Olson, *The Rise and Decline of Nations* (New Haven, Conn.: Yale University Press, 1982), p. 76.

59. Takafusa Nakamura, *The Postwar Japanese Economy* (Tokyo: University of Tokyo Press, 1981), p. 25. Nakamura does argue, however, that even this limited breakup of economic power did increase competition in Japan.

60. Johnson, *MITI and the Japanese Miracle*, p. 173.

61. T. A. Bisson, "The Economic Purge in Japan," *Far Eastern Quarterly*, vol. 12 (May 1953), pp. 279–99. Quotation is from page 299. Similar points are made in Michael Schaller, *The American Occupation of Japan* (New York: Oxford University Press, 1985), pp. 43–44.

62. Nippon Tekko Renmei, *Sengo Tekkoshi*, p. 14.

63. Seiichiro Yonekura, "Entrepreneurship and Innovative Behavior of Kawasaki Steel: The Post World War II Period," Hitotsubashi University Discussion Paper 120, 1984.

64. Kakuma Takashi, *Dokyumento Tsusansho, II: Kasumigaseki no Yuutsu* (Tokyo: PHP, 1979), p. 6.

65. T. A. Bisson, *Zaibatsu Dissolution in Japan* (Berkeley: University of California Press, 1954), pp. 191–96.

66. Nippon Tekko Renmei, *Sengo Tekkoshi*, pp. 5–8.

67. The Manager's Association had been established in May 1946 to counter the newly legalized labor unions. Its chairman was also the president of Nippon Steel. Ibid., p. 44.

68. Kozai Club, *Kozai Kurabu Sanjugonen Shi* (Tokyo: Kozai Club, 1982), p. 1. In this official history, the Kozai Club traces its roots to the cartels of the late 1920s, the wartime sales control companies, and the Iron and Steel Control Association.

69. According to Kawahito, the total subsidy amounted to as much as 87.5 percent of production cost in the case of pig iron and 76.4 percent in the case of steel bars at one point. See Kiyoshi Kawahito, *The Japanese Steel Industry* (New York: Praeger, 1972), p. 11. Other material in this section is from Kozai Club, *Kozai Kurabu Sanjugonen Shi*, pp. 2–3.

70. Ken'ichi Imai, "Iron and Steel," pp. 191–244 in Kazuo Sato, ed., *Industry and Business in Japan* (White Plains: M.E. Sharpe, Inc., 1980), p. 224.

71. Johnson, *MITI and the Japanese Miracle*, p. 226.

72. Except where noted, this account is taken from the Japan Machine Tool Builders Association, *"Haha Naru Kikai" 30-Nen no Ayumi*. The descriptions of legal changes during the 1930s are primarily from Institute of Pacific Relations, *Industrial Japan: Aspects of Recent Economic Change as Viewed by Japanese Writers* (New York: IPR, 1941).

73. To be designated, a firm had to have some 200 machine tools. Only five of these firms had existed a decade earlier.

74. Johnson, *MITI*, p. 133.

75. Vogel, *Comeback*, p. 61.

76. Ibid.

77. Japan Machinery Exporters Association, *Nippon Kikai Yushutsu Kumiai Sanjunenshi* (Tokyo: JMEA, 1982).

78. Ironically, Richard Samuels and others have found that the Japanese government had considerable difficulty mobilizing key industries during World War II. See Richard Samuels, *The Business of the Japanese State* (Ithaca, N.Y.: Cornell University Press, forthcoming). Perhaps the Japanese Ministry of Commerce and Industry caused a reflexive resistance by always seeming to seek control over industry.

79. Philippe C. Schmitter, "Still the Century of Corporatism?" in Philippe C. Schmitter and Gerhard Lehmbruch, eds., *Trends toward Corporatist Intermediation* (Beverly Hills, Calif.: SAGE Publications, 1979), p. 37. For an application of this thesis to the Japanese case, see T. J. Pempel and Keiichi Tsunekawa, "Corporatism without Labor? The Japanese Anomaly," in Schmitter and Lehmbruch, *Trends toward Corporatist Intermediation*.

80. *Business of the Japanese State*. Samuels describes similar reorganizations of trade associations in the energy-related industries.

81. Nakamura, *Postwar Japanese Economy*, pp. 28–30.

82. Olson, *Rise and Decline of Nations*.

3
The Antitrust Environment
for Trade Associations

The laws governing trade associations in Japan and the United States have a number of broad similarities, particularly since World War II. This should not be surprising, since the major postwar Japanese antitrust laws were drafted by American Occupation authorities using American models. Within the roughly similar legal structure, however, are a number of differences, which also should not be surprising, since the American model imposed on the Japanese originated in a sharply different context. The Japanese who were to administer the new laws initially had difficulty understanding them and for the first decades after the war had little reason to aggressively enforce them. Business associations had to obey clear-cut provisions of the law, but had little to fear from enforcement efforts requiring some administrative discretion. In the United States the situation has been quite different: associations have often avoided the gray areas at all cost.

After the Occupation ended, Japanese big business waged a strong campaign to soften the antitrust laws through amendments and new legislation to provide a growing list of exemptions. These efforts were frequently successful. Interestingly, however, antitrust laws appear to have taken root and developed their own constituencies in Japan, in spite of these campaigns.

This chapter describes the evolution and current status of the Japanese legal environment for trade associations and compares it with the U.S. system.

The Japanese Antimonopoly Law and Trade Associations

Before World War II Japanese government policy favored the formation of cartels, and almost every industry was cartelized. During the war, as we have seen, the system of wartime planning and control relied heavily on existing cartels. Many of Japan's prewar and wartime economic policies were precursors of postwar economic policies or were prototypes for policies that facilitated the formation and sanctioned the activities of trade associations. Although Occupation policy sought to democratize the Japanese economy and to ban the formation of cartels, many of the prewar and wartime policies were resurrected shortly after the Occupation ended, allowing exemptions from the Antimonopoly Law in such industries as machine tools and shipbuilding. Others seem prototypic of the Export-Import Transactions Law, which allowed the formation of special export and import trade associations.[1]

Development of the Antimonopoly Law. One of the key elements in the Occupation plans to democratize the Japanese economy was the Antimonopoly Law (AML) of 1947, the first antimonopoly law in the history of Japan.[2] The law was based on a draft prepared by the antitrust division of the U.S. Justice Department, which the Japanese took to be a directive. The 1947 AML combined elements borrowed from the Sherman, Clayton, and Federal Trade Commission acts, together with U.S. judicial interpretations of these acts. The final draft was more stringent than its American counterpart. It outlawed cartels completely, made monopoly illegal per se, prohibited overlapping shareholding, and required prior approval of mergers.[3]

In January 1947 the AML draft was sent to the planning office of the Ministry of Commerce and Industry to be put into proper form as a bill that could be sent to the Diet. The official in charge of translating the law, Morozumi Yoshihiko, found it to be so different from the Japanese legal tradition that he had difficulty understanding it. He later wrote: "It seems laughable today, but then we didn't really know what they were talking about."[4] Another member of the planning office staff, Komatsu Yugoro (who served as vice-minister of MITI from 1974 to 1976 and then became a director of Kobe Steel), recalled his belief that the law would result in the widespread collapse of Japanese businesses and a weakening of Japan's international competitive strength. It was widely believed that one of the major reasons for the imposition of the laws was to keep the Japanese economy weak.[5]

Despite these reactions the bill was presented to the Diet with few changes. It was passed as the Law Relating to the Prohibition of Private Monopoly and to Methods of Preserving Free Trade. To help enforce its provisions the AML provided for the establishment of the Japan Fair Trade Commission (JFTC). The role of the JFTC in policing trade associations was expanded in 1948 with the enactment of the Trade Association Law, (Jigyosha Dantai Ho), a supplementary act to the AML.[6] These laws, as discussed in chapter 2, forced considerable changes in the associations representing the steel and machine tool industries. Organizations were disbanded and reorganized with different names, different legal bases, and different statements of purpose—though often with the same executives and staff.

Japanese business leaders (sometimes with the support of American business) exerted strong pressure to weaken the provisions of the AML, and parts of the law were amended in 1949 to facilitate the flow of foreign capital into Japan and to give greater protection to patent rights.[7] Two years later the Japanese government attempted to relax the Trade Association Law, but these efforts were blocked by the Occupation authorities. In 1952 when the Occupation ended, the Export Transactions Law was passed, allowing the first major exemptions to the AML. Business leaders continued to advocate the repeal of the Trade Association Law and the severe curtailment of the AML. The Japan Iron and Steel Federation (JISF) was in the forefront of this movement. It proposed amendments to the AML and the repeal of the trade association law to the JFTC and MITI.[8] Throughout 1953 both JISF and Keidanren petitioned the Diet to permit depression and rationalization cartels.[9]

In 1953 the Diet amended the AML and abolished the Trade Association Law, although elements of it were incorporated in amendments to the AML. Depression and rationalization cartels were now allowed when the "competent ministry," most often MITI, deemed it necessary to cope with a recession or to promote the "rationalization" of an industry. Either a ministry or industry group could initiate the cartel, but if the initiator was an industry group, the concurrence of the responsible ministry was needed. Whether the initiator was a ministry or an industry group, the cartel had to be approved by the JFTC.[10]

A 1977 amendment strengthened the AML, partly in response to the public disclosure in the mid-1970s that petroleum wholesalers (and their trade association) had been involved in a large-scale price-fixing scheme to take advantage of the OPEC crisis of 1973. We describe this episode in greater detail in chapter 4.

Exemptions from the AML and Special Trade Associations. After the passage of the Export Transactions Law, other laws were passed that gave trade associations further exemptions from the AML. Trade associations of small and medium-sized businesses were exempted to allow their members to benefit from economies of scale, thereby to better compete with large firms. Special laws provided other exemptions to promote exports, encourage the development of "strategic industries," and encourage collaborative research.[11]

Depression cartels. One of the 1953 amendments to the AML allows associations of manufacturing firms to form depression cartels.

If the JFTC and the appropriate ministry approve the cartel, it can set production and sales quantities, for example, or impose restrictions on the equipment used by its members. Under some conditions it may even be allowed to set prices. The cartels are permitted for limited periods, usually six months, but can be extended for three months. Nonparticipating firms can not be legally coerced by the government to join.[12]

The JFTC's rationale for allowing depression cartels is that they are needed to cope with situations in which the sales price of a product falls below its average production cost, threatening the survival of many of the manufacturers in the industry. Ideally, the cartel would give the industry the time and resources needed to restructure. An industry that is depressed because it has excess capacity, for example, could scrap its least efficient facilities. The result (if all went according to plan) would be an industry with adequate markets to sustain itself and a higher level of average efficiency than before. Obviously, there are serious difficulties in deciding which firm's facilities should be scrapped and in enticing (or coercing) the firm to go along with the agreement. Powerful firms through their dominance of a depression cartel could conceivably force weaker competitors to scrap efficient capacity. Conversely, less efficient smaller competitors could campaign for an "equitable" scrapping policy that might result in obsolete facilities remaining in service while more efficient facilities are scrapped.

The provisions for depression cartels were widely used during economic downturns. Between the implementation of the amendment in 1953 and 1984, some seventy-one exemptions had been granted for depression cartels, with twenty-one receiving permission in 1975. Far fewer exemptions have been given in recent years. Two depression cartels, covering the ethylene and cement industries, were granted permission to engage in joint action in 1983. In the fiscal year ending in March 1984, no new depression cartels were given permission to form.[13]

In 1978 the Japanese government promulgated a special law to offer more comprehensive help to depressed industries. The law, which was renewed in 1983 and will be in effect until 1988, exempts groups of firms in depressed industries from the AML, to allow a restructuring. It also offers low-interest government loans for firms scrapping capacity. In the polyethylene film industry, firms remaining in the industry provide financing to help other firms leave it.[14]

As might be expected, trade associations are closely involved in the planning and administration of coordinated action in this process of restructuring. The trade association of a designated industry works

41

closely with the government via the Industrial Structure Advisory Council in drafting a "basic stabilization plan" *(antei kihon keikaku)*, and later in some cases may administer the depression cartel agreement.[15]

Capacity reductions were particularly extreme in the aluminum and shipbuilding industries. Under the first basic stabilization plan drafted by the aluminum subcommittee of the industrial structure advisory council, over half the 1.6 million tons per year of Japanese aluminum production capacity was scrapped. As a result, smelters were able to operate at nearly full capacity in 1980. In 1981, however, the industry ran into difficulties again, and the industrial structure advisory council planned a further reduction of capacity down to 700,000 tons per year. In 1984 the council drew up yet another plan, this time to reduce capacity to 350,000 tons per year. Meanwhile, Japanese aluminum firms invested offshore to get a share of the growing Japanese market for importing aluminum. The government encouraged them to do this by offering reduced tariffs to aluminum producers that replaced their production with imports.[16]

It is difficult to evaluate the overall efficacy of the depression cartels. A recent assessment concludes that ". . . in its context it has achieved reasonably satisfactory results."[17] The electric furnace steelmaking industry, however, did not succeed in reducing capacity, and all but three of the fourteen industries designated under the 1978 law were also designated when the law was renewed in 1983.

Rationalization cartels. According to the 1953 amendment incorporating the Trade Association Law into the AML, the JFTC can permit trade associations made up of manufacturers to impose restrictions both on the technologies used by their members and on the types of products made by them. These so-called rationalization cartels are supposed to help their members improve technology or product quality, reduce prices, increase efficiency, or obtain raw materials.

One of the earliest uses of this device was in the steel industry. Article 24:4:2 of the AML allows producers in an industry to act jointly in the purchase of raw materials. This amendment, for which the Japan Iron and Steel Federation had been a leading campaigner, was promulgated in 1953. The steelmakers then submitted an application to the JFTC for permission to form a scrap cartel, the first postwar industrial cartel. In December 1953 the Japan Scrap Federation (Nippon Tetsugusa Renmei) was established despite considerable public opposition.[18] Yanaga describes these events as being the beginning of the "cartel trend."[19]

Rationalization cartels have not been heavily used. Indeed between the enactment of the amendment in 1953 and 1983 only thirteen exemptions had been granted for rationalization cartels. No exemptions were granted in the fiscal year ending in March 1984.[20]

Other exemptions from the AML. Another set of important laws permitting exemptions from the AML was targeted at specific industries that were given high priority by the Japanese government. These laws, which were sponsored by MITI, were resurrected versions of laws passed during the 1930s as Japan sought to build up its military capabilities.[21] One of the industries so favored has been machine tools through the Emergency Act for the Promotion of the Machine Tool Industry. Other industries targeted by these laws include electronics, textile machinery, and petroleum.

Japanese law permits other exemptions to the AML, though most are less relevant to the issues of trade and research. Exemptions may be permitted, for example, to "prevent unreasonable customer enticement through giveaways or unreasonable claims." Resale price maintenance is permitted, primarily to prevent unjust price cutting and loss leader sales. As of 1983 the provisions had primarily been used in the cosmetics and drug industries.[22] Other exemptions are designed specifically to help small businesses, to allow "natural" monopolies, or to promote the rationalization of specific industries, such as the coal industry in the 1950s.

Administration of the Japanese Antimonopoly Law. The Japanese AML is administered by the Japan Fair Trade Commission (JFTC), a quasi-judicial body that is supposed to be independent of all ministries and directly responsible to the prime minister. The prime minister appoints its chairman and four commissioners with the consent of both houses of the Diet. Commissioners are supported by a secretariat under a secretary general.

The JFTC has several responsibilities that directly or indirectly affect the activities of trade associations. Under the provisions of the AML, trade associations must register with the JFTC within thirty days of their formation or dissolution. As we have seen, the JFTC is also responsible for deliberating on the formation of export associations, recession cartels, and other associations exempted from various provisions of the AML.

The JFTC receives complaints and investigates violations of the AML and can issue cease-and-desist orders enforceable by criminal proceedings.[23] Although aspects of the Japanese AML resemble those of U.S. antitrust law, there are some very important differences. The Japanese law has no provision for treble damages, and private litigants are not allowed to bring suit until after the JFTC has done so.

43

Discovery is much more limited in Japan than in the United States. As a result of these differences, private antitrust suits are rare. Indeed as of 1983 no plaintiff had ever won a private antitrust suit in Japan.[24]

A key issue is how much power the JFTC has to curtail the activities of business in general and trade associations in particular. Since the JFTC does not have cabinet rank, it is sometimes at a disadvantage when competing with MITI and is often depicted in the English language literature as half-heartedly waging a lonely battle against big business and MITI to enforce the Antimonopoly Law. Many observers have characterized the JFTC as a weak organization with only a limited will and ability to carry out its responsibilities. Eleanor Hadley quotes a report from the 1960s that says: "The chief activity of the Fair Trade Commission seems to be the sanctioning and registering of exceptions to the Law, rather than the enforcing of it."[25] Hadley also notes the weakness of its political base. Caves and Uekusa note that "conflict with the Fair Trade Commission has, of course, been endemic, but MITI's position as an administrative agency has in general given it the upper hand."[26]

The weakness and general decline of the JFTC from its founding in 1948 continued until the 1960s. In 1948 the secretariat of the JFTC had some 327 employees. This number declined to just 237 in 1954. It started growing again in the 1960s and by 1970 had reached 351.[27] Beyond this, its first staff members were transferred from other branches of the government that were not particularly sympathetic to the goals of the AML. Morozumi Yoshihiko, for example, came from the Ministry of Commerce and Industry, and later returned to MITI where, in 1971, he became the administrative vice-minister. Morozumi's view on the regulation of collusive activities by big business are made clear in a 1962 article quoted by Eleanor Hadley: The classic belief that the public welfare will be promoted by the invisible hand of free competition is held even today, but actually [this is not true]. Free competition means excessive equipment and low profits.[28] The first director of the JFTC was himself a representative of big business, the chairman of Daido Steel.[29] Moreover, Japan had little experience with antitrust and there was some confusion as to exactly what the JFTC should do. These factors became particularly important when the JFTC lost the support of the Occupation authorities after 1952.[30]

A member of the JFTC secretariat suggests, however, that this image of weakness has been overstated, and that particularly since the late 1960s the JFTC has greatly increased its power. First, the JFTC— despite its nominal independence from the ministries—has ties with the Ministry of Finance, an agency that receives less attention in the West than MITI, but which some scholars suggest is much more

44

powerful than MITI.[31] The JFTC therefore has enough of a bureaucratic base that it does not have to be overly concerned with the
actions of MITI. Second, while MITI has been generally declining in
influence, the JFTC has been increasing in both influence and prestige. One apparent turning point was around 1968–1970 when the
JFTC managed to impose some conditions before allowing the merger
of Yawata and Fuji Steel. The resulting publicity clarified the JFTC's
mission for the public with the result that many new university
graduates with higher scores on the civil service exams began apply-
ing for jobs with the JFTC. Many of their predecessors had been
demoralized by the weakness of the JFTC in the late 1950s and early
1960s and thus had left, allowing many of the bright new people to be
rapidly promoted.

In 1972 Prime Minister Tanaka named a former chief of the
Ministry of Finance's Banking Bureau, Takahashi Torihide, as chairman of the JFTC. This chairman was highly combative with MITI. In
1973 the JFTC raided the offices of the Petroleum Association of Japan,
later charging it with operating an illegal price cartel, even though the
petroleum executives said they had acted in accordance with MITI's
instructions. Since this was the first challenge to MITI's administrative
guidance, the JFTC received considerable attention. In the aftermath
JFTC was able to strengthen the Antimonopoly Law, but not to the
extent it wanted. The petroleum case was in the courts until 1980
when the Tokyo High Court ruled that MITI had indeed overstepped
its authority.[32]

In 1983 the JFTC had a staff of 427 and five divisions. In the
economics division an associations section has primary responsibility
for monitoring the activities of trade associations. In October 1983 this
section had twelve members.[33] Between the enactment of the amendments to the AML affecting trade associations in 1953 and 1983, the
JFTC had issued 350 decisions on AML violations by trade associations.[34]

American Trade Associations and the Antitrust Laws

Trade associations in the United States are subject to a wide variety of
laws and regulations that also affect the operations of other taxpayers,
other employers, and other actors in the political arena. They can
create organizations—foundations, "captive" insurance companies,
political action committees, profit-making subsidiaries—which are
also subject to the laws governing those particular forms of activity.
Just as there is no federal incorporation law in the United States, there
is no national trade association law analogous to that enacted in Japan

and later incorporated into the Antimonopoly Law; however, some forms of collective action by business groups are explicitly permitted by federal statutes. Regulations, court cases, and congressional colloquies have established other rules guiding the activities of U.S. associations.[35]

The most relevant statutes pertaining to a trade association's operations are those that directly affect its mission of providing an organizational vehicle for collective action by its members, of either an economic or a political nature. In the economic sphere, this means primarily the antitrust laws—the Sherman Act, the Clayton Act, the Robinson-Patman Act, the Federal Trade Commission Act—as well as highly specific legislation pertaining to the ability of trade associations to set up export trading companies or to establish joint ventures in research and development. In the political sphere, limitations on lobbying activities and campaign contributions, and reporting requirements for such activities, are of particular relevance.

The fact that trade associations provide a setting in which members of competing firms come together and exchange views obviously creates the potential for abuse. "Because associations are, by their very nature, combinations, their actions are generally subject to special scrutiny under the antitrust laws."[36] Members could conceivably use the opportunities for meeting to establish agreements over prices and outputs. Trade associations could also conceivably institute practices and establish rules or standards that could significantly restrict competition. These long-standing concerns about the price-fixing potential of trade association activities are best exemplified by the famous Monograph #18 of the Temporary National Economic Committee of the U.S. Congress (1940). This report was concerned with "concentration of economic power," but defined its interest largely in terms of concerns about collusion on price, output, and restriction of entry.[37] Monograph #18 devoted chapters to trade practices, the trade practices of a particular trade association (the Sugar Institute), trade statistics and bid and price information, and uniform accounting. Lumped together in a chapter labeled "other activities" were consideration of technical research and advice, standard setting, labor relations, government relations, and trade promotion.[38]

U.S. federal court decisions have created policies to deal with specific anticompetitive contingencies. Although most of what associations do is probably relevant to some aspect of antitrust law, four issues are of particular concern: price fixing, information sharing (particularly statistical reporting), standard setting, and defining membership and providing services to nonmembers.

The American antitrust laws provide an extremely hostile en-

46

vironment for price fixing. To violate the law, parties do not actually have to agree on specific prices per se; in *U.S.* v. *Socony-Vacuum Oil Co.* (1940) the Supreme Court held that any agreement that uses scales or formulas, or that otherwise limits the range within which sales or purchases are to be made, constitutes price fixing. In a 1968 advisory opinion the Federal Trade Commission (FTC) also ruled that competitors may not agree on wages they will pay to workers where the product price is closely related to labor costs.[39] A trade association handbook advises that, *"Any* discussion of prices is dangerous" (emphasis in original).[40] Unlike the situation in Japan, there are no exceptions to this policy recognized for small business, for depressed conditions, or for excess capacity.

Important cases on information sharing were decided by the Supreme Court in the 1920s and 1930s. In *American Column Lumber Co.* v. *U.S.* (1921) and *Maple Flooring Manufacturers Association* v. *U.S.* (1924), the Court ruled against information exchanges that provided member firms with highly detailed data about the specific transactions of specific competitors, but permitted more general and more highly aggregated information exchanges. In *Sugar Institute* v. *United States* (1936), the Court did not object to a plan requiring companies to disclose future prices for sugar, but did object to the institute's attempt to compel adherence to the information disclosure policy. More recently, the FTC has stated that "an association's price reporting plan which involves future or advance prices, particularly when that plan invites an industry wide pricing policy, may provide the basis of an agreement or combination to fix prices."[41] The Supreme Court in *U.S.* v. *Container Corp. of America* (1969) further restricted the scope of permissible price information exchanges in markets where a concentration of sellers and product uniformity create propitious preconditions for collusion.[42] Current legal advice to trade associations on reporting plans is to avoid collecting data on future prices or production plans, to report data only in aggregate form, and to forgo any attempt to require participation in information reporting programs.[43]

Standardization and certification activities by trade associations generally involve setting performance requirements for products or practices and, in the case of certification, passing judgment on which specific firms meet the given standards. Such activities may run afoul of antitrust law to the extent that they possibly restrict entry or fix prices. In the 1982 case of *American Society of Mechanical Engineers, Inc.* v. *Hydrolevel Corp.*, the Supreme Court held the association liable for antitrust violations committed by its volunteer staff. One staff member who was an officer in an established firm in the industry had abused the standard-setting process by having ASME issue an "informal" letter stating that a new product developed by a competitor, Hydrolevel Corp., did not meet ASME standards. Subsequently, ASME published all written technical inquiries and interpretative replies and reviewed its interpretations upon receipt of additional information.[44] In an advisory opinion the FTC has stated that no applicant for certification may be denied on the grounds that he is a nonmember of the relevant association, is a foreign competitor, or is unable to pay certification fees.[45] These rulings make the American standard-setting process more transparent and make it difficult for American firms to restrict entry by foreign companies. This situation has stood in marked contrast to that in Japan, where industrial standards are set under a program administered by MITI's Agency for Industrial Science and Technology. After widespread criticism that the Japanese system was closed to foreigners and served as a trade barrier, reforms were made in 1985 to allow foreign participation in standard setting.[46]

Trade associations must comply with antitrust requirements restricting their ability to deny membership. If association activities confer a competitive advantage to members, then any policy that denies competitors access on reasonable terms to these benefits may be construed as a concerted refusal to deal and therefore as a violation of the Sherman Act. American trade associations would thus face legal difficulties if they attempted to exclude foreign producers from membership, unless they offered access to association services to nonmembers for a fee that bore reasonable relation to actual costs of providing the service.[47]

Trade associations today are generally aware of the scrutiny under which their activities may be placed and in some cases are rather nervous about continued monitoring of their activities. Many of the larger associations have specific written policies for maintaining compliance with antitrust laws. Our inspection of the guidelines of a small number (fewer than one dozen) of large American trade associations suggests the following are typical of antitrust compliance rules:

• Prohibition of any discussion of individual members' prices, costs, or factors that might affect prices or costs, sales, inventory, or production data; prohibitions against discussion of allocation of customers or markets or of refusals to serve

• Explicit requirement for formal agenda for every association meeting and for written minutes of every meeting. Prohibitions against off-the-record sessions, secret meetings, or discussion of association business at social gatherings

• Requirement that association staff member be present for every meeting of an association committee

- Requirement that counsel approve the minutes of every meeting so that any association actions that might have anticompetitive effects can be halted
- Discussion of certain areas—eligibility for membership; certain codes and standards; statistical programs; association of cooperative research programs—only in the presence of counsel

Formal guidelines of course do not guarantee that an association will not experience any antitrust difficulties. Guidelines that are highly general might not anticipate unusual but troubling eventualities; guidelines that are too detailed can be perceived as too bureaucratic and as a result are often ignored. In such instances, the existence of the guidelines creates a false sense of security. Trade association counsel may also send documents or information on antitrust to counsel of member firms. The member firms of trade associations in an industry such as steel, which contains several large, oligopolistic firms and which has had a history of disputes over antitrust are already sophisticated about antitrust and do not require much help from association counsel.[48]

Legal Constraints on Beneficial Collective Action? A subsidiary but persistent American concern about trade associations has been that they engage in *too little* collective action. Beginning about the time of World War I, some notables have argued that social problems could be more readily solved if cooperation between government and industry and within the private sector were to increase. Trade associations were often seen as the primary organizational vehicle for developing these cooperative relationships. This point of view was particularly strongly held by Herbert Hoover, who during his tenure as secretary of commerce promoted the formation of trade associations and sought to involve trade associations in close and frequent contact with federal government decision makers.[49] Among some New Deal Democrats (James F. Byrnes, Cordell Hull, and Roosevelt's first secretary of commerce Daniel Roper), the experience of the Wilson administration's War Industries Board—the first substantial episode of close cooperation between government and trade associations—provided an attractive precedent for government-industry cooperation in the face of another national emergency.[50] The National Recovery Act, which legally mandated industry associations to set prices and output, represented the high tide of formal government-industry cooperation; however, it was ruled unconstitutional in 1935.

In the current era, concerns about a lack of opportunity for beneficial collective action have manifested themselves in recent legislation providing for a less stringent antitrust environment for cooperative research and development projects, and for export trading companies. (These developments are addressed in chapters 6 and 7.) It should be remembered that these recent legislative initiatives overturn only a small portion of previous antitrust policy as applied to trade associations. A broader effort to develop a more "corporatist" working relationship among businesses, or between U.S. businesses and the federal government, still would face a large number of antitrust barriers, even if a new effort managed to avoid NRA's fate of being found unconstitutional.

The Antitrust Environment for Trade Associations

In both Japan and the United States many individuals and institutions have expressed concern about the costs to the economy and to consumers of joint action by trade associations. Others in both countries are convinced that opportunities are being missed to solve social problems and increase economic performance through the exchange of information and other joint actions by trade associations. Because antitrust forces have traditionally been much stronger in the United States than in Japan, American trade associations and businesses try to avoid any activity that might be interpreted as collusive. Even written opinions from government officials that certain activities are legal are not seen as providing adequate protection. And the relative ease and the size of potential rewards from private antitrust suits in the United States require businesses to act with far more circumspection here than in Japan.

Until the early 1970s, Japanese businesses felt free to act collectively as long as they had approval to do so from the Ministry of International Trade and Industry. The strength of antitrust constraints in Japan should not be underestimated, however. Directly after the war Americans strongly committed to preventing the abuses and inefficiencies of joint action were able to help design institutions in Japan to control cartels. As with many Occupation-introduced reforms some of these institutions took root, despite an early lack of understanding of their purpose by the Japanese. Japanese in government and business were far more concerned about "excess" than about restricted competition.[51]

Our account shows how many of the antitrust reforms were eliminated or scaled back after the end of the Occupation. We have seen that some of the reforms have never had as much strength in Japan as in the United States because of differences in legal practices (such as the common use of private antitrust suits in the United

States, but not Japan). Although these factors may have weakened the antitrust regime in Japan compared with its U.S. counterpart, the idea that the government should take action against practices in restraint of trade has gained widespread legitimacy. We see a general trend continuing in this direction.

There has also been some institutional diffusion in the opposite direction as many Americans concerned about Japan's economic success have concluded that the roots of this success lie in the ability of industry and government to work together. We describe in chapters 6 and 7 some of the efforts to curtail antitrust laws to allow more collaborative research or collaborative action in trade, following the Japanese model. In general, Japanese and American antitrust policies are now evolving in ways that tend to reduce the differences between the two nations, and there is little evidence that these trends will be reversed in the near future. There are grounds for optimism that any frictions in U.S.-Japanese relations created by differences in antitrust policy will gradually fade in importance.

Notes

1. Yoshio Kanazawa, "The Regulation of Corporate Enterprise: The Law of Unfair Competition and the Control of Monopoly Power," in Arthur Taylor von Mehren, ed., *Law in Japan: The Legal Order in a Changing Society* (Cambridge, Mass.: Harvard University Press, 1963), pp. 480–506.

2. Much of this account is drawn from Kanazawa, "Regulation of Corporate Enterprise." Kozo Yamamura also provides a useful description in *Economic Policy in Postwar Japan* (Berkeley: University of California Press, 1967) as well as a translation of the AML.

3. Dan Fenno Henderson, *Foreign Enterprise in Japan* (Chapel Hill, N.C.: University of North Carolina Press, 1973).

4. Chalmers Johnson, *MITI and the Japanese Miracle* (Stanford, Calif.: Stanford University Press, 1982), p. 275. Morozumi later was sent to the Japan Fair Trade Commission as a staff member. From 1971–1973 he was vice minister of MITI.

5. Kakuma Takashi, *Dokyumento Tsusansho. II: Kasumigaseki no Yuutsu* (Tokyo: PHP, 1979), pp. 10–11.

6. This law, which was based on recommendations made by the U.S. Temporary National Economic Committee in 1941, required all trade associations to file copies of their articles of association, information about any changes in their organization or dissolution, and other information with the JFTC. It restricted the activities allowed to trade associations. A major purpose of the law was to dissolve many of the trade associations that had survived World War II and the early postwar years. See Johnson, *MITI and the Japanese Miracle*, p. 222.

7. Yamamura, *Economic Policy*, pp. 29–30.

8. Chitoshi Yanaga, *Big Business in Japanese Politics*, (New Haven, Conn.: Yale University Press, 1968), cites Kobayashi, *Shakai Kagaku Kiyo*, no. 3, p. 39. See also JISF, *Sengo Tekko-shi*, p. 177.

9. Johnson, *MITI*, p. 225.

10. Yamamura, *Economic Policy*, p. 56.

11. Japan Fair Trade Commission, "Guidelines Concerning the Activities of Trade Associations under the Antimonopoly Law," *Law in Japan*, vol. 12 (1979), pp. 118–61. These amendments were patterned after a draft of the Law Against Restriction of Competition that was then pending and later adopted in West Germany. See Kanazawa, "The Regulation of Corporate Enterprise," p. 488.

12. Japan Economic Institute, "Current Antitrust Policy in Japan," *JEI Report* 12A (April 1, 1983).

13. Japan Fair Trade Commission, *Kosei Torihiki Iinkai Nenji Hohkoku—Showa 59-Nen Ban*, (Tokyo: JFTC, 1984), p. 154.

14. Merton J. Peck, Richard C. Levin, and Akira Goto, "Picking Losers: Public Policy toward Declining Industries in Japan," *The Journal of Japanese Studies*, vol. 13 (Winter 1987), pp. 79–123. See also Gary R. Saxonhouse, "Industrial Restructuring in Japan," *The Journal of Japanese Studies*, vol. 5 (Summer 1978), pp. 273–320.

15. Among the members of the council for the aluminum industry were the chairman and a vice-chairman of the Japan Aluminum Federation (both of whom were also senior managers of major firms in the industry and one of whom, Komatsu Yugoro, was a former vice-minister of MITI), and the chairman of Sumitomo Light Metals, the largest aluminum roller in Japan.

16. Richard J. Samuels, "The Industrial Destructuring of the Japanese Aluminum Industry," *Pacific Affairs*, vol. 56 (Fall 1983), pp. 495–509; Tsukawa Furukawa, "Japan's MITI to Restructure Aluminum Smelting, Fabrication," *American Metal Market*, December 14, 1984; and Industrial Bank of Japan, *Nihon Sangyo no Shin Tenkai* (Tokyo: Nihon Keizai Shinbun, 1982).

17. Ibid., Peck et al., p. 123.

18. Nippon Tekko Renmei, *Sengo Tekkoshi*, pp. 177–78.

19. Yanaga, *Big Business in Japanese Politics*, pp. 171–72.

20. Japan Fair Trade Commission, *Kosei Torihiki Iinkai Nenji Hohkoku—Showa 59-Nen Ban*, p. 157.

21. Johnson, *MITI*, pp. 132, 226.

22. Masanao Nakagawa, ed., *Antimonopoly Legislation of Japan* (Tokyo: Kosei Torihiki Kyokai, 1984), p. 325.

23. Its decisions can be appealed to the Tokyo High Court. Yoshio Kanazawa, "Regulation of Corporate Enterprise," p. 487.

24. U.S. International Trade Commission, *Foreign Industrial Targeting and its Effects on U.S. Industries, Phase I: Japan* (Washington, D.C.: International Trade Commission, 1983), p. 115.

25. Eleanor Hadley, *Antitrust in Japan* (Princeton, N.J.: Princeton University Press, 1970), p. 39.

26. Richard Caves and Masu Uekusa, *Industrial Organization in Japan* (Washington, D.C.: The Brookings Institution, 1976).

27. Kyoikusha, *Keizai Kikakucho/Kosei Torihiki Iinkai* (Tokyo: Kyoikusha, 1981), p. 217.

28. See Hadley, *Antitrust in Japan*, p. 397; Johnson, *MITI*, p. 72; and Kyoikusha, *Keizaikikakucho*, p. 134. Morozumi was the MCI bureaucrat who had difficulty translating the draft of the AML into proper legal Japanese.

29. Subsequent directors were all from the public sector, all but two from the Ministry of Finance.

30. See, for example, Iwao Hoshii, *The Dynamics of Japan's Business Evolution* (Tokyo: Orient/West Incorporated, 1966), p. 78.

31. Many of the chairmen of the JFTC have been Ministry of Finance bureaucrats. A staff member mentioned, however, that the JFTC is reluctant to cross the Ministry of Finance by prosecuting banks. Interview with author, December 1984.

32. Johnson, *MITI*, pp. 299–301. We will return to this case when we discuss "administrative guidance" in chapter 5.

33. Information from Japan Fair Trade Commission.

34. Japan Fair Trade Commission, *Kosei Torihiki Iinkai Nenji Hohkoku—Showa 59-Nen Ban*, pp. 236–37.

35. The following areas of law are covered in a standard legal handbook for trade association lawyers: contracting for hotel or exhibit space; employment contracts; incorporation; subsidiary corporations; foundations; political action committees; statistical reporting; codes of ethics; price information; antitrust; advertisements, standards, seals of approval; collective buying and selling; government requests for information; federal tax law; offshore captive insurance companies; postal regulations; federal advisory committees; group legal services; mergers of trade associations; legislative and regulatory activity. See George D. Webster, *The Law of Associations* (New York: Matthew Bender, 1983).

36. Ibid., sec. 17.32.2.

37. Another monograph in the T.N.E.C. series, #10, was concerned with the relation between economic concentration and the ability to attain tariff protection and thus anticipated latter-day concerns about rent-seeking behavior.

38. U.S. Congress, Temporary National Economic Committee, *Investigation of Concentration of Economic Power*, Monograph #18, 76th Congress, 3rd session (Washington: U.S. Government Printing Office, 1940).

39. Advisory Opinion Digest No. 1662, 73 FTC 1292, 16 C.F.R. section 15.162 (1968).

40. Basil J. Mezines, *Trade Associations and the Antitrust Laws* (Washington, D.C.: Bureau of National Affairs, 1983), p. A-8.

41. Advisory Opinion Digest No. 306, 74 FTC 1679, 16 C.F.R. section 15.306 (1968).

42. Richard A. Posner, *Antitrust Law: An Economic Perspective* (Chicago: University of Chicago Press, 1976), pp. 144–45.

43. Mezines, *Trade Associations*, p. A-11.

44. Ibid., p. A-17.

45. Advisory Opinion Digest No. 152, 72 FTC 1053, 16 C.F.R., section 15.152 (1967), cited in Mezines, *Trade Associations*, p. A-18.

46. Thomas Pepper, Merit E. Janow, and Jimmy W. Wheeler, *The Competition: Dealing with Japan* (New York: Praeger, 1985), pp. 198–99; U.S. Department of Commerce, "JIS Drafting Committees Open to Foreign Participation," *TBT News: Technical Barriers to Trade* (September 1985), p. 1.

47. Mezines, *Trade Associations*, p. A-12.

48. Interview with Barton Green, American Iron and Steel Institute, January 17, 1985, Washington, D.C.

49. Ellis W. Hawley, *The New Deal and the Problem of Monopoly* (Princeton, N.J.: Princeton University Press, 1966); Ellis W. Hawley, "Herbert Hoover, the Commerce Secretariat, and the Vision of an Associative State, 1921–1925," *Journal of American History*, vol. 61 (June 1974), pp. 116–40.

50. Kim McQuaid, "The Business Advisory Council of the Department of Commerce, 1933–1961: A Study in Corporate–Government Relations," in Paul Uselding, ed., *Research in Economic History*, vol. I, (Greenwich, Conn.: JAI, 1976), pp. 171–97.

51. Recall our description of government promotion of cartels in the prewar iron and steel industry.

4
The Aggregation of Interests in American and Japanese Industry

In this chapter we briefly describe what trade associations are, how they are governed and financed, and what they do. We then provide a more specific description of associations in the steel and machine tool industries. Finally, we discuss peak associations representing business as a whole.

The goals, organization, and activities of U.S. and Japanese trade associations are broadly similar. There are vast differences, however, in the composition and specific missions of associations representing the same industries and in the relationships between these associations. In Japan, associations tend to be organized into hierarchies offering various levels at which interests can be aggregated and effectively promoted. There are also semigovernmental quasi-trade associations that allow the government to encourage certain activities.

Where possible we have attempted to present balanced information from the two countries. We do, however, present more general information on U.S. trade associations because of the availability of wide-ranging data from several surveys made by the National Association of Manufacturers.[1] Conversely, we give more detail on specific Japanese trade associations because this information is more easily available in Japan than in the United States. In describing the industries in the two countries, we give more detail on Japan, simply because U.S. readers are likely to know less about Japanese industries. Finally, we spend considerable space discussing quasi-trade associations in Japan and the links between associations in that country, because these appear to be more important than in the United States.

Trade Association Governance, Finance, and Activities

Trade associations in both the United States and Japan are generally nonprofit organizations (though some in the United States may possess profit-making subsidiaries). They commonly have a constitution,

which sets forth in highly general terms the purposes of the association, defines membership or classes of members, and authorizes
governance by a governing board and a set of officers. The bylaws are
generally unremarkable specifications of membership classes, officers, their duties, and their selection process, annual meetings,
standing committees, and the like. The most remarkable aspect of
trade association constitutions and bylaws, particularly in the United
States, is that some associations regard them as confidential. Probably
the only significant change in these documents over the past few
decades has been the disappearance of any language that could be
construed as meaning that the purposes or the activities of the association are anticompetitive. This, as we have seen in chapter 3, is of far
less concern in Japan.

The fact that U.S. firms can often leave their association at relatively low cost if the association takes policy positions with which
they disagree no doubt limits the extent to which associations take
policy positions. Even so, association positions have not always been
the product of consensus. In the U.S. steel industry, for example, the
president of Wheeling-Pittsburgh Steel testified before Congress in
opposition to the publicly stated position on industrial policy of the
American Iron and Steel Institute, of which his firm was a member.[2]
In the machine tool industry, an observer estimated that 15 percent of
the association's membership (many of whom have Japanese or other
foreign owners) disagreed with the NMTBA's decision to petition for
import relief; one of the leading producers in the industry, Ingersoll
Milling Machine Co., resigned from the NMTBA because of its disagreement with NMTBA trade policy.[3] Such public disagreements are
uncommon in Japan, but they do occur. In a celebrated incident in
1965, Sumitomo Metals defied the efforts of the Japan Iron and Steel
Federation and the Ministry of International Trade and Industry to
limit capacity expansions.[4]

Governance of associations in both the United States and Japan is
generally in the hands of a board of directors, who in turn hire an
executive director. The executive director supervises the paid staff; in
addition, much day-to-day work by associations is performed by
committees composed of industry executives who are not paid association staff. Association staff provide administrative support for these
committees. In the United States, smaller associations, or those in
industries that desire only limited common activity, may contract out
the actual work of the association to a firm that specializes in managing associations. (The U.S. specialty steel industry contracts out to a
law firm for its association work; the Electric Bar Mill Association
contracts to a firm that manages associations). Although we did not

perform a systematic quantitative study of association staff size or budgets for all U.S. associations, our impression, from scanning association directories and information supplied by the NAM for manufacturing associations and by the associations in the two industries we contacted, is that the staff of most U.S. trade associations is relatively small. The American Iron and Steel Institute, the association of most of the steel producers in the United States, as well as some from Canada and South America, has a staff of about sixty-five; the National Machine Tool Builders Association has a staff of about sixty. These staffs are quite large by American standards. Much more typical is an association with 5–10 staff members. The Japan Iron and Steel Federation has a much larger staff than the AISI, about 170 employees, but the Japan Machine Tool Builders Association staff numbers only twelve, and many associations listed in Japanese directories have fewer than five employees.[5]

Associations in the United States typically derive most of their income from members' dues.[6] For the smallest manufacturing associations—those with annual budgets of less than $250,000—dues constitute over 80 percent of total income, while for no size category of association does dues income constitute less than 40 percent of total income.[7] When economic conditions deteriorate, member firms under financial pressure often reduce or drop their commitment to trade associations, which has an obvious effect on association incomes and activities. Many of the American associations on which we obtained information reported declines in dues payments and memberships in the 1981–1983 period; published reports in the business press suggest that this observation is probably valid for more than just the sample we contacted.[8] Surveys of manufacturing trade associations conducted by the National Association of Manufacturers in 1982 and 1985 provide more systematic evidence on the effects of economic conditions on association finances. In the 1982 survey 32 percent of the associations reported declines in staff during that year; for 27 percent of the associations, the decline was 10 percent or greater. Only 28 percent of the responding associations reported any increase in staff size, and only 15 percent reported an increase of 10 percent or more.[9] The 1985 survey showed only 10 percent of the associations reporting any decline in staff, and 32 percent reporting increases; for 18 percent the increases were 10 percent or greater.[10]

There are notable interindustry variations in the financial performance of manufacturing associations. The 1982 NAM survey found that associations in the following SIC (Standard Industrial Classification) groups had experienced greater than average declines in income: lumber and wood products (SIC 24); furniture and fixtures (SIC 25);

paper and allied products (SIC 26); chemicals and allied products (SIC 28); machinery, except electrical (SIC 35); and transportation equipment (SIC 37).[11] In the 1985 survey, the six weakest performers were lumber and wood products; paper and allied products; stone, clay, glass, and concrete products (SIC 32); rubber and miscellaneous plastic products (SIC 30); chemicals and allied products; and miscellaneous manufacturing industries (SIC 39).[12] The industry associations that reported above-average growth in 1982 were in food and kindred products (SIC 20); textile mill products (SIC 22); apparel (SIC 23); printing and publishing (SIC 27); stone, clay, and glass products; fabricated metal products, except machinery (SIC 34); miscellaneous manufacturing industries; and electric, gas, and sanitary services (SIC 49).[13] The associations reporting above-average growth in 1985 were in food and kindred products; electrical and electronic machinery (SIC 36); petroleum refining and related industries (SIC 29); machinery, except electrical; wholesale trade–durable goods (SIC 50); and apparel.[14]

In addition to dues, U.S. associations rely extensively on their income from trade shows and exhibitions. About 31 percent of U.S. manufacturing trade associations held shows in 1980; by 1985, this proportion had increased to about 44 percent.[15] Other common sources of income are membership meetings, sales of publications, technical and consulting services, and revenue from seminars and training sessions. In a few instances an association may receive funds or in-kind assistance from another association with which it is working. In Japan, unlike in America, governmental organizations often subsidize certain trade association activities.

Thanks to the NAM surveys, some quantitative information is available regarding the range of activities performed by manufacturing associations in the United States in the period 1980–1985. Although comparable survey information is not available for Japan, similar activities are mentioned in the histories and other materials for trade associations in the Japanese steel and machine tool industries.[16]

Table 4–1 reports on the activities of associations of various size. There is not a great deal of variation in activities across budget size, and the small number of cases of each type makes statistical analysis problematic in any event. A more revealing analysis is presented in table 4–2, which displays changes in the percentage of the survey respondents engaging in the reported activities over the period 1980–1985.

Over the five-year period, the most dramatic declines are recorded in consumer programs (down 47 percent) and in research and development (down 28 percent). There is substantial evidence that

TABLE 4–1

U.S. Manufacturing Association Activities by Association Budget Size, 1985

Budget ($ million)	Number of Associations	Activity					
		Standard Setting	Data Collection	Educational Services	Public Relations	Health and Safety	Advertising and Marketing
0–.25	7	4	4	5	4	2	1
.25–.5	9	5	8	5	5	4	1
.5–1.0	9	4	7	7	5	5	3
1.–2.0	9	3	8	8	7	6	5
2.–5.0	11	7	10	11	10	5	6
5.0+	9	4	9	8	6	6	4
Unknown	12	4	11	9	10	5	7
Total	66	31	57	53	47	33	27
% of Total		47	87	80	71	50	41

Source: National Association of Manufacturers, *Manufacturing Trade Associations*, 1985, p. 77.

TABLE 4–2
U.S. Manufacturing Association Activities, 1980–1985

Activity	Percentage Performing Activity		
	1980	1982	1985
Standard setting	59	42	47
Data collection	91	87	86
Educational services	77	77	80
Public relations	86	69	71
Product and process testing	20	17	20
Certification of personnel or practices	13	15	20
Insurance	23	31	24
Consumer programs	61	12	14
Advertising and marketing	33	52	41
Research and development	69	60	41
Safety	46	60	50

Source: National Association of Manufacturers, *Manufacturing Trade Associations*, 1985, p. 35.

resources that formerly would have been devoted to these activities are now being used for government relations functions. This development is discussed in more detail in chapter 5.

Trade Associations in the U.S. and Japanese Iron and Steel Industries

Both the U.S. and Japanese steel industries include integrated steelmakers, ferrous scrap-based electric steelmakers, and specialty steelmakers. Despite this broad similarity, there are important differences in the structures of the two industries.

The leading firm is far more dominant in the Japanese than in the contemporary U.S. steel industry. Nippon Steel by itself accounts for about 30 percent of Japan's steel production and has no serious competitor for leadership in the industry. Three smaller firms, Nippon Kokan, Kawasaki, and Sumitomo Metals, fight it out for second place in the industry, each accounting for about 12 percent of production. The last of the major five integrated steelmakers is Kobe Steel, which produces about 7 percent of Japan's steel. There are three smaller integrated steelmakers, Nisshin, Godo, and Nakayama. Nisshin and Godo are both members of the Nippon Steel group (Nippon Steel is the largest shareholder, and the top management of these firms comes from Nippon Steel). Nakayama also has recently established ties with Nippon Steel. Between them, these smaller integrated firms are responsible for about 5 percent of Japan's steel production. Nippon Steel and its affiliates then account for more than 35 percent of Japanese steel production.[17] In contrast, U.S. Steel in 1983 accounted for only 17 percent of U.S. steel production.[18] The five major integrated Japanese steelmakers produce approximately 80 percent of Japan's ordinary steel. In 1983 the top seven U.S. integrated steel firms accounted for about 66 percent of raw steel produced.[19]

In Japan the integrated steelmakers, particularly Nippon Steel, also dominate the other two sectors of the industry. The five major integrated Japanese steelmakers produce more than 60 percent of Japan's specialty steel. Moreover, Nippon Steel affiliates are the two largest of the firms that are exclusively specialty steel producers.[20] The third largest Japanese specialty steel firm, Aichi (4.6 percent market share in 1978) is a Toyota affiliate, but also has strong ties to Nippon Steel. Nippon Kokan, Sumitomo Metals, and Kobe Steel also have affiliates in this sector.

The integrated Japanese steelmakers, most notably Nippon Steel, also control many of Japan's scrap-based firms, the mini-mills. There are nearly sixty firms in this segment of the industry in Japan. The largest two, Tokyo Steel and Toshin Steel, can produce as much steel as the smaller U.S. integrated producers, up to 3 million tons per year in the case of Tokyo Steel. Tokyo Steel is an independent firm, but Toshin Steel is an affiliate of Nippon Kokan. In all, around a dozen of the mini-mills are affiliates of Nippon Steel, three or four are associated with Nippon Kokan, and an additional three or four with Sumitomo Metals. Although American integrated firms have some presence in specialty steels, they have historically not been involved in the mini-mill sector. Indeed, the mini-mill sector of the U.S. industry experienced substantial foreign participation well before several Japanese firms became involved with the large, integrated producers: at least thirteen of thirty-six mini-mill firms in the United States are or have been partly or completely foreign-owned.[21]

Another major difference between the two steel industries is that the Japanese industry has for a generation relied heavily on exports. In mid-1985 some 35–40 percent of the sales of the major integrated Japanese steelmakers was accounted for by exports. The U.S. industry, of course, has seldom exported significant tonnages of steel in recent years.

The American Iron and Steel Institute and the Japan Iron and Steel Federation. The American Iron and Steel Institute (AISI) and the

Japan Iron and Steel Federation (JISF) are the major trade associations representing their industries. Unlike most of the numerous other trade and business associations in their industries, they are loosely comparable in their activities, and each has a membership that claims to produce 90 percent or more of the steel in its country.

The American Iron and Steel Institute is the largest and the oldest association in the U.S. steel industry, its ancestry extending to the mid-nineteenth century. Its sixty-three member companies include firms in Canada, Latin America, and the United States and specialty steel and mini-mill firms, but it historically has served as the flagship association of the large U.S. integrated carbon steel producers.[22]

The titles of current AISI divisions give a good general picture of the association's breadth of interests: manufacturing and research; government relations; international trade and economics; communications and administrative services; industrial relations; environment and energy; and product application research and construction engineering. The association operates standing or special committees on subjects of industry concern: accounting, taxation, and statistics; critical materials supply; energy; engineering; environment; general research; government relations; industrial relations; international trade; manufacturing; promoting the use of steel; public relations; and traffic. In addition, its committees deal with a variety of technical issues (such as blast furnace practice and tube manufacturing); product promotion (for steel plate producers for example); and product technical methods (for pipes, steel bars). It has a paid staff of about sixty-five, down from nearly 100 in the early 1980s.

The major association representing Japanese producers of iron and steel is the Japan Iron and Steel Federation (JISF). As was noted earlier, JISF was established in 1948 with roots in various prewar and wartime bodies. It now includes some fifty members, forty-eight steel producers and two smaller associations of steel producers. Given its dominance over the Japanese steel industry, Nippon Steel has considerable power in the JISF. At least eighteen of the corporate members of the JISF are in the Nippon Steel Group (see table 4–3).[23]

The JISF is governed by a general assembly of its members, which meets twice a year to elect officers, make changes in the constitution, and decide on the budget. Although the directors elect as the chairman one of their own, they have always chosen the chairman of the board of Nippon Steel. A board of directors meets every two months to hear reports made by its policy board. The policy board is assisted in its deliberations by the executive council, a body composed of executives of the companies to which members of the policy board belong. Under this top management structure are some twenty-five standing committees and four "conferences." The standing committees specialize in such diverse activities as public relations, raw materials policy, transportation, iron and steel statistics, industrial engineering, and international policies for the industry. The four conferences focus on pig iron (with representatives from the eight integrated iron and steelmakers); ordinary steel (which has subcommittees representing, respectively, the eight integrated steel producers, the sixteen electric furnace steel producers, and the four specialized rolling mills); specialty steel (with representatives from twenty-two independent specialty and alloy steel producers); and industrial relations (with general managers in charge of industrial relations at forty-seven companies).[24]

JISF represents its members to the government, to other industries, and to the public and handles some of the Japanese steel industry's relations with other countries. The federation also has several information collection functions: collecting and disseminating statistics on production and sales; studying the supply and demand for steel; and making surveys and other studies related to equipment, raw materials, labor, and technology. Its annual budget is around 2½ billion yen (nearly $16 million at the exchange rate current in 1986) and it has a staff of about 170 (more than double the size of the staff of AISI). Some of JISF's activities in foreign trade and research are described in chapters 6 and 7.

Other National Associations in the U.S. Steel Industry. A directory of associations lists forty-six organizations, which we classify as trade associations, in its summary of organizations in the U.S. iron and steel industry. Table 4–4 shows the distribution of staff and budget sizes for these organizations. In analyzing the budget data, it is important to keep in mind that trade associations may administer activities that are off-budget but that are nonetheless costly and collective. They may create special product or activity groups that conduct their own self-supporting activities. We have made no attempt to estimate the magnitude of these expenditures.

Most of the associations included in table 4–4 are in industries that are steel users (various fabricators, the construction industry) or intermediate purchasers (steel importers, steel service centers). Producers of raw iron and steel make up only three associations.[25]

The Specialty Steel Industry of the United States, an association organized in 1962, represents about twenty companies in the industry. The association's activities are performed by a Washington law firm, which provides administrative and statistical services to the

TABLE 4-3
CORPORATE LINKS BETWEEN COMPANY MEMBERS OF THE JAPAN IRON AND STEEL FEDERATION, 1984

Firms Associated with Nippon Steel
(percent equity owned)

Aichi Steel Works (10.8)	Nippon Kinzoku Co. (13.8)
Chubu Steel Plate Co.[a]	Nippon Steel Corporation
Daido Steel Co. (12.5)	Nisshin Steel Co. (11.3)
Daido Steel Sheet (49.0)[b]	Osaka Steel Co. (43.7)[e]
Godo Steel (7.5)	Pacific Metals Co. (13.6)[b]
Japan Metals & Chemicals Co. (8.2)	Sanyo Special Steel Co. (18.6)
Kokko Steel Works[c]	Taiyo Steel Co. (34.7)[e]
Nakayama Steel[d]	Tokai Steel Works (10.0)
Nippon Denko Co. (7.3)	Topy Industries (10.8)

Firms Associated with Nippon Kokan
(percent equity owned)

Azuma Steel Co. (41.4)	Nippon Kokan
Nippon Chuzo (32.3)[b]	Toshin Steel (42.0)
Nippon Metal Ind. (4.3)	Toyo Kohan (5.6)

Firms Associated with Sumitomo Metals
(percent equity owned)

Chuo Denki Kogyo (20.0)[b]	Nippon Yakin Kogyo[f]
Kanto Special Steel Works (33.6)[b]	Sumitomo Electric[g]
Nippon Stainless Steel (37.5)[b]	Sumitomo Metal Industries

Firms Associated with Kobe Steel
(percent equity owned)

Kobe Steel	Nippon Koshuha Steel (50.0)

Other Member Firms and Associations[h]
(percent equity owned by other steelmaker)

Funabashi Steel Works	Seibu Chemical Ind.
Hitachi Metals	Tohoku Steel
Japan Steel Works	Tokyo Steel Mfg.
Kansai Steel Corp.	Yahagi Iron Co. (Daido 1.6)
Kawasaki Steel	Yasuda Kogyo
Kubota, Ltd.	Yodogawa Steel Works (NSC 2.0)
Kyoei Steel	Zenkoku Shintetsu Kogyo Kumiai
Mitsubishi Steel (NSC 1.6)	Steel Castings and Forgings Assn.
Fujikoshi	
Nakayama Steel Products	

a. Associated with Nippon Steel.
b. Other affiliated firms hold additional equity.
c. Closely related to Nippon Steel.

(Notes continue)

64

association, including the services of two in-house economists. Its recent efforts have focused on influencing U.S. trade policy, although it is also concerned with environmental laws and regulations and the supply of critical materials.[26] The budget of this association has increased substantially since the early 1980s.

The Steel Bar Mills Association, founded in 1911, serves small electric furnace operators (mini-mills) and steel rollers. More than twenty companies fund a modest staff (1–2 full-time-equivalent positions) and budget ($50,000–100,000). Until very recently this association's activities had been limited to a modest statistical collection service and conferences for the sharing of technical information; in early 1986 the group considered for the first time the filing of unfair trade practice charges. It has begun activity on issues related to hazardous waste disposal and is considering other expansions of its activities. No integrated steelmakers currently belong to this association.[27]

Other National Associations in the Japanese Steel Industry. Aside from JISF, numerous associations represent producers of special types of steel or steel products, for example, the Galvanized Sheet Association, the Can Manufacturers Institute, and the Japan Reinforcing Bar Industry Association. Many of these associations have staffs of only one or two and a budget below $100,000, but a few do have budgets of over half a million dollars (the Japan Steel-Rib Fabricators Association, the Steel Castings and Forgings Association of Japan, the Japan Stainless Steel Association).

Japan has powerful associations for firms involved in the sale and distribution of steel, both in Japan and overseas. The largest is the Kozai Club, which includes some 119 members, thirty-two steelmakers, and eighty-seven steel distributors. As is the case with JISF, the Kozai Club is strongly influenced by Nippon Steel. Nearly half of the steelmakers among its membership are associated with Nippon Steel, as are some of the distributors. In addition to providing a forum

---

d. Has received management assistance from Nippon Steel and Sanwa Bank.
e. Not on first section of stock market. Percentage of equity is taken from Okamoto Hirokimi, *Gendai Tekko Kigyo no Ruikei Bunseki* (Kyoto: Minerva Shobo, 1984), pp. 314–15, 1980 data.
f. Related to Sumitomo Metals.
g. Fellow member of Sumitomo group.
h. Many of the firms in the "Other Members" category are not listed on the Tokyo Stock Exchange, so we do not have information on their ownership.
SOURCE: Toyo Keizai Shinposha, *Japan Company Handbook*, 1st Half 1984.

TABLE 4–4
U.S. Iron and Steel Trade Associations:
Staff and Budget Sizes, 1984

Staff Size	Number of Associations	Budget (thousands of dollars)	Number of Associations
61–70	1	2,000–5,000	1
51–60	1	1,000–2,000	4
41–50	0	500–1,000	5
31–40	0	250–500	12
21–30	1	100–250	11
16–20	1	50–100	5
11–15	3	25–50	2
6–10	5	10–25	2
2–5	28	Less than 10	2
1	5	Unknown	2
0	1		

NOTE: The list excludes labor unions and engineering societies or other groups that enroll individuals rather than firms.
SOURCE: Craig Colgate, Jr., ed., *National Trade and Professional Associations of the United States and Canada & Labor Unions*, 20th edition (Washington, D.C.: Columbia Books, 1985).

for the exchange of views of these member firms, the Kozai Club compiles statistics on steel products, engages in survey research, and makes recommendations in response to inquiries from the government. To carry out these activities the Kozai Club has an annual budget of around 1.4 billion yen (a little less than $9 million at 1986 exchange rates) and a staff of 115.

The Kozai Club is governed by a chairman (the chairman of the board at Nippon Steel) and five deputy chairmen. In 1982 the deputy chairmen were from Nippon Steel, Sumitomo Metals, Kawasaki Steel, Mitsubishi Trading, and C. Itoh Trading. Other members of the top management came from the other major integrated steelmakers and the major trading firms. The club is governed by a general assembly and a board of directors, under which are fifteen standing committees.[28]

Additional associations of firms concerned with the sale of steel products include the Japan Iron and Steel Wholesalers Association and the League of Iron Steel Products Association (which itself includes some twenty-one associations concerned with iron and steel products).

Japanese steel exporters belong to the Japan Iron and Steel Exporters Association (JISEA), a type of organization provided for under Japanese law.[29] This organization has always been closely linked to the Kozai Club and in some sense can be thought of as the foreign affairs division of the Kozai Club. JISEA and the Kozai Club share the same executive director, the same chairman, and the same office building, although their memberships are different. The major stated mission of the JISEA is to prevent unfair practices in the steel export trade, to conduct surveys on the status of exports, and to help develop export markets through public relations activities. JISEA has overseas offices in Paris, Washington, New York, and Los Angeles. In recent years the budget of the JISEA has been a little under 1 billion yen—a little more than $6 million at 1986 exchange rates. Other export associations in the steel industry represent the producers of galvanized sheet, wire products, and electric wire and cable.

Other associations in the Japanese steel industry are primarily concerned with securing raw materials. The eight integrated steelmakers belong to the Committee for Overseas Iron and Steel Raw Materials; sixty-five firms belong to the National Scrap Conference, and 100 firms belong to the Japan Steel Scrap Reserves Association. The Association for the Promotion of the Recovery and Use of Iron Resources, which was founded in 1975, is affiliated with the Japan Iron and Steel Federation and has more than 100 members. Still other associations are concerned with the byproducts of steel production, for example, the Nippon Slag Association and the Steel Industry Foundation for the Advancement of Environmental Protection Technology.

Professional associations provide yet another forum for contact between the members of the various steel companies. Foremost among these is the Iron and Steel Institute of Japan (ISIJ). Founded in 1916, this organization has nearly 10,000 individual members and a budget of nearly 1 billion yen. ISIJ publishes technical journals and sponsors technical conferences and lectures.

One major difference between trade associations in Japan and the United States is that the links between organizations are generally denser in Japan. Japanese associations frequently become members of other associations and sometimes engage in formally organized joint activities. One of the standing committees of the JISF, the Research Committee on Overseas Markets, works with the Kozai Club to collect basic data and information on the worldwide distribution of steel.

This information is used to plan the industry's international trade policy.[30] Although these arrangements are also found in the United States our data suggest they are less common.

Japanese associations are also linked geographically, often occupying offices in the same building. The Tekko Kaikan, or Iron and Steel Building, houses all the steel industry export associations as well as such sales-oriented associations as the Kozai Club, the Japan Iron and Steel Wholesalers Association, the League of Iron and Steel Products Associations, the Galvanized Sheet Association, the Japan Reinforcing Bar Association, and the Specialty Steel Association of Japan. It is also home to the Japan Project Industry Council.[31] Two of the peak associations in the steel industry, the Japan Iron and Steel Federation and the Iron and Steel Institute of Japan, are located near each other in the Keidanren Building. The chairman of Keidanren until 1986, Inayama Yoshihiro, is a former chairman of the Japan Iron and Steel Federation, the Kozai Club, and Nippon Steel.

A third link is provided by Nippon Steel, the major producer in the industry. Senior executives of this firm are chairmen of most of the national trade associations in the Japanese iron and steel industry. Nippon Steel's chairman of the board is chairman of the Japan Iron and Steel Federation, the Kozai Club, the Japan Iron and Steel Exporters Association, and the Japan Project Industry Council. Nippon Steel's president is chairman of the Japan Stainless Steel Exporters Association and the Cooperative Association for Iron and Steel Exports to the United States. Various vice-presidents are chairmen of the Iron and Steel Institute of Japan, the Galvanized Sheet Association, the Japan Galvanized Iron Sheet Exporters Association, and the Nippon Slag Association. Senior advisers oversee the Committee for Overseas Iron and Steel Raw Materials and the Japan Steel Scrap Reserves Association.

In a few instances, top managers from other steel firms hold the top position in a national trade association, generally in specialized sectors of the industry. The chairman of the Specialty Steel Association of Japan in 1984, for example, was Takeda Kizo, chairman of Daido Steel—but Daido is a Nippon Steel affiliate and Takeda is a former senior managing director at Nippon Steel.

In addition to chairmen and interlocking boards of advisers, the trade associations occasionally share staff members. Hasegawa Kiyoshi, the executive director of Kozai Club, is also executive director of the Japan Iron and Steel Exporters Association and a director of the Japan Project Industry Council. He began his career with the Ministry of Finance. During the war years he was involved in the apparatus to ration the distribution of iron and steel, and at the end of the war he was with the Iron and Steel Control Council. In 1947 he started working for the Kozai Club.

Hasegawa is not the only person to be simultaneously executive director of more than one trade association. Kurosawa Hiroyasu is executive director of the Association for the Promotion of the Recovery and Use of Iron Resources, the Japan Steel Scrap Reserves Association, and the Electric Furnace Structure Improvement Association. Yabe Shigeo is executive director of the Japan Galvanized Iron Sheet Exporters Association and the Galvanized Sheet Association, as well as chairman of the League of Iron and Steel Producers Associations. Horie Ken'ichi is executive director of the League of Iron and Steel Producers Associations and general affairs manager of the Japan Galvanized Iron Sheet Exporters Association.

It should be noted as well that many of the associations come under the jurisdiction of the same departments of the government. MITI's Basic Industries Bureau officially oversees the Japan Iron and Steel Federation, the Kozai Club, the Committee for Overseas Iron and Steel Raw Materials, the Japanese Scrap Industry Association, the Association for the Recovery and Use of Iron Resources, the Can Manufacturers Institute of Japan, the Japan Cold Finished Steel Bar Industry Trade Association, and the Special Steel Association of Japan. The export associations all fall under the jurisdiction of MITI's International Trade Administration Bureau.

Trade Associations in the
U.S. and Japanese Machine Tool Industries

The U.S. machine tool industry has long occupied a position of technological strength as is shown by its ability to export a substantial share of its output. But its strength has been eclipsed during the 1980s by the rapid rise of the Japanese machine tool industry, which since 1982 has been the world's largest. Only two years earlier Japan ranked behind West Germany, the United States, and the USSR. In 1983 around one-fourth of its sales were exports, with the United States taking well over one-third. The technological strength of the Japanese industry is shown by the fact that more than 60 percent of the Japanese machine tools sold in 1983 were numerically controlled.[32] As we noted in chapter 2, only a generation ago the Japanese machine tool producers tended to be small firms only able to produce non-competitive low-technology products.

Many small, less technology-intensive firms remain in Japan. While approximately 1,900 establishments produce metal fabricating machine tools in Japan, only about 180 have more than fifty employees. Much of the recent growth of the industry has been accounted for by the larger firms. The market share of the five largest firms rose from 22.7 percent in 1977 to 29.3 percent in 1980; that of the ten largest firms went from 43.9 percent to 47.7 percent. Some of the larger firms in this industry are diversified giants such as Mitsubishi Heavy Industries and Citizen Watch, but most of the industry leaders are smaller, more specialized firms. Okuma Machinery, for example, leads Japan in machine tool sales, but has only about 1,700 employees. Another major firm, Mori Seiki, has just over 1,000 employees. Most of the firms are concentrated in areas where they have many customers: near the auto producers (primarily located in Aichi, Shizuoka, and Hiroshima prefectures) or in the Tokyo area. There are also producers, however, in the Hokuriku district (on the western side of central Japan), an area with a long tradition in the machinery industry.

The Central Associations in the U.S. and Japanese Machine Tool Industries. The two largest associations in the U.S. machine tool sector are the National Machine Tool Builders Association (NMTBA), which represents machine tool producers in the United States, and the National Tooling & Machining Association (NTMA), which represents the contract special tooling and precision machining industry. Both associations were formerly located in Cleveland, an important manufacturing center for the machine tool industry, but moved to Washington, D.C., in the 1960s. The NMTBA, founded in 1902, represents about 400 firms and claims to account for about 90 percent of U.S. machine tool output.[33] It is governed by a fourteen-person board of directors elected to staggered three-year terms and operates twenty-six committees.[34] In addition, the association operates product groups for seventeen products, and has its own political action committee.

The National Tooling and Machining Association was founded in 1943. Its approximately 3,700 member firms (average size: 22 employees) support a staff of about sixty, of which thirteen are based in regional offices. The rest are housed in suburban Washington, D.C. The association offers business management assistance; training centers and training aids for workers; assistance to the sixty local chapters of the organization; various promotional items, such as certificates, cards, bumper stickers; publications detailing industry news and legislative developments; national meetings and seminars; assistance in marketing; group insurance/safety programs. Five NTMA employees are involved in administering a federally funded CETA apprenticeship training program. NTMA also operates its own political action committee. Its promotional literature emphasizes the importance of collective action in the political arena.

Two major national associations serve a constituency in Japan that is roughly analogous to that of the National Machine Tool Builders Association in the United States. The more prominent and important of these associations is the 112-member Japan Machine Tool Builders Association (JMTBA) Most, but not all, of the major machine tool producers belong to JMTBA.[35] With an annual budget of not quite half a billion yen (around $3 million at 1986 exchange rates) and a staff of twelve, it is far smaller than the NMTBA. As we shall see, however, JMTBA seems to be well linked with other organizations that give it the ability to do more than these numbers would indicate.

There is no dominant firm comparable to Nippon Steel in the machine tool industry, and so the position of chairman of the JMTBA has been held for two-year terms by the chief executives of several of the major firms as well as of some that are relatively small. The chairman in 1984 was Degawa Kinroku, president of Hitachi Seiki (a leading producer of machine tools). Under the chairman are four vice-chairmen, an administrative managing director, and a board of directors *(rijikai)* made up of twenty-six directors and three auditors. The directors and auditors are senior executives from some of the member firms—though not all of them.

The JMTBA pursues a wide range of activities through committees *(iinkai)* for technology, trade, markets, economic surveys, and finance/taxation. There is also a special committee for the Japan International Machine Tool Trade Exhibition. Each of these committees also includes subcommittees.[36]

One of JMTBA's major continuing concerns has been industrial standards. The organization has taken part in framing export inspection standards, Japan Industrial Standards (JIS), JMTBA standards, and parts standards, as well as the translation of JIS standards into English. JMTBA also publishes the *Technology Data Handbook* and monitors standards proposed to the International Standards Organization (ISO). As part of its public relations activities, JMTBA has arranged for lectures to be given all over Japan. It has also jointly sponsored conferences on machine tool–related technologies with other organizations such as the Japan Productivity Center. JMTBA has also cooperated with groups representing industries that use machine tools. In 1962 JMTBA and eight other associations organized the Machine Tool and Related Products Committee (Kosaku Kikai Kanren Dantai Kyogikai).

The JMTBA has undertaken several activities to raise the level of

71

machine tool technology in Japan. (These activities are described in detail in chapter 7.) In at least one area the purview of its activities is broader than that of such organizations as the Japan Iron and Steel Federation: it incorporates trade functions that would be carried out on behalf of the steel industry by the Japan Iron and Steel Exporters Association. (These activities are described in detail in chapter 6.) The JMTBA gained considerable attention in the United States in 1982 when in a petition to the president of the United States, Houdaille Industries charged that it was part of a cartel used by the Japanese government to reorganize the Japanese machine tool industry.[37] Houdaille points out that after the Machine Tool Law was enacted in 1956, MITI issued its Basic Rationalization Plan for the metal cutting machine tool manufacturing industry (MITI Notification no. 112). The plan called for firms to be more specialized in the manufacturing of products and to collaborate more on research. In what Houdaille says was "most probably" a response to these guidelines, the JMTBA set up a Manufacturing Shares Deliberation Committee in 1957, which led to the Agreement Regarding Concentrated Manufacturing in 1960. Subsequent agreements kept firms from entering certain markets through the 1960s, 1970s, and 1980s. Despite this apparently close relationship between MITI and the JMTBA, Ezra Vogel notes that until the 1970s the JMTBA's smaller members successfully resisted pressure to have the JMTBA take former MITI bureaucrats as staff members.[38]

The other major association representing machine tool builders in Japan is the Japan Metal Forming Machine Builders Association (JMFMBA). As was mentioned above, this association was formed in 1947 to represent firms producing mechanical and hydraulic presses. JMFMBA has relatively limited resources with a staff of only four and an annual budget of not quite 90 million yen (around $370,000). Most of the association's 115 members are relatively small firms that specialize in the production of presses, but a few are major firms from the shipbuilding or steel industries, such as Hitachi Zosen, IHI, Kobe Steel, and Nippon Kokan. Given that the NMTBA in the United States is somewhat equivalent to a combination of the JMTBA and JMFMBA, it is interesting to note that there is not much overlapping of membership between the JMFMBA and JMTBA. Only about half a dozen firms belong to both organizations.

JMFMBA offers managerial guidance to its members and organizes cooperative research between the producers and users of metal-forming equipment. It also helps arrange trade fairs and otherwise carries out overseas public relations activities. Like many other Japanese trade associations it gathers information on foreign markets and competitors for its members.

Other Associations in the U.S. and Japanese Machine Tool Industries. Other associations represent the machine tool industries in both the United States and Japan. Indeed, it is interesting to note that in the United States although the machine tool industry has never attained the size (measured in employment or sales) of the iron and steel industry, and it does not support nearly as many individual associations, the number of large associations is actually slightly greater than in the iron and steel industry (see table 4–5).

Perhaps the most interesting aspect of trade associations in the Japanese machine tool industry compared with those in the United States is that they are interconnected in a network of peak (and semi-peak) organizations, including the Japan Machinery Federation, the Japan Society for the Promotion of the Machinery Industry, and the Machine Tool and Related Products Committee. In addition, Japanese machine tool producers act collectively through export and import associations and through more specialized trade associations representing components of the industry, such as the Japan Industrial Robotics Association (JIRA).[39]

The interests of the Japanese machine tool and other machinery industries are aggregated in the Japan Machinery Federation (JMF), which include some sixty companies and fifty-nine other trade associations. JMF, which has a staff of thirty-six and an annual budget of around 270 million yen (approximately $1.7 million) is itself a member of Keidanren.

Another semi-peak association related to the machine tool industry is actually a public corporation. This organization, the Japan Society for the Promotion of the Machinery Industry (JSPMI), channels money from motorcycle and small car racing as subsidies to the machinery industries. JSPMI was established in 1964 with an endowment from the Japan Bicycle Promotion Association. In 1966 it built the Machinery Promotion Building (Kikai Shinko Kaikan), which houses dozens of trade associations in the machinery industries, including the Japan Machine Tool Builders Association, the Japan Metal Forming Machinery Builders Association, and the Japan Machinery Federation. In addition to offices, the building offers these associations a computing center, lecture halls, laboratories, meeting rooms, and a library. The building also houses the Machinery Promotion Club (Kikai Shinko Kurabu). JSPMI operates various research facilities for the machinery industries, helps them collect marketing

TABLE 4–5
U.S. MACHINE TOOL/ROBOTICS INDUSTRY:
STAFF AND BUDGET SIZES, 1984

Staff Size	Number of Associations	Budget (thousands of dollars)	Number of Associations
51–60	2	2,000–5,000	2
41–50	0	1,000–2,000	5
31–40	0	500–1,000	0
21–30	1	250–500	0
16–20	0	100–250	4
11–15	2	50–100	7
6–10	1	25–50	1
2–5	12	10–25	1
1	3	under 10	1

SOURCE: Colgate, *National Trade and Professional Associations.*

and technical information, and otherwise promotes their trade and technological capabilities. These activities are described in chapters 6 and 7. JSPMI's annual operating budget is more than 2¼ billion yen per year (about $10 million), and it has a staff of 75. The current chairman is Iwata Kazuo, the chairman of Toshiba Electric. Officials of the JSPMI frequently include chairmen of the JMF, the JMTBA, and the Japan Machinery Exporters Association. Indeed, the first chairman of JSPMI was the managing director of the Japan Machinery Exporters association.

The Japan Machinery Exporters Associations (JMEA) was identified in the Houdaille brief as an integral part of the Japanese machine tool "cartel," and mention was made of the interlocking memberships between JMEA and the JMTBA. Indeed, some of the links are fairly clear. JMEA has divisions [*bukai*] for machinery and machine tools. In 1982 the chairman of the machine tool division was Makino Tsunezo, chairman of the Makino Milling Machine Company.[40] Makino had been chairman of the division since 1957. He has also been chairman (1954–1955) and vice-chairman (1951, 1953, 1959–1962, 1969–1970) of the JMTBA, chairman of JMTBA's trade division (1959–1977), and a member of JMTBA's board (1951–1976). JMEA worked out agreements related to machine tools being exported to the United States and Canada in 1978.

Still another type of trade association in the machine tool industry, the Machine Tool and Related Products Committee (Kosaku Kikai Kanren Dantai Kyogikai), was established in 1962 to organize the first

Japanese International Machine Tool Trade Exhibition. It now consists of thirteen trade associations representing more than 1,000 firms. These trade associations include the JMTBA, the Japan Bench Machine Tool Builders Association, and the Machine Tool Unit Manufacturers Association of Japan.

The Japanese machine tool industry, like the steel industry, has also made use of the provisions of the Mining and Manufacturing Technology Research Association Law to organize research associations such as the Machinery Technology Association (Kikai Gijutsu Kyokai) which drew on MITI funds to work on technology for a fully automated factory. Other "research cartels" are discussed in greater detail in chapter 7.

Associations in the Robotics Industry. Comparing U.S. and Japanese associations in the robotics industry gives a sense of how associations are formed and of how they later interact with other organizations.

The Japanese were about three years ahead of the Americans in organizing a trade association in this sector. In 1971 thirty-five Japanese firms organized the Industrial Robotics Roundtable (Sangyoyo Robotto Kondankai). The roundtable's first chairman was Ando Hiroshi, the vice-president in charge of machinery at Kawasaki Heavy Industries (the leading firm in the industry at the time). The roundtable had its headquarters in the offices of another trade association, the Hydraulics Industry Association, within JSPMI's building in Tokyo. One of the roundtable's first activities was to carry out the 1971 Survey on Industrial Robots, which was sponsored through the small vehicle promotion subsidy of MITI.[41]

The Japanese robotics association continued to develop with the help of government. When robotics was designated a priority industry under the Electronics and Machinery Industries Temporary Measures Law [Kidensho] in 1971, the roundtable changed its legal status to become a voluntary association. At that time its forty-four corporate members established a new overseas committee to support such international activities as symposia. Ando Hiroshi continued as chairman of the reorganized body.[42] Another organizational change was made in 1973 when the association assumed its current legal form, as an incorporated private association.[43] In addition, at this time JIRA reorganized into its current seven standing committees: policy, public relations, robotics diffusion, safety, labor saving models, systems, and overseas.

In 1973 JIRA also acquired its current executive director, Yonemoto Kanji. Yonemoto, a former official in both the Ministry of International Trade and Industry and the Science and Technology

Agency, was asked to take this position by two high officials from MITI's Machinery Information Bureau. He heads a board of seventeen trustees who hold office for varying terms.

JIRA also has a chairman and two vice-chairmen from industry. The chairmen, who recently have served two-year terms, have generally been senior executives from such major firms as Kawasaki Heavy Industries, Hitachi, Mitsubishi Heavy Industries, Mitsubishi Electric, and Fuji Electric. Vice-chairmen also serve two-year terms (they do not automatically become chairman) and have generally come from major firms.

In 1984 JIRA had seventy-three regular members, 179 supporting members, and well over 1,000 individual members. Regular members are firms or incorporated associations involved in the manufacture or sale of industrial robots, robot control systems or related equipment, or research on these topics. Foreign firms based in Japan can join, as have Cincinnati Milacron Japan Ltd. and Texas Instruments Japan, Ltd. Dues are based on the size of the firm.[44] Supporting members are firms or associations holding common goals with JIRA.[45] The individual members are often academic researchers, journalists, or interested business executives.

All three categories of members receive publications and have access to JIRA's data bank (which has information on patents, technology, etc.). The regular members also receive catalogs and research reports and are eligible for MITI's *kijoho* subsidies (these are discussed in greater detail in chapter 7) and for special no-interest loans intended to promote the diffusion of robotics technology.[46]

JIRA funds come from three major sources: the association itself, the Japan Small Car Promotion Subsidy, and the general government budget. In 1982 the Small Car Promotion Subsidy was the largest of these, amounting to 38,492,000 yen (about $170,000), general government funds amounted to 8,100,000 yen (about $34,000), and the association's own funds amounted to 19,250,000 yen (about $80,000). JIRA got its first general government budget money in 1974 to conduct survey research related to the standardization of robots (about $50,000 to $60,000), although in recent years government funding has decreased. Aside from research on standardization, JIRA has supported market surveys by the Japan External Trade Organization (JETRO) (for example, in Poland and Bulgaria), developed safe automated casting and assembly systems, and performed research on intelligent robots.

The Small Car Promotion Subsidy has supported JIRA activities since its organization. In 1971 it subsidized a survey on industrial robots; in 1982 major activities included education programs on robotics for small and medium-sized firms, a forecast of the development of robotics research, efforts to promote the diffusion of robotics, and the development of certain technologies. Major items underwritten by JIRA itself included a study of the feasibility of a robot technology center, research on firefighting robot systems, and studies of the international standardization of robots.

One interesting activity of JIRA was its role in formulating MITI's famous *Vision of Trade and Industry Policies for the 1980s*. MITI drafted the basic form of the "vision" in 1979 and made an inquiry to the General Affairs Committee of the Industrial Policy Deliberation Council, which established a special subcommittee for policy in the 1980s to study the vision. At the request of MITI, the Japan Industrial Robotics Association drafted a "vision" for the industrial robotics industry. The "Robotics Industry Vision for the 1980s" it submitted in 1979 included five major items: the structure of the industrial robotics industry, the role of industrial robots in society and the economy, trends in technological development, trends in demand, and "hopes" for government policy. In March 1980 the General Affairs Committee (Sogo Bukai) of the Industrial Policy Deliberation Council reported its guidelines for trade and industry in the 1980s and submitted the Vision of Trade and Industry Policy for the 1980s to the minister of international trade and industry.

JIRA has also been involved in establishing and operating a research cartel sanctioned by the Mining and Manufacturing Technology Research Association Law of 1961.[47] The cartel, the Advanced Robot Technology Research Association, was established as part of a national research and development project and includes seventeen firms and two associations. In early 1984, after being recognized by the minister of international trade and industry, the cartel entered into an agreement with MITI's Agency for Industrial Science and Technology and started full-scale research to develop technology related to robots for restricted work environments, for example, for use in nuclear energy and ocean development and during natural disasters. The research was scheduled to continue for eight years and was budgeted at 20 billion yen. JIRA's president, Teruhisa Shimizu, is its president. JIRA also provides its members with other research-related surveys, has organized nine overseas tours of research facilities concerned with robotics, translated technical reports, and invited foreign researchers to give lectures in Japan.

In the United States the Robotics Industry Association (RIA) was begun, not as a trade association, but as a committee of a professional society, the Society of Manufacturing Engineers (SME). This was in 1974. RIA became formally autonomous only in 1983. Interestingly, given the repeated past examples of the Japanese modeling their organizations and institutions on those of Western countries, the organization of the RIA was influenced by the Japan Industrial Robotics Association. About half a dozen supplier and vendor companies saw a need for such an organization in the United States, and in 1973 SME provided seed money and staff support for the organization that became known as the Robot Institute of America. For a time the institute carried both individual and corporate members, but in 1980 the 11,000 individual members were spun off to SME, and the institute assumed a more traditional trade association role.

RIA's 320 member companies (manufacturers, distributors, and users) support a staff of ten. Its principal areas of activities are standards development; robot expositions; publications, workshops, and seminars; compilation of production statistics; and government relations. RIA has also established semiautonomous product groups for personal robots and automated vision systems.

Peak Associations in the United States and Japan

In both Japan and the United States the organization of those with common interests often continues beyond the trade association level as various industries unite in efforts to shape public policy. In Japan, however, there is a hierarchy in which industry associations are often linked in broader sectoral associations of associations, which in turn are linked in still broader organizations that represent large segments of business as a whole. In part because of this institutionalized aggregation of interests, Japanese trade associations are often judged to be more politically influential than their American counterparts.[48]

Four major national economic organizations make up the highest level of aggregation of organized business interests in Japan: Keidanren (the Federation of Economic Organizations), the Japan Chamber of Commerce and Industry (JCCI), Nikkeiren (Japan Federation of Employers Associations), and Keizai Doyukai (Japan Committee for Economic Development). These organizations formulate and articulate policy proposals from business, they are major contributors to political parties, and their leaders are powerful members of advisory councils.[49]

Keidanren. Keidanren, generally considered the most powerful business organization in Japan, includes the Japan Iron and Steel Federation, the Japan Machinery Federation, and other trade associations, as well as wholesale and retail businesses, trading houses, banks, insurance companies, securities houses, and industrial firms (including

78

Nippon Steel). The president of Keidanren is often referred to as Japan's prime minister of big business. This "prime minister" until 1986 was Inayama Yoshihiro, former president of Nippon Steel and former head of the Japan Iron and Steel Federation, the Kozai Club, and the Japan Iron and Steel Exporters Association. After Inayama retired, he was replaced by Saito Eishiro, another former Nippon Steel chairman. Directly below the chairman at Keidanren are twelve vice-chairmen, themselves chairmen of major corporations, each representing a business sector (such as machinery, textiles, chemicals, steel, energy, finance) or business groups (Mitsui, Mitsubishi, and Sumitomo). One represents the interests of the Kansai region (Osaka-Kyoto). The group elects a chairman from the vice-chairmen, with the understanding that he should not be from one of the major business groups or from finance.

Although Keidanren is immensely influential in shaping government policies, it has on occasion expressed concern about "excessive" government involvement in business. This was particularly true when Keidanren was led by Ishizaka Taizo from 1956–1968. Keidanren is credited, for example, with helping to prevent the enactment of an ambitious MITI law in the early 1960s that would have given business numerous incentives to restructure to meet foreign competition. Under president Uemura Kogoro from 1968–1974 Keidanren worked closely with government. Indeed, Uemura was himself a longtime government official. The next president of Keidanren, Doko Toshio (chairman of Toshiba), publicly stated that he favored having Keidanren cease making political donations, but it is not clear what effect his views had.

Nikkeiren. Another of the most important Japanese peak associations, Nikkeiren, is an organization of employers, whose members include regional associations of managers and other trade associations, including the Japan Iron and Steel Federation. Nikkeiren represents some 30,000 companies. It has supported firms involved in labor disputes and additionally has served an important public relations function. Before becoming head of Keidanren, Nippon Steel's Inayama was a deputy chairman of Nikkeiren. Another of the four deputy chairmen was the chairman of Daido Steel, a Nippon Steel affiliate.

Japan Chamber of Commerce and Industry. The Japan Chamber of Commerce and Industry (JCCI) is supposed to be a forum for smaller firms. In 1969, however, Nagano Shigeo (then chairman of Fuji Steel, one of Japan's largest firms, and a year later chairman of Nippon

Steel) became president of the chamber. Believing it was the responsibility of big business leaders to help small business organize to gain more political power, Nagano helped to strengthen and enlarge the Japanese Small Business Finance Corporation, thus widening the access of small firms to capital.[50] Perhaps one reason big business began feeling this responsibility is that at that time an organization controlled by the Japanese Communist Party was gaining influence with small business through an antitax campaign.

Keizai Doyukai. Keizai Doyukai, the Japan Committee for Economic Development, was established just after World War II as an organization of progressive middle-ranking executives of firms and trade associations. It now includes around 1,000 members. Keizai Doyukai has also been closely associated with the steel industry over the years. One of its founders was Otsuka Banjo (president of Japan Specialty Steel Pipe Co.). Another was Nagano Shigeo, who was director of Keizai Doyukai for two years in 1948–1949. More recently, Saito Eishiro (chairman of Nippon Steel in the early 1980s) was one of the top leaders of Keizai Doyukai. Some see the organization as a training ground for industrial statesmen. In 1966 the three top leaders of Keizai Doyukai were instrumental in forming the Sanken (Industrial Issues Study Council) which also included Nagano Shigeo. The group was established to study Japan's industrial system in an age of internationalization. It was instrumental in promoting the merger of Yawata Steel and Fuji Steel in 1970, but later became inactive.

As we have seen, the hierarchy of associations aggregrating interests in Japan is more highly developed in the machinery industry than in steel, perhaps because the machinery industry is much more fragmented and diverse than the steel industry. Steel was directly and independently linked to the government. As our discussion has shown, steel industry executives have played key roles in the management of the major Japanese peak associations, partly because of the history of close association between the industry and government. In the rebuilding of Japan immediately after World War II the development of a strong steel industry was seen as vital to all other reconstruction and industrial development. In the early postwar years, the Economic Stabilization Board, which led the rebuilding of the Japanese economy, decided that five industries should be given special priority in the allocation of resources to facilitate the rebuilding of Japan: steel, coal, fertilizer, shipbuilding, and electric power. Of these, steel and coal were given the greatest emphasis[51] and received preferential treatment in access to finance. Thus it is not surprising that the steel industry (and most particularly its leading firm) has since had a position of leadership in Japanese industry. This position will presumably decline as rising industries gain political strength commensurate with their economic importance.

In summary, in Japan individual industries belong to a sort of umbrella association that encompasses the various divisions in the industry; these associations are in turn represented by more encompassing multi-industry peak associations that work to forge consensus across industries and thereby possess substantial influence on political outcomes. The system approximates a hierarchy in which each level aggregates and reconciles the interests represented at that level.[52]

U.S. Peak Associations. Two associations in the United States have attempted to approximate this structure. The Chamber of Commerce of the United States, founded in 1912, and the National Association of Manufacturers (NAM), founded in 1895, are the two oldest national business associations in the United States. The chamber, with 180,000 member companies and several thousand state and local chamber and trade association members, had a 1985 budget of $65 million.[53] "Our main mission in life," said Richard Lesher, its president, "is to influence the United States Congress."[54] NAM represents 13,000 companies, 150 state and local associations of manufacturers, and 110 manufacturing trade associations; its 1985 budget is in excess of $10 million. Like the chamber, its activities are strongly oriented to affecting legislative outcomes.

Because both NAM and the Chamber of Commerce have long had extremely large and heterogeneous memberships, and because of conflicting interests within American business, other national associations have arisen that serve more narrowly defined segments of the business community than the two senior associations. The National Federation of Independent Business, founded in 1943, and the National Small Business Association, founded in 1937, focus on small business, while a variety of national organizations comprise the largest U.S. corporations. One early big business organization was the Special Conference Committee, a management group of very large firms established in 1919 to deal with labor. It had been created by General Electric and Jersey Standard and numbered among its members AT&T, Bethlehem Steel, DuPont, General Motors, Goodyear, International Harvester, and Westinghouse. The committee favored company unions, employee pension plans, and other "welfare capitalist" measures in the 1920s, a program that was bitterly opposed by organizations like NAM.[55]

Other national associations dominated by big business include

81

the Business Council, the Committee for Economic Development, and the Business Roundtable. The Business Council originated as a hybrid private–public organization in 1933. A small number of businessmen from the largest corporations collaborated with Secretary of Commerce Daniel Roper to create a "business cabinet." Its corporate sponsors hoped that such an organization would marry corporate expertise to federal power and then serve as a long-range economic planning council with primary responsibility for formulating industrial recovery strategy. The idea bore a certain resemblance to officially recognized "parliaments of industry," which played an advisory role to the governments of Czechoslovakia, France, and the Weimar Republic.[56] As a sort of "advisory committee without portfolio" the council obtained rent-free office space in the Commerce Department, did not have to release minutes of its meetings or allow journalists or other outsiders to attend, was free to set its own agenda, and enjoyed superior access to high level executive branch decision makers. No executive order establishing the organization was ever drafted, nor did federal officials have any significant role in selecting its membership. Its greatest influence was in shaping a number of important New Deal legislative initiatives.[57] In 1961 its close relationship to the federal government was ended, and it became a purely private organization.

Members of the Business Council and Secretary of Commerce Jesse Jones were instrumental in the establishment of the Committee for Economic Developments (CED) in 1942. Originally organized to provide a focal point for business involvement in reconversion planning during the war, CED evolved into a permanent, multi-issue organization that periodically issues reports on public policy problems of particular concern to the largest corporations.

The Business Roundtable, established in 1972, is an organization of 175–200 chief executive officers of the largest corporations in the United States. Unlike the Business Council or CED, the roundtable actively attempts to influence specific legislation. (A counterpart organization for medium-sized companies, the American Business Council, was formed in 1980.) The roundtable emerged out of two business organizations, one that had been formed to contain construction costs and a second small group of large firms (the "March Group") that had been more generally concerned with what it perceived as the political weakness of big business in national politics in the early 1970s. Former Treasury Secretary John Connally and former presidential counselor Bryce Harlow were active in the early stages of the organization's life.[58]

That the American system of associations has relatively weak hierarchical features is generally conceded. Important firms may not belong to the primary industry association in their industry; segments of an industry may maintain their own associations, which often operate independently or even antagonistically; associations such as NAM and the Chamber of Commerce attempt to play the role of peak associations, aggregating the interests of a large variety of members, but their role in shaping policy is often overshadowed by issue-specific coalitions. (Merger discussions between NAM and the Chamber of Commerce were held in the mid-1970s, but had broken off by 1977).[59] There is no direct U.S. counterpart to the kind of close-knit business elite found in Japan, where a relatively small and stable group of officials (many based in the Japanese steel industry) staffed key positions in firms, associations, and government ministries for literally decades. Political conflicts within the American business community produce shifting alignments, as new issues break up old coalitions and create new alliances.[60] To the extent that it happens, the bargaining process that reconciles opposing positions typically happens within governmental institutions such as Congress, rather than in business associations. When American associations fail to meet the needs of some segment of their membership, the disaffected members may create new associations rather than continue to attempt to change the operation of the old ones. The resulting pattern of interindustry political relations looks a good deal messier than that found in Japan. It has been suggested that the diversity of the American economy, the fragmented nature of governmental authority under a federal system, and a political culture hostile to organized interests all work against the emergence of a more centralized pattern of interest representation in the United States.[61] Although our research did not investigate this claim systematically, what we found is not inconsistent with it.

The Aggregation of Business Interests in Japan and the United States

The aggregation of interests in Japan generally seems to be a more "orderly" process than in the United States. Japanese firms are organized into trade associations, and the associations themselves are then organized into powerful sectoral organizations and then into peak organizations. This may be desirable with respect to economic growth. Mancur Olson argues that more encompassing organizations have greater incentive to make the society in which they operate more prosperous.[62] But how encompassing does an organization have to be to deliver those benefits? And how does one ensure that suborganiza-

83

tions do not seize control for their own benefit? Keidanren encompasses all Japanese big business, but in the 1980s the steel industry seems to have power within Keidanren that is disproportionate to its importance in the Japanese economy. Given the evolution of international comparative advantage, this could lead to problems in Japan; it is difficult to argue, however, that this problem has been any milder in the United States.

William Ouchi claims that the Japanese system is not only more efficient in promoting economic growth than the U.S. system (or lack of a system), but that it is also fairer. Ouchi asserts that those forced to sacrifice their own interests now are repaid later. We are skeptical about this conclusion. Kozo Yamamura quotes from an article in the Japanese daily newspaper *Asahi Shimbun* that describes an association in the electric furnace sector of the steel industry that was formed with the cooperation of MITI to help that industry recover from a serious downturn in the late 1970s.

> The indignities suffered [in 1978] are still fresh in the memory of Masanari Ikeda, president of Tokyo Steel, which was not a member of the Association. At that time, he was doing his utmost to resist MITI's efforts to coerce him to join the cartel. "I heard that an order to join the cartel might be issued if I continued to resist. First I thought 'they wouldn't dare,' then I really got angry. After I reached the conclusion that I had no alternative but to join the cartel, I felt totally defeated.[63]

We wonder if this may not be a more general problem. Nippon Steel, for example, clearly seems in a position to dominate its industry and to exert a very broad and powerful influence.

One might expect that the more central role of trade associations in Japan would be reflected in large staff sizes and budgets, and our evidence suggests that the Japanese associations probably have more resources than many of their American counterparts. As we noted, in the steel industry the difference is striking. The American Iron and Steel Institute (AISI) has a staff of only about sixty-five. The Japan Iron and Steel Federation (JISF) has a staff of 170, and in representing the interests of the Japanese steel industry JISF is joined by such organizations as the Kozai Club with a staff of 115 and the Japan Iron and Steel Exporters Association with a staff of sixty-nine. Part of this difference in staff size may reflect the wider range of interests of Japanese steelmakers, which include, for example, a need to influence public opinion in the United States and Europe. Part of it may simply reflect the greater relative importance of the steel industry in Japan than in the United States.

The U.S. National Machine Tool Builders Association has a staff of sixty. Its two major Japanese counterparts, the Japan Machine Tool Builders Association and the Japan Metal Forming Machine Builders Association are much smaller, with twenty and four staff members, respectively. In this industry, the Japanese trade associations seem to have far fewer personnel resources, but this appearance is deceptive. Many activities are carried out on behalf of the Japanese Machine tool industry by a network of other organizations: the Japan Machine Tool Trade Association (which promotes Japanese machine tool exports), the Japan Machinery Exporters Association, the Japan Machinery Federation and the Japan Society for the Promotion of the Machinery Industry. We do not have information on the staff sizes of all of these organizations, but the Japan Machinery Federation has a staff of thirty-six; the Japan Machine Tool Trade Association a staff of eleven in Japan and ten overseas; and the Japan Society for the Promotion of the Machinery Industry a staff of seventy-five.[64]

It is generally inadvisable to compare Japanese and American trade associations on a one-to-one basis, since, like the machine tool associations noted above, the performance of various tasks may be distributed differently within a set of associations in Japan than it is in the United States. Our investigation cannot settle conclusively the question of the relative resource endowments of associations in the two countries, but based on our study of these two sectors, and the more general availability of public funds for association activities in Japan than in the United States, we believe that the Japanese associations are somewhat more richly endowed than their American counterparts.

Notes

1. National Association of Manufacturers, Associations Department, *Manufacturing Trade Associations: Their Changing Focus and Management* (Washington, D.C.: NAM, 1981, 1983, 1985).

2. Testimony of Dennis J. Carney, chairman and chief executive officer, Wheeling-Pittsburgh Steel Corporation, in *The Domestic Steel Industry and the Antitrust Laws: Hearings before the Committee on the Judiciary*, United States Senate, 98th Congress, 1st session, July 1, 1983, p. 130 et seq.

3. *Industry Week*, March 5, 1984, p. 15.

4. For an English-language account of this episode, see U.S. Department of Commerce, *Japan: The Government-Business Relationship* (Washington, D.C.: U.S. Government Printing Office, 1972), pp. 146–47. It is also discussed in greater detail in chapter 5.

5. We surveyed several Japanese government and private directories of associations. One that includes data on staff sizes is Mikami Marketing, Inc., *Zenkoku Kakushu Dantai Meikan*. In Japan some association employees appear

to be seconded from member firms; others are retired employees of member firms. We did not collect information on the salary and other arrangements involved when this occurs.

6. We do not have comparable information on this topic for Japan. But more than two-thirds of the budget for the Japan Industrial Robotics Association in a recent year came from government funds. Such heavy government subsidization, we believe, would be most likely to occur in an industry such as robotics, which is being promoted by special laws.

7. National Association of Manufacturers, *Manufacturing Trade Associations*, 1985, p. 47.

8. Bruce Frazer, "Trade Groups and the Recession: Economic Recovery Comes Slowly in the Basic Industries, and Slower Still for Trade Associations in Those Sectors," *American Metal Market*, May 7, 1984, p. 11.

9. National Association of Manufacturers, *Manufacturing Trade Associations*, 1983, p. 39.

10. National Association of Manufacturers, *Manufacturing Trade Associations*, 1985, p. 74.

11. National Association of Manufacturers, *Manufacturing Trade Associations*, 1982, p. 8.

12. National Association of Manufacturers, *Manufacturing Trade Associations*, 1985, p. 15.

13. National Association of Manufacturers, *Manufacturing Trade Associations*, 1982, p. 7.

14. National Association of Manufacturers, *Manufacturing Trade Associations*, 1985, p. 14.

15. Ibid., p. 41.

16. One activity that is frequently mentioned in the larger Japanese trade associations, which seems to have no obvious counterpart in American associations, is relations with industries in foreign countries. In an English-language description the Japan Iron and Steel Federation mentions as one of its six most important sets of activities, keeping "in constant and close contact with the iron and steel industry in foreign countries." If American associations do this, they do not discuss it.

17. Most of the general information on Japan in this section was taken from Okamura Hirokumi, *Gendai Tekko Kigyo No Ruikei Bunseki* (Tokyo: Minerva Shobo, 1984).

18. American Metal Market, *Metal Statistics 1984* (New York: Fairchild Publications, 1984), p. 162.

19. Ibid. In the United States the importance of the largest firms when measured by their contribution to domestic steel consumption is of course even lower because imports have an appreciable market share.

20. These firms are Daido (8.7 percent market share in 1978) and Sanyo (5.3 percent market share in 1978).

21. Leonard Lynn, "Multinational Joint Ventures in the U.S. Steel Industry," in David C. Mowery, ed., *International Collaborative Ventures in U.S. Manufacturing* (working title) (Cambridge, Mass.: AEI/Ballinger, forthcoming).

22. The AISI had sixty-three members as of April 1985. See American Iron and Steel Institute, *Steel and America: An Annual Report* (Washington, D.C., 1985).

23. We did not collect information on JISF members that were not listed on the Japanese stock exchange. The firms we identify with steel company groups were either so identified in industrial manuals or had a major steelmaker as their largest shareholder.

24. Japan Iron and Steel Federation, *Japan Iron and Steel Federation* (Tokyo: JISF, undated).

25. This excludes associations organized around specific materials such as the Institute of Scrap Iron and Steel and the National Slag Association.

26. David A. Hartquist, telephone interview with author, Specialty Steel Industry of the United States, July 12, 1985.

27. David Kramer, "Mini-mill group may file 301 charges vs. 2 nations," *American Metal Market*, May 2, 1986, pp. 2, 8; telephone conversation with Oliver Dulle, executive vice-president, Steel Bar Mills Association, May 6, 1986.

28. Inayama Yoshihiro served as chairman of the Club from its founding in 1947 until his retirement as chairman of Nippon Steel in 1979. Kozai Club, *Kozai Kurabu Sanjugonen Shi* (Tokyo: Kozai Club, 1982).

29. More detail on export associations is given in chapter 6.

30. Japan Iron and Steel Federation, *Japan Iron and Steel Federation*.

31. The Kozai Club established the Tekko Kaikan, K.K. to build the Kaikan in 1961; the president of the new company was Inayama, the chairman of the Kozai Club.

32. "Numerically controlled" refers to a process whereby the movements of the machine are automatically regulated by means of a computer or some other device. The earliest systems used numerical information on punched tape.

33. Two of the largest producers, Cross & Trecker and Ingersoll Milling & Machine, have resigned from the association for different reasons. In the case of Cross & Trecker, disagreement over the subletting of floor space at an industry exhibition led to resignation of the firm. In the case of Ingersoll Milling, resignation followed the association's decision to file its Section 232 trade petition.

34. They are: accounting procedures; audit; distributor relations; economics and statistics; electrical standards; environmental; government relations; human resources and training; international trade; long-range planning; manufacturing; marketing communications; meetings; membership; numerically controlled software; numerical control; OSHA; product liability; public affairs; research and development; safety standards; sales management; service management; show; technical standards; transportation.

35. The largest nonmember is Mori Seiki. Mori, the largest specialty maker of numerically controlled lathes, was ranked second in the machine tool industry in a 1981 survey. See Yano Research Institute, *Current Machine Tools in Japan* (Tokyo: Yano Research Institute, 1981).

36. The technology committee, for example, had eight special subcommittees: the development of technology, standards, international standards, electrical, hydraulics, numerical control, grinding machines, and safety.

37. Houdaille Industries, Inc., Petitioner, *Petition to the President of the United States through the Office of the United States Trade Representative for the Exercise of Presidential Discretion Authorized by Section 103 of the Revenue Act of 1971, 26 USC, 48(a)(7)(D)*. Filed by Covington and Burling of Washington, D.C.

38. Ezra Vogel, *Comeback; Case by Case—Building the Resurgence of American Business* (New York: Simon and Schuster, 1985).

39. The Japan Iron and Steel Federation does not belong to any higher level sectoral organizations, but it does include two smaller trade associations among its members and is itself a member of Keidanren.

40. In 1981 Makino was Japan's seventh largest machine tool builder.

41. For a history of the robotics industry in Japan, see Robert U. Ayres, Leonard Lynn, and Steve Miller, "Technology Transfer in Robotics Between the U.S. and Japan," in Cecil Uyehara, ed., *Technological Exchange: The U.S.-Japanese Experience* (Washington, D.C.: University Press of America, 1982.)

42. Chapter 7 contains more information on this law.

43. The purpose of this reorganization was to clarify JIRA's legal responsibilities and powers. The new status was approved by the minister of international trade and industry on October 1, 1973. See JIRA, *10-Nen no Ayumi*, p. 18.

44. A firm with less than 200 million yen in capital and sales of less than 100 million yen per year would pay annual dues of 600,000 yen. A firm with more than 10 billion yen in capital and sales of over 15 billion per year would pay total annual dues of 1,700,000 yen.

45. In 1984 foreign supporting members included Apple Computer, IBM (U.K.), a couple of smaller robot companies in the United States, and other firms from Singapore, Korea, Germany, and the U.K. Other supporting members included the Kansai Information Center (in Osaka), the Tokyo Research Institution, and the Japan Productivity Center.

46. *Robotto*, vol. 42 (April 1984), pp. 84–104.

47. The information here is drawn primarily from Masakazu Kobayashi, "Kyokyugen Sagyo Robotto No Kenkyu Kaihatsu Keikaku," *Robotto*, vol. 42 (April 1984), pp. 4–8.

48. See, for example, William Ouchi, *The M-Form Society* (Reading, Mass.: Addison-Wesley, 1984).

49. A more specific discussion of the various mechanisms of influence appears in chapter 5. For more information on the four major peak associations, see Akiyama Tetsu, *Zaikai Yon Dantai No Soshiki To Katsudo* (Tokyo: Kyoikusha, 1978); Ouchi, *The M-Form Society*; and Tanaka Yonosuke, "The World of the *Zaikai*," in Murakami Hyoe and Johannes Hirschmeier, eds., *Politics and Economics in Contemporary Japan* (Tokyo: Kodansha International, 1983), pp. 64–78.

50. Some discussion of Nagano's activities appears in Richard J. Samuels,

The Politics of Regional Policy in Japan (Princeton, N.J.: Princeton University Press, 1983).

51. See Kiyoshi Kawahito, *The Japanese Steel Industry* (New York: Praeger Publishers, 1972), pp. 8–9 and Tatsuro Uchino, *Japan's Postwar Economy* (Tokyo: Kodansha International, 1978), pp. 35ff.

52. Ouchi states the point somewhat differently, but his argument for the political equivalent of "middle managers" who would synthesize the common interests of various factions is highly similar to the Japanese hierarchy we present. See William G. Ouchi, "The Microeconomic Policy Dialogue: Analysis and Recommendations," *Global Competition: The New Reality, Volume II,* Report of the President's Commission on Industrial Competitiveness (Washington, D.C.: U.S. Government Printing Office, January 1985).

53. This and other basic statistics and information about national associations in the United States is taken from Colgate, *National Trade and Professional Associations of the United States,* an annual yearbook published by Columbia Books, Washington, D.C.

54. Mark Green and Andrew Buchsbaum, *The Corporate Lobbies: Political Profiles of the Business Roundtable & the Chamber of Commerce* (Washington, D.C.: Public Citizen, 1980), p. 12.

55. Kim McQuaid, *Big Business and Presidential Power from FDR to Reagan* (New York: William Morrow, 1982), p. 34.

56. R. H. Bowen, *German Theories of the Corporative State* (New York: Whittlesey House, 1947), pp. 3–4.

57. More information on the role of the council and of the other national associations mentioned here can be found in McQuaid, *Big Business.*

58. Additional background on the Business Roundtable can be found in Green and Buchsbaum, *The Corporate Lobbies.*

59. Robert H. Salisbury, "Why No Corporatism in America?" in Philippe C. Schmitter and Gerhard Lehmbruch, eds., *Trends toward Corporatist Intermediation* (Beverly Hills, Calif.: SAGE Publications, 1979).

60. Phyllis S. McGrath, *Redefining Corporate-Federal Relations* (New York: The Conference Board, 1979), pp. 79–80.

61. Salisbury, "Why No Corporatism?"

62. Olson suggests that less encompassing organizations can profit at the expense of other parts of the society. Highly encompassing organizations are more likely to be able to profit through the growth of the society as a whole. Olson notes that encompassing organizations can also do badly for their society under some circumstances because they lack diversity of opinion and advocacy. Mancur Olson, *The Rise and Decline of Nations* (New Haven, Conn.: Yale University Press, 1982), esp. pp. 47–53.

63. Kozo Yamamura, "Success that Soured: Administrative Guidance and Cartels in Japan," in Kozo Yamamura, ed., *Policy and Trade Issues of the Japanese Economy* (Seattle: University of Washington Press, 1982), pp. 77–112.

64. Although some information on budgets has been published, reporting procedures do not seem comparable enough to allow strong conclusions to be based on them.

5
Trade Associations and Business–Government Relations

Economists have devoted considerable attention to explaining collective action in an economy composed of autonomous, profit-seeking actors.[1] Their studies have generally set the problem in a highly abstract setting, devoid of institutional features. The result has been scant recognition of one of the more historically prominent methods of facilitating collective action: governmental action to promote it and to institutionalize it.

That trade associations may be useful to government as well as to their member firms is fairly obvious. Government officials may find it more useful in the course of their dealings with the private sector to turn to a single source of information or to listen to a single voice expressing an industry position than to contend with a welter of sometimes conflicting claims. Trade associations may also assist in the implementation of certain policies. Finally, the formation of certain trade associations may solve certain political problems facing elected officials.

Some of the advantages to government of having trade associations in a given industry are revealed by the following discussion by a British research team writing in the mid-1950s; we believe the comments apply more generally:

> From the point of view of Government it is always a matter of great convenience to have a single consultative body for an industry. Sometimes the need for decision is urgent and time does not permit consultations with a great number of bodies or individual firms—a general view is required on short notice. Again, it is a great advantage for ministers and civil servants if differences of opinion in an industry can be reconciled inside an association before the question is brought before a department—the smaller the number of views the official has to deal with the simpler his task. The Government, therefore, is likely to welcome not only associations of manufacturers turning out similar products, but the federation of associations. But this in no way precludes the inter-

change of views between government departments and individual firms when this is desired by either side.[2]

The role of associations in providing information and advice to government often is significant. There are usually few people who understand well the circumstances of an industry who are not already employed by it. As a consequence, government staffs frequently must rely on industry groups for information in fashioning and implementing policy. As noted by McRobie et al.,

> Trade associations are also an invaluable source of expert knowledge and advice on industrial matters. Ministries cannot be specialists in all branches and problems of industry. . . . Specifically, when trade negotiations with other countries, or a conference on countries working together under the GATT are about to take place, the Board of Trade consults the relevant associations on the proposals likely to be discussed. Similarly, all production departments consult the appropriate trade associations on proposed regulations and legislation. This two-way traffic of information and periodic exchange of views is of considerable value to public administrators, trade association officials and businessmen alike.[3]

This chapter takes up the various organizations and arrangements that link government to business in Japan and the United States, giving particular emphasis to those involving trade associations.

The Japanese Government and Trade Associations

The relationship between trade associations and government has long been a close one in Japan. It has also been an ambiguous one. Who is in charge? Does government use the trade associations to dominate the economy? Or does big business use the trade associations to dominate the government? James Abegglen used the term "Japan, Incorporated" to describe a Japanese economy run by groups of bureaucrats and business leaders able to allocate national resources to the sectors that seemed most promising. Abegglen concluded: "It is difficult, and perhaps not useful, to attempt to define the boundary between government and business in any given major business decision."[4]

Japan is a parliamentary democracy with a parliament, the Diet, that is frequently characterized as reigning rather than ruling. It is the bureaucracy that rules. Bills before the Diet are more likely to have originated in the bureaucracy than in the Diet.[5] For this reason, much of the sort of policy-making activity that occurs in the U.S. Congress, in Japan occurs in an interplay between businesspeople and bureaucrats. Two Japanese government agencies have played primary roles in regulating and making use of trade associations: the Japan Fair Trade Commission (JFTC) and Ministry of International Trade and Industry (MITI). We have already described the JFTC; we turn here to a description of MITI and its relationship with business organizations.

MITI and Trade Associations. MITI oversees most of the trade associations in manufacturing, frequently using them to pursue its industrial policies.[6] The ministry's 13,000 employees are organized into a Ministry Secretariat, seven bureaus, and three extraministerial bureaus.[7] Several of the bureaus are involved in relationships with the various types of associations we have described in this study. The export associations work closely with the International Trade Administration Bureau's export division. Chambers of commerce and industry are licensed and given guidance and supervision by the Industrial Policy Bureau's general affairs division. The depression cartels are coordinated by another office in the Industrial Policy Bureau, the industrial organization policy office. MITI's Basic Industries Bureau has an international trade office that "approves the export of goods under the bureau's jurisdiction, e.g. iron and steel . . . ," and thus works with some of the special purpose associations set up to administer import quotas imposed by the United States and other countries.[8]

Several divisions of MITI's Machinery and Information Bureau are closely linked to trade associations in the machine tool industries. The general affairs division coordinates the enforcement of the Law on Extraordinary Measures for the Promotion and Development of Specified Machinery and Information Industries. The international trade division authorizes exports of machinery. The vehicle division sees that profits from the bicycle and motorcycle races are used to promote the machinery and other industries, providing subsidies for research done by some trade associations. MITI's Agency for Industrial Science and Technology (AIST) promotes collaborative research and drafts standards for machinery, etc. The agency is responsible for the famous national R&D projects, several of which entailed the formation of research associations in the steel and machine tool industries.[9]

Two mechanisms by which MITI influences business have attracted considerable attention from Western scholars are "administrative guidance" and the "descent" of MITI bureaucrats into the top ranks of management. One Japanese legal scholar defines "administrative guidance" as "actions taken by administrative organs that are not legally binding, but are intended to influence the action of other parties to realize an administrative aim." Although this practice is not unique to Japan, there is a widespread belief that it is more pervasive there than in the United States; it is frequently used by MITI to guide firms in making production adjustments to eliminate what is regarded as excessive competition.[10] According to Chalmers Johnson, MITI's first "totally independent action as a new ministry" involved the use of administrative guidance to limit production. This occurred in 1952 when MITI informally advised ten major fiber spinning firms to reduce production by 40 percent and assigned quotas to each firm. Firms not complying were given to understand that they might not be allocated the foreign currency they needed to buy raw cotton. This advice to limit production was later echoed in guidance given that year to the rubber and steel industries. MITI brushed aside protests from the JFTC, asserting that informal advice from the government was not subject to the Antimonopoly Law.[11]

On occasion, MITI has used administrative guidance to help trade associations control their members. In 1965 the Japan Iron and Steel Federation (JISF) established a special committee to control investments in new steelmaking facilities. MITI supported the JISF in this effort, even though it had no clear-cut legal basis for doing so.[12] MITI made a department decision under its organization law to give production quotas to eighty-five companies. The fifth largest firm in the industry, Sumitomo Metals, argued that MITI's actions represented wrongful interference in Sumitomo's management rights and refused to comply with the quota. MITI retaliated by curtailing Sumitomo's coal import quota, but before this action had any effect the demand for steel increased and a settlement was reached.[13] In 1966 the Petroleum Association of Japan asked MITI to use administrative guidance to force Idemitsu Kosan to comply with the federation's efforts to curb increases in crude petroleum production. During the same year firms in the spinning industry sought similar help to overcome Nisshin Spinning's resistance to continuing a recession cartel in the cotton spinning industry.

MITI's policy of administrative guidance received a serious blow when it was challenged by the JFTC in the petroleum association case. This first challenge from another government agency was backed up in 1980 by a decision of the Tokyo High Court, which ruled: "If the Ministry of International Trade and Industry issues administrative guidance to an industrial organization in order to have each enterprise follow the restrictive guideline on oil refining, the industry will, more often than not implement joint action. Therefore, such administrative guidance should be prohibited."[14] In 1981 the JFTC issued a memorandum in line with the court decision seeking to set limits for administrative guidance. The memorandum noted that conflicts with the Antimonopoly Law were very likely to result from administrative guidance given to trade associations.[15] In its own memorandum MITI described areas in which it claimed administrative guidance was important to the Japanese national economy—for example, in requesting voluntary control over exports to avoid trade restrictions or in recommending production increases during periods of tight supply. MITI argued: "The aim of administrative guidance is to implement an effective measure in a flexible manner on the basis of agreement and cooperation of other parties, without excessive interference. Therefore, administrative guidance has played an important role in the development of the Japanese economy and it will continue to be effective in the future."[16]

Reference has already been made to some of the personal links between MITI and industry. The prewar and wartime antecedents of MITI, as we have seen, included Yawata Steel as an agency. Thus until recently senior executives in the steel industry were often men who had spent their careers as government officials. In chapter 2 we mentioned Ojima Arakazu, who passed the higher civil service examinations in 1918 and entered the Ministry of Agriculture and Commerce (MITI's predecessor). Upon leaving office as minister of munitions (another ancestor of MITI) in 1941, he became a director of Nippon Steel. Although he retired from Nippon Steel at the end of World War II to avoid being purged, he returned to become president of Yawata Steel (one of the two firms formed out of Nippon Steel under the occupation antimonopoly policies) in 1956. He retired as chairman of the board of Yawata in 1967 and continued as an adviser. Inayama Yoshihiro, who was president of Keidanren until 1986 and honorary chairman of Nippon Steel, also began his career as a government bureaucrat.[17]

The flow of retired MITI bureaucrats to the management of business firms and trade associations provides a contemporary link between MITI and industry. MITI bureaucrats generally retire young—traditionally when a member of their or of a junior cohort becomes a bureau chief. Those retiring are often in their forties and may move into managerial positions in business firms, trade associations, or public corporations. The bureaucrats who reach the pinnacle at MITI, the bureaucratic vice-ministers, almost invariably retire into the top management of major firms. Most are still in their early fifties and so have many years to guide the destiny of the large firms. Many go into the steel industry. Indeed, of fifteen bureaucratic vice-ministers retiring between 1952 and 1976, no fewer than six retired into the top management of major steel firms. Hirai Tomisaburo (MITI vice-minister from 1953–1955) retired from MITI to become a director at Yawata Steel and later became president of Nippon Steel. Matsuo Kinzo (MITI vice-minister from 1961–1963) later became chairman of the board of Nippon Kokan, Japan's second largest steelmaker. Kumagai Yoshifumi (MITI vice-minister from 1968–1969) later became chairman of Sumitomo Metals, Japan's fourth largest steelmaker. Three other retired vice-ministers, while not becoming presidents or chairmen, became executive vice-presidents or directors of major steel firms.[18]

It is more difficult to track the movement of lower level MITI officials into businesses and trade associations, although it certainly occurs. The director of MITI's iron and steel production section in the mid 1950s, for example, was later a deputy division manager at Yawata Steel and then in charge of the data room of the Japan Iron and Steel Institute.[19] In discussing the development of the Japanese machine tool industry, Ezra Vogel notes: "To make the most of their [MITI's] influence and to facilitate communication with these [machine tool] industry associations, they use a minuscule amount of money to help the associations with organizational expenses and place former officials on their staffs. Associations, needing to keep MITI's goodwill, accept the funds and former officials."[20] Vogel does not cite specific individuals, but as was mentioned in chapter 3, Yonemoto Kanji, the executive director of the Japan Industrial Robotics Association, was an official at MITI until his retirement in 1968. Yonemoto worked for a private firm from 1968 until 1973 when he was asked to become executive director of the Japan Industrial Robot Association. Interestingly, he was approached not by industry officials, but by the director of MITI's Machinery Information Bureau.[21]

Advisory Commissions. A major formal mechanism for interaction between trade associations and government in Japan is through advisory commissions (*shingikai*). Some characterize these organizations as rubber stamp organizations routinely approving whatever the bureaucracy wants them to. Others see them as conduits for business influence on the government. Ouchi stresses the heavy involvement of trade associations in MITI's Industrial Structure Advisory Commission. He notes that twenty-eight of its eighty-two members represent trade associations. Among those from the steel industry in the Industrial Structure Advisory Commission in 1979 were:

• H. Hyuga, president of Sumitomo Metals and chairman of the Kansai Federation of Economic Organizations

- Y. Inayama, chairman of the Japan Iron and Steel Federation and former president of Nippon Steel, later president of Keidanren
- T. Okumura, executive director of the Japan Iron and Steel Federation and chairman of the International Trade and Industries Statistics Association
- E. Saito, president of Nippon Steel Corporation (also chairman of the Kozai Club, the Japan Iron and Steel Exporters Association, and the Japan Project Industry Council)
- T. Hirai, counsellor to Nippon Steel Corporation (Hirai was MITI vice-minister from 1953 to 1955)
- Y. Kumagai, president of Sumitomo Metals (Kumagai was MITI vice-minister from 1968–1969)
- H. Iwamura, president of Kawasaki Steel
- S. Kobayashi, president of Japan Steel Works
- K. Takahashi, president of Kobe Steel
- K. Takeda, president of Daido Steel (formerly a managing director at Nippon Steel, also chairman of the Special Steel Association of Japan)
- Y. Yasuda, president of Toshin Steel[22]

The Industrial Structure Advisory Council is organized into some twenty committees, one of which focuses on the steel industry, another on the machinery industry. Although the machine tool builders are not nearly as well represented as the steelmakers, the director of their trade association, the Japan Machine Tool Builders Associations, is a member of the council.

Other advisory commissions also include representatives of the machine tool and steel industries. Executives from Sumitomo Metals and Nippon Kokan, for example, are among those on the Import-Export Trade Advisory Council. A Nippon Steel vice-president is one of eleven members of the Export Insurance Advisory Council. Officials from several associations related to the machinery industries are on the Export Inspection and Design Promotion Advisory council.[23]

Those deemphasizing the role of the advisory commissions typically note that the commissions have no staff and thus must have their research and other work done for them by the bureaucracy, assuming that the trade associations and individual firms do not carry out this function. This was done in the robotics industry, and Richard Samuels notes a similar pattern in the aluminum industry. Samuels comments:

> While it is frequently acknowledged that committees in the Diet and the ruling Liberal-Democratic Party (LDP), having

limited expertise and staff, are dependent upon the bureaucracy for data and analysis, it is not as often recognized that the well-fabled Japanese bureaucracy is itself often dependent in the same way upon the industry associations and firms with which it works so closely.[24]

Samuels points out that legislative, administrative, and LDP programs related to the aluminum industry usually are in close accord with the proposals of the MITI Industrial Structure Council (where most important policy discussions take place in the Basic Problems Subcommittee of the Aluminum Industry Subcommittee). According to Samuels, detailed proposals for public and private action to restructure the badly depressed aluminum industry in 1981 "seem to have been adopted verbatim in the recommendations of the advisory commission in its subsequent report of October 1981."[25]

Advisory commissions have also been important in the implementation of the various laws promoting industries. We shall later discuss their activities with regard to the series of special laws promoting the development of the machine tool industry.

The LDP Policy Affairs Research Council. U.S. business interests focus much of their lobbying activity on legislative committees involved in the drafting of legislation. Given the long-standing dominance of the LDP in Japan, much of the comparable activity occurs not in official Diet committees, but rather within the LDP. Once the LDP leadership decides on the draft of a law, passage is often a foregone conclusion. The organizations responsible for drafting laws for the LDP are Policy Affairs Research Councils (PARCs). Since much of the lobbying activities on behalf of business are directed at these committees, we describe them in some detail here.[26]

According to Thayer, the PARC rather than the Diet is where the real deliberations on policy occur. In cases where legislation is not necessary the decisions of the PARC are announced by the cabinet as national policy. The opposition parties may make critical speeches, but the cabinet hardly ever reconsiders its decisions. Writing more recently, Izumi says that PARC directors have much greater prestige and influence than the chairmen of Diet committees.[27]

The formal basis for the power of the PARC is the LDP constitution, which requires that any bills or policy plans be examined and approved by the PARC before becoming official party policy. After the PARC approves a bill, it sends it to the Executive Council for consideration, which almost always follows the PARC's recommendations. The bill is then sent to the Diet Policy Committee (Kokkai Taisaku Iinkai), and then to the Diet, usually as a cabinet-sponsored bill.[28]

Since the LDP has dominated the Diet for a generation, the support of the party is sufficient to ensure enactment of a bill.

The top management of the LDP PARC currently includes a chairman *(kaicho)*, eight vice-chairmen *(fukukaicho)* and a deliberative council *(shingi iinkai)* with nineteen members. The PARC is organized into seventeen divisions *(bukai)* that correspond to important units of the bureaucracy. Each of the twelve ministries, for example, has an approximately corresponding division, although the Ministry of Agriculture, Forestry, and Fisheries is represented by separate divisions for agriculture, forestry, and fisheries. The other four divisions of the PARC include cabinet affairs, local affairs, science and technology, and environmental affairs. The divisions also correspond to some of the standing committees of the Diet. Aside from the divisions, the PARC now includes nearly 100 special committees.[29] This is more than double the number reported in the late 1960s by Thayer and Fukui.

Campbell describes the relationship between the LDP PARC and the bureaucracy as similar to that between the American executive departments and bureaus and congressional legislative committees.[30] According to Thayer, in the 1960s most of the work of the PARC was carried out by the bureaucrats.

> Most of the bureau directors of the various ministries are on intimate terms with their respective committees, divisions, and commissions in the policy affairs research council. They spend a great deal of time testifying, and their staffs spend a great deal of time preparing research for them. No bureaucrat who hopes to have ministry ideas translated into laws will fail to touch base early and often with the party organs. And aside from legislation, the party organs hold the ministries responsible for keeping them informed of recent developments in their respective areas of interest.[31]

The balance of knowledge appears to have shifted significantly in the past decade, and the politicians are now sometimes better informed than the bureaucrats—largely because the Tanaka faction has dominated the party for more than a decade and division chairman have acquired substantial expertise.[32]

Japanese Diet members often become identified as the mentors of certain industries. Sometimes they are former bureaucrats who have past connections with the industry, such as Hayashi Yoshiro who worked with the machine tool industry as a MITI section chief, and continued to be interested in this industry after retiring from MITI and being elected to the Diet in 1969. An industry and a politician also form links as the politician moves through the posts of division chairman in the PARC, chairman of the Joint Committee and the Houses, Parliamentary vice-minister and minister.[33]

A mentor relationship was reportedly established in the robotics industry in 1979 when Yonemoto Kanji, the executive director of the Japan Industrial Robot Association, managed to convince Watanabe Kozo of the importance of his industry. Watanabe was then the chairman of the PARC's commerce and industry division [shoko bukai]. Watanabe is described as having been instrumental in the fiscal year 1980 budget allocation of some 40 million yen for the promotion of the robotics industry. This included public funds to support a leasing system, special depreciation allowances, and later (in 1983) support for the AIST National Advanced Robot Technology R&D Project.[34]

Mentors for the steel industry have included Akita Daisuke (a vice-speaker of the House of Representatives) and Shintani Torasaburo (a former bureaucrat of the Ministry of Post and Telecommunications). The study we draw on for this account lists some sixty-five people who could be considered mentors for various industrial sectors.[35]

The U.S. Government and Trade Associations

Recent policy debate has emphasized the Japanese government's use of business associations to coordinate business activities in an effort to make business more efficient. Such efforts are seen as alien from an American point of view. It is frequently forgotten that the U.S. government has also in its history attempted to use business associations as policy instruments.

Efforts to organize a national chamber of commerce in the United States can be traced back as far as 1859, and an organization that attempted to function as a national chamber (the National Board of Trade) began to operate in 1868.[36] The growth in membership of this national organization did not keep pace with the increasing number of commercial organizations in the United States, which led to internal efforts beginning in 1910 to reorganize it. The first such initiative came from the Department of Commerce and Labor and its secretary, Oscar Straus, in 1907. The department created a National Council of Commerce from boards of trade and chambers of commerce of the forty largest U.S. cities. The council was to act as an intermediary between local commercial bodies and the department in making available the information collected by the department concerning foreign trade.[37] Straus's successor, Charles Nagel, however, made it clear that he considered the council just another private organization, not a semipublic body. One month after the New York *Journal Of Commerce* attributed to Nagel critical views of the council's activity, its chief officers resigned.[38] The council dissolved in 1912 upon the organization of the U.S. Chamber of Commerce.

Because of the vigorous antitrust policy of Taft's Justice Department, the administration's relations with big business were strained. Nagel was therefore anxious to develop rapport with small business and also was wary of the "trusts." Nagel and Taft came to support a national chamber of commerce to represent a broad business constituency and find support within business for the administration. In 1911 Taft announced publicly in a message to Congress that he supported a "central organization" of businessmen that would represent "different phases of commercial affairs."[39] Taft advocated the new group in the part of his message dealing with foreign policy, probably because he saw the expansion of trade as one of the most obvious areas of common interest in the business community.

Nagel and his department were directly involved in forming the chamber. Indeed the initial letter proposing such a body was drafted by A. H. Baldwin, head of the Bureau of Manufacturers. Nagel sent Baldwin to commercial associations across the country, especially to those made up of smaller manufacturers and merchants who exhibited the greatest interest in a national group. The largest industrial concerns were not interested at first and were somewhat skeptical about the prospects for the success of such a group.

The first substantial formal interaction between trade associations and the federal government in the United States took place during World War I. The Wilson administration created the War Industries Board to supervise the production of goods for the war effort. Because of the legal difficulties caused by having business people serve in an organization that had a voice in the allocation of government contracts, the administration turned to trade association officials as their connections to the private sector. Although Woodrow Wilson was unenthusiastic about trade associations, viewing them as an unwarranted concentration of power, circumstances compelled the administration to create "war service committees" in each industry to cooperate with the War Industries Board.[40]

During the 1920s Herbert Hoover's tenure as secretary of commerce witnessed a determined effort by that agency to create a system whereby:

> America would benefit from scientific rationalization and social engineering without sacrificing the energy and creativity inherent in individual effort, "grassroots" involvement, and private enterprise. Such a synthesis, [Hoover]

argued, would make the "American system" superior to any other, particularly in its ability to raise living standards, harmonize industrial relationships and integrate conflicting social elements into a harmonious community of interests. And the key to its achievement, he had concluded on the basis of his wartime engineering and personal experience, lay in the development of cooperative institutions, particularly trade associations, professional societies, and similar organizations among farmers and laborers. These, Hoover and other associationists believed, would form a type of private government, one that would meet the need for national reform, greater stability, and steady expansion, yet avoid the evils long associated with "capital consolidations," politicized cartels, and governmental bureaucracies.[41]

Hoover envisioned a network of associations that would interact with a Department of Commerce systematically reorganized as a department of economic development and international trade—not unlike MITI and certainly not unlike some recent proposals for reorganizations of the federal executive branch.[42] Although his ambitious reorganization plan was not realized, Hoover did make internal changes in the Commerce Department: he reorganized the Bureau of Foreign and Domestic Commerce along commodity lines, and established cooperating private enterprise groups, typically chosen by the relevant trade associations.[43]

In the steel and machine tool industries, a number of smaller U.S. associations were formed under the stimulus of the National Recovery Act legislation or from a desire of the federal government to influence the federal government's allocation of materials during World War II.[44] But the only direct governmental encouragement of trade association formation in iron and steel or in machine tools we uncovered was in the case of the American Institute for Imported Steel. During the Korean War, Department of Commerce officials encouraged several steel importing firms to form this association. The American Institute for Imported Steel still exists to represent the interests of firms that import about 70 percent of total import tonnage. Although in the early 1950s steel imports were a very small proportion of total U.S. domestic consumption, wartime pressure on steel supplies led the government to seek a reliable source of information about importing activities. Of course, as steel imports have risen over the years, their economic importance and their political significance have increased. The institute, in addition to its information gathering activities, represents the industry before political bodies on import-related matters, serves as the chief channel of communication between American importers and exporters and foreign steel producers and suppliers, and works to maintain adherence to quality and product standards and existing trade customs and practices.[45]

The nature of appropriate association–government relations has not surfaced as an important issue in recent decades. The only significant policy initiative relevant to association–government relations in recent years has been the controversy of the early 1970s regarding the proper constitution and conduct of federal government advisory committees. (Since trade associations are only one potential source of members for U.S. advisory committees, this controversy was not about associations per se, but rather about the definition of "special interests" and the legitimacy of their involvement in the policy formation process in such a fashion.) The claim that association activities currently lack legitimacy because of their cartelistic activities in the nineteenth century is difficult to reconcile with the continued treatment of association involvement in the public sphere as a nonissue.[46]

The survey of trade associations carried out in 1938–1939 by the Temporary National Economic Committee (TNEC) found that the most common activity of trade associations was involvement in government relations: 82 percent of the responding associations reported activity in this area. Not all government relations is lobbying; some large part consists simply of informing association members of current laws and policies or responding to information requests from government agencies and legislators. Some 45 percent of those responding stated, however, that they had contacted members of legislative bodies, presumably with the intent to influence legislation.[47] A study of British trade associations in 1957 revealed a similar centrality for government relations activity in associations, but no systematic survey results were published.[48] Our examination of U.S. trade association activities in the iron and steel and machine tool sectors showed a similar importance of governmental relations, and the NAM surveys reported in chapter 4 suggest that government relations is important in American industry more generally as well. The results of a 1980 survey show that about one of four U.S. trade associations spends more than one-third of its budget on government relations, and one of ten spends more than 60 percent. The activities of associations that do not attempt to fulfill a broader, general purpose role for their members are most frequently government relations and public relations.[49]

As a glance at the list of witnesses appearing before Congress on many bills will show, trade associations are ubiquitous in their legislative presence. Moreover, since trade association staffs sometimes mobilize individual company members to testify in addition to (or instead of) the association, the official hearing record in such cases may lead the observer to underestimate the importance of the informal, behind the scenes coordinating activity in shaping legislative outcomes.

Trade associations in the American political system can and do intervene at any level of government—in the legislative, executive, or judicial branches. Unlike in Japan, the U.S. federal structure of government and the lack of continuous one-party dominance create a situation where there is no single obvious entry point for access to the political system. The NMTBA, for example, has been involved in policy debates ranging from the decision by the Chicago area Metropolitan Fair and Exposition Authority and Illinois state legislature to spend $250 million to expand McCormick Place convention center to congressional votes on legislation easing export controls on high-technology products to a presidential decision on whether to grant NMTBA's petition restricting imports of machine tools on national security grounds.[50] A central trade association in a large industry—such as AISI in the steel industry—may at any given time be involved in close to a dozen political initiatives. The 1984 annual report of the AISI lists the following activities:

• monitoring closely the implementation of the steel agreements between the United States and the European Economic Community
• lobbying for the Fair Trade in Steel Act
• helping to found and participating in the Trade Reform Action Coalition—sixty-seven trade associations and labor unions
• supporting a trade bill sponsored by U.S. Rep. Sam Gibbons
• working to eliminate export financing by the Organization for Economic Cooperation and Development (OECD) in the less-developed countries; halting Export-Import Bank financing of the Kwangyung Bay facility in South Korea
• monitoring foreign trade zone applications; becoming involved in foreign trade zone applications in the Chicago area
• joining with other groups in a successful effort to persuade the federal government to reconsider plans to impose incremental pricing rules on natural gas used in important industrial operations; seeking rule changes so that pipeline companies would carry "self-help" gas at reasonable rates

In addition, AISI had joined with Chevron, General Motors, and other plaintiffs in a successful bid to have the Supreme Court rule that manufacturers can count an entire factory as a single emissions source with respect to federal clean air standards.[51] An AISI staff member served on the steel advisory committee, and AISI staff played a prominent role in the organization of the committee. In the spring of

1985 AISI lobbied to reduce or eliminate reductions in federal funding for customs inspectors and chemists in the U.S. Customs Service.[52]

In addition to its interests in product liability, NMTBA has been involved in shaping federal tax policy, particularly inasmuch as changes in the tax code affect capital spending plans of manufacturers. Its staff also are concerned with export controls on trade with east bloc countries and monitor regulatory developments in areas such as occupational safety and health.

The high level of government relations activity of the above associations is not atypical. The 1985 NAM survey of manufacturing associations found that 86 percent of them performed at least one government relations function. In general, the activity of business in government relations, which was much noticed in the mid- and late 1970s, has continued to grow. Compared with the 1982 survey results, the 1985 NAM survey showed higher levels of trade association involvement in all government relations functions but one: the operation of political action committees. Compared with nongovernmental activities of the same associations, only statistics, education, and public relations are more common activities than involvement in regulatory affairs or retaining Washington representation.

What political issues are trade associations involved in? The National Association of Manufacturers Computerized Associations Resources Index (CARI) annually compiles a summary of member associations' interests and the legislative coalitions that they join. Based on the CARI data, product safety, labor relations, and international trade, in that order, are currently the most widespread political concerns among manufacturing trade associations.

Political Action Committees and Other Electoral Expenditures. The involvement of associations in the operation of political action committees appears to have peaked in the late 1970s or early 1980s. The 1985 NAM survey of manufacturing trade associations reveals that operation of a PAC is one of only two government affairs activities to have declined in popularity in recent years (see table 5–1). According to the survey narrative, the main reason for their decreasing popularity is the difficulty in raising sufficient money to make a PAC viable. One fourth of the NAM survey respondents, primarily associations with budgets over $1 million, reported having PACs. Of all the associations having PACs, 24 percent reported they were unable to raise more than $5,000 in a full two-year election cycle, and only another 24 percent were able to raise $25,000 or more.[53]

Although most of the large, integrated producers have had their own PACs for some time, the AISI does not operate a political action

TABLE 5-1
U.S. MANUFACTURING ASSOCIATIONS PERFORMING
VARIOUS GOVERNMENT RELATIONS FUNCTIONS,
1982 AND 1985
(percent)

Function	1982	1985
Congressional affairs	69	70
Regulatory affairs	78	79
Government affairs committee	71	76
Legislative response network	57	71
Political education	20	15
Political action committees	33	26
Government relations conference	39	45
Washington representation	67	86

SOURCE: National Association of Manufacturers, *Manufacturing Trade Associations: Their Changing Focus and Management* (Washington, D.C.: NAM, 1985), p. 37.

committee. Aside from its own employees, AISI could raise funds only by soliciting from employees of member companies, and if they operate a PAC, they no doubt are reluctant to share their contributions pool with the industry association PAC. In the steel industry, Bethlehem, U.S. Steel, Armco, Inland, LTV, Republic, Wheeling-Pittsburgh, and National all operated PACs in 1982.[54] The machine tool builder firms generally employ fewer people than the integrated steel companies, and the industry also contains many small companies for which a firm PAC would not be worthwhile to operate. Even the industry leaders, however, tend not to have PACs, and the corporate PACs in the machine tool industry are not particularly large. Of eleven leading machine tool builders listed by *Forbes*, only four had PACs operating at the time of the 1980 election; of those four, the largest PAC contributed only $35,000;[55] this compares to political contributions of $183,906 by the U.S. Steel PAC for the same time period.[56] Total contributions by Machine ToolPAC of NMTBA for 1984 were $41,757; the Tooling & Machining PAC, operated the National Tooling and Machining Association (the trade association for machine shops) contributed $165,400 in that same year.[57] Such expenditure levels are quite modest when compared not only with those of large "ideological" PACs or with those of the realtors and physicians (in the million dollar range), but are even smaller than those given by many individual Fortune 500 corporations.[58]

TABLE 5-2
Salience of Political Issues
to U.S. Manufacturing Trade Associations, 1984–1986

Issue	1984 Ranking	1985 Ranking	1986 Ranking	Percent mention, 1986
Product safety	1	1	1	97
Labor relations	2	3	2	88
Taxation	6	4	3	86
International trade	3	2	4	84
Environment	5	6	5	83
Association management	14	5	6	74
Innovation/technology	10	8	6	74
Regulation and competition	4	7	8	72
Deficits/budget	7	9	9	64
Employee benefits	11	11	10	43
Energy	9	10	11	40
State and local issues	17	14	11	40
Antitrust	8	13	13	38
International finance	12	12	13	38
Transportation	13	16	15	33
Resources	15	15	16	21
Agriculture	16	17	17	12

Source: National Association of Manufacturers, Association Council, *CARI: Guide to the Computerized Associations' Resources Index* (Washington, D.C.: NAM, 1986), p. 7.

Some trade association expenditures, although not explicitly targeted at aiding candidates, are nonetheless intended to influence the course of an election, set the agenda for candidates' discussion of issues, and shape public opinion on new legislative proposals by officeholders. During 1980 the five most frequent "public policy" advertisers were all trade associations.[59] A survey by *Industrial Marketing* reported that companies supported such association efforts for two reasons: "One, the expense needed to even dent public opinion is staggering. Two, more than a few . . . companies have some serious credibility problems because of . . . years of bad press." Association ads give companies "more bang for the buck:"[60] the pooling of expenditures makes an association campaign to influence public policy much more attractive than a campaign led by a firm of a few hundred employees.

Policy-Making Networks. There are also political resources that are nonfinancial. Networks of personal connections and friendships, involvement in party politics, and prior government service can be important political assets. In contrast to the Japanese situation, our interviews with trade association personnel in the United States revealed that trade association staff members generally did not have prior government service and were generally not active in party politics. (We suspect that trade association political affairs directors may be a partial exception to this observation, but we did not interview enough of them to allow us to generalize about them.) The only remotely "Japanese style" career path we found was that of one vice-president of AISI who had served as a subcabinet officer in the Commerce Department in the Kennedy-Johnson years. The most common career path in the associations we contacted was simply a move from employment in one of the industry's firms to employment in the trade association.[61] In many smaller associations, staff positions are often filled by association professionals whose career path consists primarily of movement from one association position to another. Such individuals are not in the position to build the same kind of personal networks as those moving between government and business.

Comments about the political connections and activities of trade association staff do not necessarily apply to the board members or company-delegated executives. Chief executive officers of large firms, for example, may be quite well connected politically and use their connections to benefit their industry. It is neither analytically nor practically useful, however, to attempt to apportion their influence into personal, corporate, and association components.

Industry Activity and Bargaining with the Executive Branch: The Case of the Steel Industry. The steel industry and the machine tool industry both have a long history of interaction with the federal government. The steel industry historically has employed many more people than the machine tool industry and has been faced with a different set of political concerns than has the machine tool industry. The industry has long been the object of attention of the highest levels of the executive branch. Kim McQuaid has recounted some of the details of the bargaining in 1938 between Franklin Roosevelt and Myron Taylor and Edward Stettinius of U.S. Steel in which the White House offered various inducements and threats in an attempt to persuade the company to maintain wage rates rather than reduce them.[62] The 1962 confrontation between the industry and the Kennedy White House is well known.[63] Another important high-level bargaining session occurred in 1984, when the Reagan administration and top level executives of the domestic steel industry concluded a "memorandum of understanding" setting forth government policy on trade, taxes, antitrust, and the environment. The text of the memo seems to commit the Reagan administration to taking a negotiating position in talks with steel exporting countries that would limit exports to not more than 18.5 percent of apparent domestic consumption; it also commits the administration to introducing and supporting legislation that will make any such arrangements enforceable by customs. The administration pledges to uphold these limits for at least five years, but there is a "presumption" of renewals of the program. The industry in turn agreed not to file unfair trade cases, except against semifinished steel imports, against a country as long as it makes "satisfactory progress" toward meeting the objectives of this program.[64] The agreement was worked out by steel industry leaders interacting directly with the White House.

Employment of Outside Political Lobbyists. Although both NMTBA and AISI are relatively large associations, their political affairs staffs are small—fewer than half a dozen in both cases.[65] Neither association, however, relies solely on its own staff for its political activities. Member firms often have their own governmental affairs departments and those of large firms typically dwarf those of associations. Sometimes government affairs personnel wear the hat of association representative in testimony or other governmental relations activities. In addition, associations may retain a professional lobbying or public relations firm to assist the association on specific political tasks. Reliance on outside lobbyists, coupled with the frequent rotation of association officers and staff tenures generally not much longer than ten–fifteen years, means that American associations, unlike their Japanese counterparts, cannot capitalize on the long-term presence of top association officials in the political system. Since the representatives of the association change more quickly, they do not have a chance to build up the extensive personal networks that some Japanese trade association officials seem to possess.

Advisory Committees in the United States: The Case of the Steel Advisory Committee. Although in the United States the civilian side of the federal government has not recently performed any activities to promote trade associations analogous to those of MITI that we have discussed, there is one federal government institution with a close analogue in Japan: the federal advisory committee.[66] It has been suggested that the policy-making process in the United States could be improved by strengthening the advisory committee system so that committees could be used as a forum for mid-level bargaining among all affected interest groups to create policy consensus.[67] The steel advisory committee created by the Reagan administration bore some of the desired characteristics of this strengthened advisory committee system—there was an attempt to include all of the relevant interests and to reach genuine consensus, and staff resources and the attention of high-level government officials were devoted to ensuring that the effort was successful.

The steel advisory committee was initiated by discussions in 1983 involving Robert Peabody and James Collins of AISI, Jack Sheehan and Ed Ayoub of the United Steelworkers, and Clarence J. Brown, deputy secretary of commerce. The committee structure that developed out of this and subsequent discussions established a work plan for the committee and each of its five subcommittees (on the state of the industry; trade issues; industry rationalization; capital formation; employment, productivity, and adjustment). Each subcommittee was chaired by an official from a government department (the Commerce Dept., the Labor Dept. the Office of the U.S. Trade Representative, and the Council of Economic Advisers) and included in addition three government, three union, and three industry members. Public comments were taken by the full committee when the committee reviewed the reports of the individual subcommittees.[68]

The committee spent its first six months preparing the overall "state of the industry" document; the other committee reports occupied the next five months.[69] The committee on capital formation did not produce a unified statement: instead, separate comments were filed by Treasury, the industry, and the union. The only overall agreement was on a broad recommendation to support "policies conducive to sustained economic growth and continued expansion of plant and equipment." The committee on rationalization focused solely on antitrust policy; most of its recommendations endorsed existing policy. The subcommittee on employment generated seven policy recommendations pertaining to labor-management participation teams, employment health costs, adjustment assistance policies, and employment security. Its recommendations were usually general, nontechnical statements of desired governmental action. The recommendations of the subcommittee on trade amounted to an endorsement of the current Reagan administration policy initiatives in trade in steel. Its report on the state of the industry was the lengthiest component of the committee's report, providing a baseline for additional advisory committee recommendations and serving as the "threshold document" for the interagency group on the steel industry established by the Reagan administration in 1984.[70]

AISI staff who were interviewed regarding the steel advisory committee found it to be a mildly useful exercise, but managed to keep their enthusiasm for their experience well within bounds. They (and to some extent other Commerce Department staff on the committee) perceived it as a favor to labor, because the late Lloyd McBride of the United Steelworkers had been the most vocal advocate of such a committee. One high official of AISI saw the advisory committee as providing the benefit of educating government and labor staffs about industry capital needs and elements of the trade problems facing the industry. He was not optimistic that significant tangible policy changes would emerge from the advisory committee process. He explained that industry expectations of the results of such committees were now lower than they had been before their participation in the Carter administration tripartite committee system.[71]

The advisory committee process in this case simply provided an occasion where (1) existing policy initiatives were further ratified and legitimized; (2) some general suggestions for changes in some specific policies were made; (3) agreement on the current state of the world was fashioned; (4) discussion was limited to *public sector* actions that would improve the industry's health. Private sector actions were treated either as corporate prerogatives or as subjects for collective bargaining and were not on the agenda of the committee. Since the output of such a committee is literally advisory and not formally binding on any actor, and since agreement with labor and government is necessary before a recommendation can emerge from the committee structure, it is not surprising that industry officials would prefer to work directly with state officials in a traditional political relationship, where these limitations are not present.

Coalitions in the Trade Issue. Lacking a network of aggregating associations, and faced with peak associations (the National Association of Manufacturers and the U.S. Chamber of Commerce) that are frequently viewed by association staff as too large and cumbersome to manage much collective action, U.S. associations have come to rely heavily on informal, ad hoc coalitions to attain their public policy objectives. In this section we discuss the formation of coalitions in international trade.

Although large associations like NMTBA and AISI have enough resources to work alone on many issues, they may also join legislative coalitions—a product liability coalition in the case of NMTBA, the Trade Reform Action Coalition in the case of AISI. AISI was instrumental in founding the coalition and performs much of the coalition's work in its own offices. The coalition is composed of several smaller groups of firms, unions, and associations: The American Fiber, Textile, and Apparel Coalition (eighteen trade associations and two labor unions); the American Furniture Manufacturers Association; the Automotive Service Industry Association; the Group of 33 (twenty-eight trade associations and five unions in industries such as footwear, leather products, chemicals, lead and zinc, textile machinery, industrial equipment, various textile and apparel products, and agricultural products); the Metalworking Fair Trade Coalition (thirty-six trade associations in the metalworking industry); the National Coal Association; and the Steel Service Center Institute.[72] The Committee to Preserve American Color Television (three manufacturers and eleven labor unions) was a member in 1983 but subsequently left the coalition. The members of the Trade Reform Action Coalition claim to employ more than 5.25 million workers and generate annual sales of over $312 billion.[73] AISI is also a member of the Deficit Reduction Coalition, a group of 325 companies and trade associations that worked to promote passage of the 1985 budget compromise between the Reagan White House and the Republican leadership in the Senate.[74]

The Trade Reform Action Coalition (TRAC) and an industry proposal for a steel quota were born simultaneously. The staff of AISI had always been aware of which industries were experiencing difficulties due to imports; when they sought to form a coalition they did not have to spend much time searching for coalition partners. Natural agreement within TRAC has been described as high, with little need for substantial bargaining. One staffer described the organization as having a "silent majority" and a core of active participants who are necessarily sensitive to the preferences of those who are silent. The coalition has a loose-knit, informal operating style, with much of its activity being conducted by ad hoc groups. Most differences within the coalition are handled informally and off the record. The formation of the coalition was not connected to any actions by the Congressional Steel Caucus or other group of office holders.[75]

Coalition building on the trade issue experienced a sizable increase in activity in 1983–1984. Partly in response to the formation of the Trade Reform Action Coalition and its efforts to pass a Fair Trade in Steel Act, a group known as Steel Users and Suppliers of America formed in the autumn of 1984. Another group formed at that time was Steel Products Manufacturers Committee, composed of seven major metalworking industry concerns.[76] Consumers for World Trade, a group of agricultural, consumer and retailing groups as well as metalworking firms and at least one steel company (Nucor), urged President Reagan in August 1984 to reject steel quotas.[77] Another group,

111

the American Council for International Business, composed of over 200 firms and trade associations, also lobbied in 1984 against protectionist measures in tariff legislation.[78] In early 1985 four congressional caucuses—those for steel, autos, copper, and textiles—announced plans to work together to support measures aimed at attaining protection for each sector.[79] An AISI staff person working on TRAC interviewed at the time this coalition was announced, remarked that his organization had not anticipated this development; thus it is possible the impetus for the coalition came largely from Congress.[80]

Business–Government Relations in Japan and the United States

One of the most noticeable differences in business–government relations between the United States and Japan is that in Japan they are much more highly structured and long-lasting. This, of course, is consistent with our observation in chapter 3 that Japanese business interests are much more systematically aggregated than are business interests in the United States. Other Japanese institutions show a similar orderliness and stability when compared with their American counterparts.

Part of the stability of the Japanese business–government relationship is probably due to the unbroken control of government by the Liberal-Democratic Party for a generation. Some might also be attributed to the greater likelihood that Japanese government, trade association, and corporate officials have longer tenure in their positions. American political and economic systems experience more rapid turnover of both elected and appointed officials.[81] Such rapid turnover in itself is probably an important cause of less cooperative relations in the United States.[82]

This contrast is reflected in the advisory councils in the two countries. In the United States, advisory councils tend to be ad hoc groups with an ad hoc agenda and ad hoc mission. In Japan advisory councils tend to be long-lasting bodies with a formal charter; a prominent example is the Industrial Structure Council, which was formally established in 1964 under provisions of the MITI Establishment Law. It has well-defined rules for membership, a highly structured system of committees and subcommittees, and regularly issues reports in response to government requests.

The relative orderliness in Japan is also reflected in the organization of political contributions. According to one recent account, the five major integrated steelmakers were all among the twenty largest donors to the Liberal-Democratic Party. Indeed, Nippon Steel was the second largest corporate donor (after Nissan). But both the Japan Iron and Steel Federation and the Kozai Club made larger contributions than Nippon Steel.[83] By contrast, in the United States it is unusual for a trade association to operate a larger political action committee than its member firms, unless the members are so small (for example, realtors, auto dealers) that their individual efforts would carry insignificant weight.

A common question is whether the balance of power between business and government in the United States differs from that in Japan. Phrasing the comparison in this way is probably not very useful. Clearly the Japanese government, through MITI and some of the laws described elsewhere in this study, has more formal authority than do comparable U.S. government agencies. But business organizations such as Keidanren and others also are more influential than comparable organizations in the United States. The greater capacities of business and government to help or harm each other's interests, in conjunction with the relative weakness of nonbusiness political groups in Japan and their exclusion from the policy-making process, has led to a more cooperative relationship between the two than has generally occurred in the United States. Relations between business and the state in either society cannot be fully understood without also comprehending the political strength of nonbusiness forces.

In Japan there is reason to believe the historical pattern of close and cordial relations between business and government is now weakening. As new industries rise and as all industries establish new international ties, it becomes harder to maintain a single common business interest. Nippon Steel has less power within the steel industry than it used to, and the steel industry has less power in the Japanese business community. In government too, cleavages are appearing. Some of the new high-technology industries fall outside the traditional areas that MITI has overseen. Other ministries have advanced their claims to jurisdiction over computer software, biotechnology, telecommunications, and other emergent technologies. The internationalization of Japanese business has made it less dependent on finance from Japanese sources and less constrained by laws governing imports of raw materials and exports than was true in the past. This weakens a historically important method of state "guidance" for private business decisions.

Since the early 1970s there has been a noticeable trend toward increased collective political action by business associations in the United States. Various sources of the trend toward collective action in the United States have been hypothesized: the rise of the public interest movement and its initial victories; the increasingly decentralized Congress and the growing inability of key members to head off legislation that business did not want; declining economic performance, which brought lower corporate profits and increased public receptivity to arguments that major reforms were too heavy a burden for a fragile economy.[84] The trend toward collective action can be likened to an arms race or a tariff war, in which action by one or a few actors alters the incentives for others to act, causing the process to snowball. As sections of the business community become more active politically, the unorganized sectors risk losing some benefits because the political and economic costs of various policies fall on the unorganzied actors.

Although in the United States business has become more politically active, it has not adopted the Japanese-style norms and institutions promoting business cohesion. In spite of temporary business unity around Reagan administration tax and budget proposals, and the rise of the Business Roundtable and other new organizations, strong consensus-building organizations comparable to Keidanren to mediate between American business organizations do not seem to be emerging. A study of how a business "general interest" is fashioned in the United States found that particularistic norms and practices are entrenched; although top-level business organizations such as the Committee for Economic Development may take an interest in system-wide issues, those interests generally do not extend to sector-specific associations.[85] To the extent that business groups expend effort merely in rent-seeking and in neutralizing one another's political influence, they divert resources away from more socially useful activities. The possibility raised by Mancur Olson and others—that the policies that emerge as a result of these pressures might retard rather than enhance economic performance—is a very real one.

Notes

1. A treatment of this topic that is accessible to the lay reader is Russell Hardin's *Collective Action* (Baltimore, Md.: Johns Hopkins University Press, 1982).

2. George McRobie et al., *Industrial Trade Associations* (London: Political and Economic Planning, 1957), pp. 66–67.

3. Ibid., p. 67.

4. James Abegglen, ed., *Business Strategies for Japan* (Tokyo: Sophia University Press, 1970), p. 72.

5. Several reasons for the relative strength of the bureaucracy have been given: the traditional closeness of the Liberal-Democratic Party (many of whose leaders are former bureaucrats) to the bureaucracy; the small staff size of Diet members, requiring them to seek help from bureaucrats and others in drafting bills; the respect bureaucrats, as opposed to politicians, are accorded in Japan.

6. Other ministries oversee those in their own domains, such as finance, construction, and transportation.

7. In 1983 MITI had 12,892 personnel of whom 9,808 were attached to the ministry proper, making it one of the smaller government ministries. The Ministry of Finance, for example, had some 76,310 personnel, of whom 23,485 were attached to the ministry proper. See Japan Administrative Management Bureau, *Organization of the Government of Japan 1983*, (Tokyo: Institute of Administrative Management, 1983).

8. The quotations and overall descriptions in this section are drawn from Japan Trade and Industry Publicity, Inc., *MITI Handbook* (Tokyo: Japan Trade and Industry Publicity, annual).

9. The activities and organizations mentioned here are discussed in detail in chapter 7.

10. Narita Yoshiaki, "Gyosei Shido," in Hideo Tanaka, ed., *The Japanese Legal System* (Tokyo: Tokyo University Pres, 1976), pp. 353–90.

11. Johnson, *MITI and the Japanese Miracle* (Stanford, Calif.: Stanford University Press, 1982), pp. 224–25.

12. Some parts of the steel industry were doing well, so a recession cartel could not be formed.

13. Eugene Kaplan, *Japan: the Government-Business Relationship* (Washington, D.C.: U.S. Department of Commerce, 1972), pp. 147–48.

14. Hiroshi Shiono, "Administrative Guidance," in Kiyoaki Tsuji, ed., *Public Administration in Japan* (Tokyo: Tokyo University Press, 1984), pp. 203–215. See also Johnson, *MITI*, p. 300.

15. Masanao Nakagawa, ed., *Antimonopoly Legislation of Japan* (Tokyo: Kosei Torikhiki Kyokai, 1984), p. 171.

16. Shiono, "Administrative Guidance."

17. Inayama passed the higher civil service examinations in 1928 and entered the Ministry of Commerce. He then started working at the government-owned Yawata steel works.

18. Johnson, *MITI*, lists the *amakudari* positions of retired MITI vice-ministers as of 1978. p. 72.

19. Leonard Lynn, *How Japan Innovates: A Comparison with the U.S. in the Case of Oxygen Steelmaking* (Boulder, Colo.: Westview Press, 1982), p. 53.

20. Ezra Vogel, *Comeback: Case by Case—Building the Resurgence of American Business* (New York: Simon and Schuster, 1985), p. 64.

21. JIRA, Japan Industrial Robot Association, *10-Nen No Ayumi* (Tokyo: JIRA, 1982), p. 62.

22. William G. Ouchi, *The M-Form Society* (Reading, Mass.: Addison-Wesley, 1984), pp. 236–39.

23. Gyosei Kanricho, ed., *Shingikai Soran*, 1983 (Tokyo: Ministry of Finance Printing Bureau, 1983).

24. Richard J. Samuels, "The Industrial Destructuring of the Japanese Aluminum Industry," *Pacific Affairs*, vol. 56 (Fall 1983), pp. 495–509. As we saw in chapter 4, in developing its vision for the 1980s, MITI turned to an advisory council which in turn asked the Japan Industrial Robotics Association to draft a vision for the robotics industry.

25. Ibid., pp. 501–02.

26. General sources on the PARCs include Nathaniel Thayer, *How the Conservatives Rule Japan* (Princeton, N.J.: Princeton University Press, 1969); Koji Kakizawa, "The Diet and the Bureaucracy: The Budget as a Case Study," in Francis Valeo and Charles Morrison, eds., *The Japanese Diet and the U.S. Congress* (Boulder, Colo.: Westview Press, 1983).

27. Shoichi Izumi, "Diet Members," in Francis R. Valeo and Charles F. Morrison, eds., *The Japanese Diet and the U.S. Congress*, (Boulder, Colo.: Westview Press, 1983), pp. 61–78.

28. Haruhiro Fukui, *Party in Power: The Japanese Liberal-Democrats and Policymaking* (Berkeley: University of California Press, 1970), p. 83.

29. *Seikan Yoran 1984* (Tokyo: Seisaku Jihosha, 1984).

30. John Campbell, *Contemporary Japanese Budget Politics* (Berkeley: University of California Press, 1977), pp. 122–25.

31. Thayer, *How the Conservatives Rule Japan*, p. 226.

32. Chalmers Johnson, "Tanaka Kakuei, Structural Corruption, and the Advent of Machine Politics in Japan," *Journal of Japanese Studies*, vol. 12 (Winter 1986), pp. 1–28.

33. Nihon Keizai Shimbun, *Jiminto Seichokai* (Tokyo: Nihon Keizai Shinbum, 1983), p. 24.

34. Ibid., pp. 23–24, 27.

35. Ibid., p. 25.

36. Kenneth Sturges, *American Chambers of Commerce* (New York: Moffat, Dard and Company, 1915), p. 56.

37. Sturges, *American Chambers of Commerce*, pp. 60–61.

38. Becker, *The Dynamics of Business-Government Relations: Industry and Exports, 1893–1921* (Chicago: University of Chicago Press, 1982), p. 120.

39. Ibid., p. 121.

40. Daniel R. Beaver, *Newton D. Baker and the American War Effort, 1917–1919* (Lincoln, Neb.: University of Nebraska Press, 1966), pp. 74–76; Robert D.Cuff, *The War Industries Board: Business–Government Relations During World War I* (Baltimore, Md.: Johns Hopkins University Press, 1973).

41. Ellis W. Hawley, "Herbert Hoover, the Commerce Secetariat, and the Vision of an 'Associative State,' 1921–1928," *The Journal of American History*, vol. 61 (June 1974), pp. 117.

42. Ibid., p. 121.

43. Ibid., p. 124.

44. Although a discussion of NRA as well as business–government relations in World Wars I and II is certainly relevant to understanding the evolution of government–business relations in the United States, space limitations prohibit a fuller discussion. For more background on the NRA and trade associations, see in particular Robert Himmelberg, *The Origins of the National Recovery Administration: Business, Government, and the Trade Association Issue, 1921–1933* (New York: Fordham University Press, 1976).

45. American Institute for Imported Steel, "Fact Sheet: American Institute for Imported Steel," December 5, 1983.

46. See William G. Ouchi, "The Microeconomic Policy Dialogue: Analysis

116

and Recommendations," *Global Competition: The New Reality, Volume II*, Report of the Presidents Commission on Industrial Competitiveness (Washington, D.C.: U.S. Government Printing Office, January 1985), p. 364.

47. Temporary National Economic Committee, *Investigation of Concentration of Economic Power*, Monograph #18, Trade Association Survey, 76th Congress, 3rd session (Washington, D.C.: U.S. Government Printing Office, 1940), pp. 334, 336.

48. McRobie, *Industrial Trade Associations*.

49. Udo H. Staber, "The Organizational Properties of Trade Associations" (Ph.D. diss., Cornell University, 1982), pp. 265–68.

50. *American Metal Market*, "Tool Imports Get 41.5% of 1st Qtr. Sales," September 3, 1984.

51. Mark Bomster, "Top Court Rules for AISI on Pollution Control Issue," *American Metal Market*, June 26, 1984.

52. Jan Green, "Steel Industry Fights Customs Staff Cuts," *American Metal Market*, April 9, 1985, p. 6.

53. National Association of Manufacturers, *Manufacturing Trade Associations*, p. 39.

54. Marvin J. Weinberger, *The Pac Directory: A Complete Guide to Political Action Committees* (Cambridge, Mass.: Ballinger, 1982).

55. Jill Bettner, "Industrial Equipment and Services," *Forbes*, January 2, 1984, p. 195.

56. Edward Roeder, *PACS Americana* (Washington, D.C.: Sunshine Services Corp., 1982).

57. Figures supplied by staff of Federal Election Commission.

58. Focusing only on trade association PAC donations can give a misleading picture of total industry electoral spending. In addition to donations by PACs of individual firms in the industry, one must also count the individual contributions of managers and owners as at least partly an "industry" rather than a purely individual expenditure—the interest of such individuals in policies which aid the industry in which they have a substantial personal stake is obvious. Finally, some sizable "soft money" expenditures by individuals or by PACs may not fall under the reporting requirements. See, for example, Elizabeth Drew, *Politics and Money: The New Road to Corruption* (New York: Macmillan, 1983).

59. The five were the American Gas Association, the American Council on Life Insurance, the Chemical Manufacturers' Association, the American Insurance Association, and the Association of American Railroads. See William C. Frederick and Mildred S. Myers, "Public Policy Advertising and the 1980 Presidential Election," in *Research in Corporate Social Performance and Policy*, vol. 5 (Greenwich, Conn.: JAI Press, 1983), p. 69.

60. Ibid., pp. 70–71.

61. An interesting sidelight to this generalization is that two of the AISI vice-presidents are British.

62. Kim McQuaid, *Big Business and Presidential Power From FDR to Reagan* (New York: William Morrow, 1982), pp. 11–17.

63. A leading industry executive presents his perspective on the confronta-

117

tion in Roger Blough, *The Washington Embrace of Business* (Pittsburgh, Penn.: Carnegie-Mellon University; and Columbia University Press, 1975).

64. Martyn Chase, "Government Steel Trade Policy Documented," *American Metal Market*, October 25, 1984, pp. 1, 7.

65. Counting who is concerned with government affairs in a trade association staff is a tricky business, since many areas of association concern, from research and development to standards and regulations to broader concerns such as fiscal policy, all will entail some consideration of and interaction with the government. If, however, we restrict consideration to those staff who have as a primary responsibility government relations, the number generally is small.

66. As is often noted, the most relevant analogue to MITI in the American political system is probably the U.S Department of Defense. We did not investigate the relations between associations and the Department of Defense in this study.

67. Ouchi, "The Microeconomic Policy Dialogue," Appendix E.

68. Interview with Robert Brumley, U.S. Dept. of Commerce, Washington, D.C., November 29, 1984.

69. Ibid.

70. Remarks of Clarence J. Brown, deputy secretary, U.S. Department of Commerce, Steel Advisory Committee meeting, November 1984.

71. Interviews conducted by the authors with Robert Peabody and James Collins of AISI, and with Robert Brumley, and Timothy Roth, Dept. of Commerce, Washington, D.C., November 30, 1984.

72. One association conspicuous by it absence from the coalition is the National Machine Tool Builders Association.

73. Members of the Trade Reform Action Coalition (mimeo), February 1985.

74. "Business Coalition Spurs Deficit Cutting Budget," *American Metal Market*, June 3, 1985, p. 38. Other trade association members of the coalition in the metal and metalworking industries include the American Hardware Manufacturers Association, the American Mining Congress, the Construction Industry Manufacturers Association, the Cutting Tool Manufacturers Association, and the Valve Manufacturers Association.

75. Interviews by the authors with Frank Fenton and Barry Solarz, AISI, Washington, D.C., April 18, 1985.

76. Martyn Chase, "Coalition of Steel Consuming Firms Established to Fight Quotas," *American Metal Market*, September 6, 1984, p. 16.

77. Martyn Chase, "Ranks of Companies Opposed to Steel Quotas Reinforced," *American Metal Market*, September 14, 1984, p. 5.

78. "Business Group Urges Veto," *Pittsburgh Post-Gazette*, October 3, 1984, p. 20.

79. David Kramer, "4 Congressional Caucuses Plan Import Alliance," *American Metal Market*, March 27, 1985, p. 1.

80. Solarz interview.

81. There are fewer political appointees at the top of the Japanese bureaucracy than in the United States The prime minister appoints a cabinet

minister and one parliamentary vice-minister for each minister. Below this level all officials come up through the civil service.

82. Robert Axelrod, "The Emergence of Cooperation among Egoists," *American Political Science Review,* vol. 75, no. 2 (1981), pp. 306–18.

83. Nihon Keizai Shimbun, *Jiminto Seichokai,* pp. 230–34.

84. David Vogel, "The Power of Business in America: A Re-appraisal," British Journal of Political Science, vol. 13 (1983), pp. 19–43.

85. Staber, "Organizational Properties of Trade Associations." A useful comparison of the U.S. and British patterns of government relations with top-level business groups is provided by Michael Useem, *The Inner Circle: Large Corporations and the Rise of Business Political Activity in the United States and United Kingdom* (New York: Oxford University Press, 1984).

6
Trade Associations and Foreign Trade

A common and important role for trade associations in both the United States and Japan has been the promotion of exports for member firms and the protection of local markets against foreign competitors. These activities have intensified in recent years. In Japan there has been a widespread legal recognition and formalization of these activities. The various provisions of the Export-Import Transactions Law permit exemptions from the Antimonopoly Law to allow firms to engage in a wide range of collective action to promote exports: research on overseas markets and political environments, agreements on quality standards to protect the image of the Japanese industry, price agreements, overseas public relations and lobbying, etc. Sometimes special associations have been formed to carry out these activities or have spun off from existing trade associations to cope with demands from foreign governments that the volume of exports to their markets be reduced.[1]

Americans have seen many of these Japanese activities as a threat to U.S. industry. This argument was put forth strongly by Houdaille Industries in its petition to President Reagan in 1982. Some have argued that the United States should change its laws to allow U.S. firms to compete with the Japanese in export markets on a more equal footing. This chapter describes recent activities to promote exports (and protect domestic markets) by U.S. trade associations and gives some attention to efforts to learn from the Japanese in this area. Then, to put these efforts into context, the chapter describes some of the Japanese business associations that have been created to promote the interests of Japanese exporters.

Activities of U.S. Associations Related to Trade

Much of the attention given to trade association action related to foreign trade has been devoted to the efforts of groups hurt by import

120

competition to obtain relief through executive branch action or by persuading Congress to pass legislation establishing import quotas or increasing tariffs. In the United States the recent depression witnessed a surge in the filing of unfair trade petitions with the International Trade Commission (ITC). Domestic steel producers alone filed more than 150 such petitions in 1982.[2] (Most of these cases came under the antidumping and countervailing duty statutes.) One case that has attracted considerable attention was filed by Bethlehem Steel and the United Steelworkers under section 201 of the Trade Act of 1974. After a favorable ruling by the ITC, the Reagan administration agreed to seek voluntary export restraint agreements from various trading partners in exchange for the industry's pledge not to bring any more petitions against these countries.

The Specialty Steel Industry of the United States, which has largely eschewed coalition activities and collaboration with the carbon steel producers, has sought and attained some protection from imports. A four-year import restraint program begun in 1983 made the industry the "guinea pig" for the idea that import protection would be linked to modernizing investments.[3] In 1984 the association asked the Reagan administration to impose quotas on imports of stainless steel sheet and strip. Existing tariffs on flat-rolled products did not prevent increases in import market penetration for these products from occurring in 1984; the industry group desired that these products be treated like bar, rod, and wire products. The Reagan administration rejected their plea.[4]

In the machine tool industry, attention has focused on the petition filed by Houdaille Industries in 1982 under section 103 of the Revenue Act of 1971, which gives the president authority to withdraw investment tax credits from U.S. purchasers of equipment produced by a foreign cartel. Although it is a member of NMTBA (and was so at the time that it filed), the firm did not coordinate its strategy with NMTBA on trade matters and notified NMTBA of its intended filing only a few days before it took official action.[5] After the denial of its petition in 1983, Houdaille sought a working relationship with Okuma Machinery Works, a Japanese machine tool firm, the first step in a "more comprehensive" relationship.[6]

Another important case in the machine tool sector was the petition by the National Machine Tool Builders Association under section 232 of the Trade Expansion Act of 1962 for protection from imports on national security grounds. By mid-1983 NMTBA was estimated to have spent $800,000 on the 232 effort. They hired a leading Washington lobbying firm, one of whose partners is a close friend of the Reagan family. They met with many high-level Reagan administration

121

officials at the cabinet and the subcabinet level.[7] The business press reported that about 15 percent of the association members, many of whom have Japanese or other foreign owners, did not support the effort.[8]

At the NMTBA convention in the autumn of 1984 Walter Mondale announced support for NMTBA's 232 petition but NMTBA Executive Director James Gray said that "by January [1985] it may be too late—by then every major builder may have made an arrangement to source its machinery overseas."[9] Since the category of machinery, computers, and peripherals has constituted one of the most active sectors for the formation of joint ventures in recent years, and since many joint ventures involve links with foreign firms, Gray may have been correct.[10] A strategy similar to the one adopted by Houdaille can be readily emulated by other builders.[11] Such a development, in conjunction with the continued lack of success of such efforts as the 232 petition, could eventually lead to a shift in the political preferences of the association on matters of trade policy. Indeed, one industry observer has suggested that the shift is already under way.[12] In 1984 discussions were held between the association and officials of the Department of Defense Office of International Economics, Trade, and Security Policy. That office presented to the NMTBA Government Relations committee various possible policies for reviving the industry without relying on import quotas. The list ranged from ending the DOD waiver of buy-American rules for European machine tools, to accelerating defense purchases of machine tools for government-owned plants, to investing DOD Manufacturing Technology Program funds in machine tool development projects.[13]

In addition to appeals to the executive branch for relief of import pressure, trade associations have sought legislation from Congress on imports. The requests often have been for quotas or tariffs, but additional trade-related concerns are also on association agendas.

Trade rules involving Communist countries have received considerable attention from trade associations. AISI has testified on legislation to alter the way Communist country imports are treated in unfair trade cases.[14] NMTBA has long been concerned with the regulations regarding the export of critical technology to east bloc countries. Industries such as the machine tool builders are concerned that current Defense Department rules regarding exports to Communist countries are unduly restrictive, conferring a competitive advantage on producers in other Western countries that do not have to operate under such restrictions. The machine tool builders have advocated a measure that would restrict U.S. imports from any country that violates agreed restrictions on the export of goods to communist nations.[15] The specialty steel industry sought to extend an import ban on Soviet nickel to cover finished specialty steel products produced in third countries using Soviet nickel or nickel-bearing materials, but the Treasury Department rejected the petition.[16]

Also significant are association efforts to monitor administrative implementation of trade policy measures and to alter that implementation process when it appears to be working against their interests. The American Institute for Imported Steel took legal action to reverse a November 1984 Customs Service decision to embargo cargoes of pipe and tube imports from the European Economic Community while they were at sea. (The Customs Service had determined that imports of these commodities had already exceeded 1984 quotas and ordered the cargoes to be held in bonded warehouses until the end of 1984.)[17] The Metal Cutting Tool Institute and the Cutting Tool Manufacturers Association have asked for and received identifying markings on machines instead of on the packing boxes.[18] AISI has lobbied Congress against budget cuts for customs inspectors because of concern that a reduced staff would be less able to enforce existing trade regulations.[19]

Trade associations also participate in government advisory committees on trade policy. William Ouchi's study of federal advisory committees for the President's Commission on Industrial Competitiveness briefly examined the president's Export Council and the Industry Sector Advisory Committees for paper and paper products, aerospace equipment, capital goods, electronics and instrumentation, and ferrous ores and metals.[20] Ouchi concluded that these committees had served the nation well during the Tokyo Round trade negotiations, but that since then interest in these committees has declined, along with their effectiveness. Trade association representatives typically constitute a small percentage (about 10 percent) of the membership of such committees. Interviews with trade association representatives who had served on such committees revealed that trade association representatives do not play any special role as aggregators or brokers of interests and that official communication among industry advisory committee members outside of meetings is not common.[21] Thus, even if Ouchi's suggestions for improving the representativeness of advisory committees were adopted, a lack of lateral communication among members could inhibit the kind of "M-form" consensus-seeking process that he envisions.

Interest in these committees probably has declined because there has not been another set of trade negotiations comparable to the Tokyo Round. During the Tokyo Round, negotiators did consult with committee members, even at times calling committees directly from the negotiations site to confer about negotiating positions.[22] Trade association staff have also visited negotiations sites while negotiations were in progress to confer with negotiators.[23] With no negotiations going on, however, it is not surprising that participants in the committee invest less effort in the committee's work.

Export Promotion. An industry such as the U.S. carbon steel industry, which is import competitive, has little reason to devote effort to export promotion. Much of the steel the United States has exported in the past fifteen years has been due to foreign countries' fulfillment of "buy American" clauses in U.S. aid packages.[24] The machine tool industry, which manages to export substantial amounts of products even in the face of import competition, is in a different situation. The NMTBA has promoted exports since the 1960s, when the original motivation was simply to develop a market not wholly captive to the U.S. business cycle; it proudly proclaims that it was the first trade association to receive an award from the Department of Commerce for its efforts to promote exports.[25]

A major vehicle for promoting the sale of American machine tools abroad is the industrial exposition. Machine tool builders have recognized the value of expositions since the early 1900s, and NMTBA continues to organize and participate in them. An NMTBA-organized show in Shanghai in 1985 attracted 33,000 visitors and generated $10 million in sales and an anticipated $30 million in follow-on orders.[26] NMTBA also performs market surveys, inspects local metalworking plants to determine machinery needs, holds presentations of various sorts (catalog shows, video tape shows, applications-oriented technical presentations), leads industry-organized, government-approved trade missions, assists member firms in obtaining export licenses and holds seminars on exporting techniques, hosts foreign machine tool purchasing delegations, forwards product inquiries to appropriate member firms, and assists overseas buyers in planning large projects such as the equipping of entire plants.

In connection with a large transaction involving the Indonesian government, NMTBA performed the following functions:

• served as go-between for the Indonesian government in its initial contacts with American firms
• sent an NMTBA trade mission to Indonesia to discuss the technology needed to start up basic machine tool production
• indirectly assisted in putting together an attractive package of terms and conditions for its members to offer on the project (An export trading company was the actual negotiating agent.)

The National Tooling and Machining Association (NTMA) has also been active to some degree in promoting foreign business. The

People's Republic of China has asked NMTA to conduct technical seminars and to tour China's end users to determine their needs.[27] NTMA would demonstrate training programs and advise Chinese companies on how to set up their own programs.

Market Protection: The Case of AISI. As an association in an import-competitive industry, AISI has developed an extensive formal organizational structure to deal with trade issues. An international trade committee of AISI meets monthly; the vice-president for international trade and economics and his three subordinates staff that committee. The committee from time to time forms task forces on special subjects. Quasi-permanent task forces deal with executive branch appointments to relevant agencies (International Trade Commission, State Department, Commerce Department, U.S. Trade Representative); with "buy American" legislation at the state and federal levels; with foreign trade zones (monitoring their creation and objecting when they are seen as injurious to the U.S. industry); and with the customs service (monitoring performance and providing training seminars to customs personnel when needed). (When the association develops a position on a trade issue, the lobbying on the issue is then implemented by the government relations committee.)

AISI has been briefed by government officials on the status of negotiations on voluntary export restraints and given its reaction to those briefings. (At the same time the government briefed individual companies with petitions before the ITC and queried them as to what voluntary restraint agreement would constitute equivalent relief. It did not pose this question to AISI.)

AISI's decision in the spring of 1983 to seek legislative quotas on steel imports was the product of industry consensus, the trigger price mechanism of the Carter administration, and Reagan administration efforts to negotiate "voluntary" restrictions with foreign governments. Until 1982 the desire within the industry for quotas was not strong, but when a second attempt at using trigger prices collapsed and voluntary export restraints came to be perceived as ineffective, a clear preference for quotas began to emerge among AISI members. Since the Tokyo Round agreements constrain tariffs, and since the industry judged that tariffs would have to be very high to be effective, quotas became the preferred policy of the U.S. producers.[28]

Export Promotion Associations in the United States

Webb-Pomerene Associations. To a limited extent, U.S. companies may engage in some concerted export activities under the Webb-

Pomerene Act of 1918. The act permits associations of U.S. companies to obtain antitrust immunity for their activities and agreements made solely in pursuit of export trade as long as they do not restrain trade within the United States or restrain the export trade of U.S. competitors; these associations are roughly comparable to Japanese export associations. The Webb-Pomerene Act probably affords protection for price, export volume, and territorial agreements in pursuit of export trade.[29] As noted by Atwood and Brewster, "As far as can be determined from legislative history, [Federal Trade] Commission practice, and court decision, an association may be loose or close and it is at liberty to allocate quotas, fix prices, or determine other terms of its members' export sales."[30] Under the act, however, export trade as defined does not include such activities as provision of services, technology licensing, or foreign investment. Under the Webb-Pomerene Act, U.S. companies are not permitted to act in concert to restructure their industry, allocate product manufacturing specialities, or otherwise engage in domestic anticompetitive activities.

To date, few companies have sought the immunity afforded by the Webb-Pomerene Act, partly because the scope of immunity is unclear. "No definite standards are prescribed for permissible activities, and no explicit procedure is stipulated for prior review of a Webb-Pomerene association's operations. The inevitable result of this uncertainty has been administrative and judicial rulemaking which has done more to restrain than to advance the intent of the Act."[31] The activities of a Webb-Pomerene association could also be challenged under the antitrust or other laws of a foreign nation, even though the same practices are permitted by U.S. law. Such a challenge occurred in 1982 in the European Economic Community against a Webb-Pomerene association engaged in the export of paper products.[32] In addition, the Webb-Pomerene Act only exempts goods, but not services. Thus, marketing, financing, transportation, insurance, or other service activties required by foreign trade would not be covered by this act.[33]

Although in 1978 there was one Webb-Pomerene association with members from the machine tool industry (the American Machine Tool Consortium), it did not engage in the sale of any numerically controlled machine tools and has since been dissolved. As of 1982 there were no Webb-Pomerene Associations in the machine tool industry, and only thirty-nine such associations in all.[34]

Export Trading Companies. Legislation in 1982 removed legal impediments to collective action by U.S. firms engaged in foreign commerce, which eased legal restrictions on export trading companies. Export trading companies are not trade associations; nor are they entirely new institutions in the American economy. (A study of the law notes that export trading companies were common in the American economy throughout the first hundred years of independence from Britain.[35]) They are, however, the closest American parallel to either the famed Japanese general trading companies, the *sogo shosha*, or the export trade associations discussed below.

The Export Trading Company Act of 1982 was intended by Congress to remedy the fragmented nature of the export trade service industry in the United States and the lack of financial leverage of the sector. It is the stated purpose of the act to increase U.S. exports of products and services by encouraging more efficient provision of export trade services to U.S. producers and suppliers. It establishes an office within the Department of Commerce to promote formation of export trade associations and export trading companies, permits holdings by various financial institutions in export trading companies, reduces restrictions on trade financing provided by financial institutions, and modifies the application of the antitrust laws to export trade. The act allows persons interested in establishing export trading companies to apply to the Department of Commerce for a "certificate of review," which certifies that the export company will not engage in activities that lessen competition or restrain trade in the domestic market or that restrain trade of any competitor and that its activities will not "unreasonably" affect prices of the goods being exported, will not constitute an "unfair" method of competition, and will not create a situation in which the exported goods are reasonably expected to be reimported to the United States. The certificate of review protects the bearer from antitrust suits.[36]

As of June 1985, fifty-four certificates of review had been issued by the Commerce Department's Office of Export Trading Company Affairs.[37] Nearly two years after passage of the Act, the *Wall Street Journal* reported that most such companies were not yet profitable and had not attained high sales volumes. Observers attributed the weak performance of these companies partly to economic conditions nationally and worldwide, and partly to the inexperience and lack of expertise of the American companies.[38] A later report on export trading companies operated by banks painted a picture of mixed results and predicted a shakeout among the thirty-eight bank-affiliated export trading companies.[39]

It is possible that under the more permissive legal environment created by the 1982 legislation novel institutional forms may emerge and become significant actors in American foreign commerce. Joint ventures in providing services and permanent joint ventures in overseas manufacturing and construction are now legally feasible. It is also possible that the new act will encourage U.S. competitors to form joint ventures to allow exchanges of pricing data that would be relevant to fashioning a coordinated bidding strategy for overseas transactions. Such a practice would begin to approach that of the traditional export cartel. Another possibility is represented by nonprofit trading companies established by private or public agencies to maximize the volume of exports from a given geographic region. The Port Authority of New York has expressed interest in establishing such a company to benefit the economy of the region and to improve load factors on the authority's transportation system.[40]

Foreign Trade and Japanese Associations

As we saw in chapter 2, the effects of foreign competition and possibilities for exports were central factors in the organization of Japanese trade associations. Indeed, coping with foreign trade has generally been of more immediate importance to Japanese than to American business. The Japanese were far more remote, both geographically and culturally, from the sources of their imports and from many of their richer foreign markets. Europeans and even Americans could operate in each other's economies much more easily than could the Japanese. As exporters the Japanese frequently found themselves faced with demands to raise their prices or establish quotas, demands they were able to meet more easily through collective action. The Japanese were also quite concerned with import competition. In steel and machine tools this has been a far more historically prevalent focus of attention than the relatively recent prospect of substantial export sales.

Through the first half of this century Japanese iron and steel were not internationally competitive, and there was little effort on the part of industry associations to export. The problem, rather, was competing with foreign steel in the Japanese market. While 1936 saw a prewar peak of exports amounting to 500,000 tons of steel, more than half was to Manchuria and the other Japanese-controlled areas of China.[41] One of the functions of the Iron and Steel Council was to study the steel industries of other countries on behalf of the industry, but the focus of study was the capacity of foreigners to export to Japan rather than the capacity of foreign markets to absorb Japanese exports. This situation changed drastically in the 1950s. Although in the early 1950s, the Japanese steel industry was not as advanced as those in many other parts of the world, it could find overseas markets during periods of steel shortages. Foreign markets in the Far East that were not easily served by their European and American rivals particularly benefited them, especially during the Korean War years.

The major postwar association for steel producers and traders, the Kozai Club, was quick to help Japanese steelmakers identify and move into export markets. It began making overseas market surveys in 1949, collecting, compiling, and distributing reports and information from Europe and North America. A Japanese university professor sent back reports from Antwerp, Belgium, on developments in Europe. In 1950 the Kozai Club began publishing periodicals on the iron industry in Europe, the United States, and other countries. It began collecting major foreign trade journals and by the mid-1950s was producing specialized reports on aspects of the economic environment of the steel industry in foreign countries. Japanese studies in the early 1960s took up labor–management relations in the U.S. steel industry, U.S. market structure, trade, and other topics to give Japanese industry officials more information on U.S. attitudes and policies regarding dumping.[42]

Before World War II Japan had been overwhelmingly dependent on imported machine tools. Its own firms were small and scattered and survived by concentrating on narrow niches for less advanced equipment. There not only was little question of machine tool manufacturers organizing export drives, but also little point in attempting to lobby for import protection. During the war years government policy had channeled resources into the industry in an effort to build it up, but as discussed in chapter 2, the industry was in dire straits in the first few years after the war. Machine tools that had been used in the military economy glutted the market. In the 1960s the Japan Machine Tool Builders Association became more active in promoting exports, but before discussing these activities it is important to be aware of some legal changes that occurred in the early 1950s.

A major impetus for collective action in both the steel and the machine tool industries, as well as in many other industries, was the enactment of the Export Transactions Law of 1952. This was the first Japanese effort to attenuate the strict Antimonopoly Law imposed during the Occupation.[43]

The Export Transactions Law was enacted and implemented with notable speed as soon as the Occupation authorities were out of the way. MITI's International Trade Bureau, with the cooperation of the Japan Fair Trade Commission, drafted a bill providing for the law and just three weeks after the end of the Occupation submitted it to the Diet. Four months later, in September 1952, the new law was enacted. By the end of 1952 several exporters' associations had been established, including the Japan Machinery Exporters Association.[44] In at least some cases, the new export associations were former departments of existing trade associations. This was the case with Japan Iron and Steel Exporters Association (JISEA), for example. JISEA was essentially the overseas trade department of the Kozai Club. In 1986 the two organizations continued to share the same executive director and to occupy offices in the same building.

In its initial form the Export Transactions Law (*Yushutsu Torihiki Ho*, Law #299 of 1952) did not apply to imports, but the law was soon amended to cover imports and was given its present name, the Export-Import Transactions Law (EITL) (*Yushutsu Yunyu Torihiki Ho*, Law #188 of 1953). Provisions of the law were further extended in amendments proclaimed in 1955, 1957, and 1965, in the implementation order (*yushutsunyu torihikiho jikkorei*, 1955), and in ministerial orders (*shorei*) issued in subsequent years. The EITL provided a legal basis for businesses to form export trade associations (*yushutsu kumiai*) that could engage in many activities that otherwise would have been illegal under the AML. According to the EITL, export trade associations are specifically intended to:

- prevent unfair export trading by members
- develop and maintain export markets through the use of surveys, publicity, the provision of introductions, etc.
- improve the price, quality, design, etc. of export products
- handle foreign complaints and disputes related to exports
- establish facilities to promote the common interests of members
- lend funds to members and borrow on their behalf

Export associations are also allowed to establish standards of price, quality, design, and the like for products being exported to specific foreign markets, but must file a notification with MITI before doing so.[45] While these activities are couched in general terms, they clearly open the door to behavior that could restrain competition.

A point that has caught the attention of some critics of Japanese trade policies is that EITL provides for MITI and the export associations to share responsibilities. Under certain conditions, for example, MITI can issue a ministerial ordinance supporting the standards of price, quantity, design, and quality set by associations. Violators may be ordered by MITI to suspend exports of specified commodities for up to a year. The minister of international trade and industry may also entrust the administration of its ministerial ordinances to export associations, including the handling of applications for permission to export. Such applications are required for certain designated commodities. Among the ten groups of commodities designated in the ministerial order implementing the EITL were such items as bicycles, cigarette lighters, and flatware. In the case of bicycles the major concern was the volume of exports going to North America, and the Japan Bicycle Exporters Association administered the application process. In the case of cigarette lighters the concern was the design of products going all over the world, and authority over the application process was given to the Japan Light Industry Products Exporters Association. With flatware the concern was both the design and the volume of products being exported, and again the Japan Light Industry Products Exporters Association administered the process. Quality, price, and contract terms were of concern in other areas as well, and in all but one instance an export association was designated to handle the application process. More recently five associations have taken over this responsibility: the Japan Automobile Export Association, the Japan Electric Wire and Cable Exporters Association, the Japan Machinery Exporters Association, the Japan Pottery Exporters Association, and the Japan Pearl Exporters Association.[46]

Several of the exporters' associations are very active in the United States and other countries through their overseas offices. The Japan Iron and Steel Exporters Association has offices in Los Angeles, New York, and Paris. The Japan Machinery Exporters Association has offices in Brussels and New York. The Ship Exporters maintain an office in London, and the Textile Products Exporters Association one in New York.

The EITL is administered jointly by three divisions of MITI's International Trade Administration Bureau, the export division, the import division, and the general affairs division. Industry has an opportunity to shape the law through the Fair Export Import Trade Advisory Commission (Yushutsunyu Torihiki Shingikai). The commission, which was established in 1953, advises MITI on possible changes in ministerial ordinances related to the EITL. Members of the commission in 1983 included top executives from leading manufacturing firms, trading companies, and banks. Other members were senior executives from Keidanren, the Japan Chemical Industry Association, the Japan Light Industry Products Export Association, and a few scholars, journalists, and representatives of citizens groups.[47]

The Japanese Response to the U.S. Demand for Quotas in Steel. A recent example of the political activities of Japanese export associations is provided by the Japanese response to the 1984 petition of Bethlehem Steel and the United Steelworkers of America calling for a 15 percent market share limit on imported steel products over a five-year period. The petition was opposed at a public hearing in Washington by three export trade associations, the Japanese Iron and Steel

Exporters Association, the Japan Galvanized Iron Sheet Exporters Association, and the Japan Wire Products Exporters Association.[48]

Despite the efforts of these organizations, in June 1984 the U.S. International Trade Commission recommended that quotas be imposed. President Reagan rejected the recommendation but announced a plan to seek "voluntary" restraints from nations selling steel in the United States. Reagan sought to limit imports to 18.5 percent of the U.S. market. After difficult negotiations, officials from MITI accepted a quota of 5.8 percent of the U.S. market share for Japan. (The agreement was conditional on the cessation of trade or antitrust legal action in the United States against Japanese firms.) The quota required Japan to reduce its steel exports to the United States by roughly half a million tons. One problem was deciding how much each firm would have to reduce its exports to achieve the overall reduction. Should each firm's quota be based on its exports to the United States in the year before the quotas were imposed? Or should the quota be based on an average of each firm's exports over a period of several years? Many of the electric furnace "mini-mills" had been increasing their market share and would get larger quotas under a system based on exports in the most recent year. The integrated steelmakers would get larger quotas under a system based on an average of several years. Another issue was whether the appropriate law to use in allocating the reductions was the Foreign Trade Law or the Export–Import Transactions Law. Under the Foreign Trade Law the government would directly allocate quotas. Under the Export–Import Transactions Law the industry would form an export cartel and govern itself in setting the quotas. Since the major integrated firms dominated the trade associations, the export cartel would presumably work against the interests of the electric furnace steelmakers.[49]

As it turned out, MITI had the industry organize two export cartels under the Export-Import Transactions Law to coordinate Japanese compliance with the quota. One of these new organizations, the Cooperative Association for Iron and Steel Exports to the United States (Beikoku-muke Tekko Kyoryokukai) has some 200 firms as members. Its chairman is Takeda Yutaka, the president of Nippon Steel. This association allocates quota rights to steelmakers. Another association, the Japan Iron and Steel Exporters Association for the United States of America (Beikoku-muke Tekko Yushutsu Kumiai) then grants them export licenses. The latter association is a kind of joint venture of the three existing Japanese steel industry trade associations. Its members include thirty-eight trading companies, 121 manufacturers, and the three steel industry export associations. Its head is

Saito Yutaka, a Nippon Steel executive vice-president, and the chair of its executive committee is yet another Nippon Steel executive.[50] As with so many other activities in the Japanese economy, it is difficult to assess the relative weight of the roles of MITI and leading firms in allocating quotas. Japanese accounts describe MITI as exercising supervision, but do not go into detail. As in other instances where the United States forced "voluntary" restraint agreements on the Japanese, there are indications that the steel quota system put pressures on the Japanese system of antitrust. For that matter, MITI felt it necessary to get assurances from the U.S. Justice Department that the Japanese quota allocation system would not be the target of U.S. antitrust actions.[51]

Export Promotion in the Japanese Machine Tool Industry. The main export association serving the Japanese machine tool industry under the Export-Import Transactions Law is the Japan Machinery Exporters Association (JMEA). It serves a wide range of industries from automobiles to electronic communications equipment and cameras. One of the twenty-six divisions of JMEA is devoted to machine tools. As with the other export trade associations, JMEA has been active in collecting overseas market information, carrying out public relations activities, setting up trade fairs, etc. Beginning in 1963 with an office in Brussels, it has since set up offices in New York and Bangkok. In the late 1960s it had well over 600 members, but this number has since declined to about 550. In addition to promoting machine tool and other machinery exports, the JMEA also promotes "orderly exports" to various markets. In 1978 JMEA organized an agreement regarding price and volume of exports of certain machine tools to the United States. This agreement was extended year by year into the mid-1980s with the expectation that it would continue as long as there were trade problems. Other agreements followed in the late 1970s and 1980s.

The Japan Machine Tool Builders Association (JMTBA), of course, also plays a leading role in promoting Japanese machine tool exports. The JMTBA includes among its six committees two that are related to foreign trade: the Trade Committee and the Special Japan International Machine Tool Show Committee. The Trade Committee includes working groups focusing on export prospects, "orderly" exports, and government requests. For a while many of JMTBA's activities in this area were carried out by an affiliate organization, the Japan Machine Tool Export Promotion Association (Nippon Kikai Yushutsu Shingikai). This organization was established in 1962 as a spin-off of the Japan Machine Tool Builders Association during an export drive being promoted under the extension to the Extraordinary Measures Law for the Promotion of the Machinery Industry.[52] The new organization quickly opened branches in Chicago, Düsseldorf, São Paolo, and Vienna to handle public relations, conduct market surveys, set up exhibits, and perform other activities. In 1978 the society was merged into the JMTBA; the São Paolo office was closed, but the others continue to operate under the management of the JMTBA and the Japan External Trade Organization.[53]

Trade Associations and Foreign Trade: Summary

Our comparison of the roles of trade associations in Japan and the United States has shown that many apparently similar legal and organizational forms in fact have important differences.

The United States has long permitted the formation of export cartels through the Webb-Pomerene Act, but this institution has seldom been used. More recent legislation has eased financial and antitrust restrictions on collective action in foreign commerce, but it is too soon to know how important these changes will be. The Japanese government has gone considerably farther, not just permitting certain joint activities, but actually encouraging them. Japanese export associations are granted certain exemptions from antitrust law and also are delegated certain government responsibilities. They engage in direct efforts to sell the products of their members and in lobbying to shape laws in foreign countries, to control the quality of Japanese products being exported, and (often in response to demands from foreign governments) to control prices by their members. In comparison, American chambers of commerce in fifty-six foreign countries can perform many of these activities, but they are organized along territorial rather than product lines and enjoy no official U.S. government sanction.

It is not difficult to identify factors that have contributed to the much more prominent governmental role in Japan. Since Japan is poor in mineral resources and has little arable land relative to its population, it was required to expand drastically its imports of fuels and raw materials to carry out its expansion of industrial production. With industrial expansion came an increase in consumer incomes in Japan, and a consequent increase in the demand for food and other imports. Japanese policy makers faced several constraints in their ability to increase imports to allow industrial expansion. During the 1950s and 1960s they lacked international reserve assets. The government was committed to maintaining the value of the yen. It also decided not to admit significant foreign direct investment and restricted long-term Japanese borrowing abroad. Japanese economic expansion was thus limited by the extent to which the Japanese could expand their exports and restrain imports.[54]

Government's responsibility for promoting exports naturally coincided with the interests of business. The Japanese historically had unusual difficulties selling in the Western countries because of geographic, linguistic, and cultural barriers. Europeans and even Americans could operate in each other's economies much more easily than could the Japanese. These circumstances provided a strong incentive for Japanese business to pool its efforts. This incentive was substantially amplified by frequent outbreaks of negative reactions to the sudden and large-scale sale of low-priced Japanese goods in various countries. The Japanese were faced with demands for quotas or higher prices and could most easily meet the demands through collective action. They were historically plagued by an image of selling poor quality products (sometimes as they attempted to sell cheap merchandise made for Asian markets in the West). Through export associations and other organizations loosely affiliated with the trade associations and backed by law, it was possible to impose quality standards that would make it easier to sell Japanese products in general.

The United States has been in a substantially different situation and has perceived less need to develop institutions for joint action of the sort used by the Japanese. While some trade associations such as the NMTBA have devoted considerable resources to export promotion, it is fair to say that this activity has been much more emphasized in Japanese associations. Even when American business organizations were formed to promote exports, they have generally offered only a few of the advantages of their Japanese counterparts. The Japanese export associations now offer their members political and market information, as well as coordinated public relations activities in important foreign countries. American firms might benefit from having their trade associations perform more functions in their behalf, but because of the different pattern of government–business relations in this country, it is doubtful that American associations will ever perform the same mix of functions their Japanese counterparts do.

Notes

1. Japanese law has also sanctioned the formation of import cartels for various purposes. Some of these in earlier periods, for example, promoted the import of certain types of machines that the Japanese could not yet produce that were seen as vital to Japanese industry.

2. American Iron and Steel Institute, Steel in America—1983 (Washington, D.C.: AISI, 1983), p. 10.

3. Martyn Chase, "Specialty Steel Chief: Industry Plans Billion Dollar Outlay in 5 Years," *American Metal Market*, July 20, 1984, p. 1.

4. "Specialty Steel Fights for Protection," *American Metal Market*, September 7, 1984, p. 2; Mark Sfiligoj, "Trade Group Urges Quotas on Stainless," *American Metal Market*, March 5, 1985, p. 3.

5. Interview, Joe Franklin, National Machine Tool Builders Association, McLean, Va., November 30, 1984.

6. "Houdaille gets Japan Know-How to Produce Screw-Type Pumps," *American Metal Market*, November 15, 1984; "Houdaille, Okuma Reach Deal," *American Metal Market*, November 19, 1984; and "Houdaille to Build Machines for Okuma," *American Machinist*, January 1985, p. 25.

7. "NMTBA Mounts Huge Lobby," *American Metal Market*, September 5, 1983.

8. *Industry Week*, March 5, 1984, p. 15.

· 9. Nancy Kingman, "Mondale Tells Builders He Backs Import Relief," *American Metal Market*, September 17, 1984, pp. 4, 10.

10. "Joint Ventures: For Better or for Worse?" *Industry Week*, February 20, 1984, p. 39.

11. A similar strategy is being pursued in the steel industry. See Donald B. Thompson, "Can a Cause of a Problem Solve it? Japanese Connections Spreading through Steel Industry," *Industry Week*, May 14, 1984, p. 19.

12. Patricia L. Walker, "U.S. Tool Builders Gird to Compete Head-On," *American Metal Market*, May 13, 1985, p. 30.

13. "Hopes for NMTBA's 232 Petition Diminish," *American Metal Market*, November 1, 1984, p. 1.

14. "Reform Sought on Grievances versus Communists," *American Metal Market*, May 7, 1984, pp. 1, 8.

15. Alan Murray, "High-Tech U.S. Exports Pose Dilemma for Policy-Makers," *Congressional Quarterly*, March 26, 1983, p. 609; Rosanne Brooks, "Industrialists' Hopes Dashed for Easing of Export Rules," *American Metal Market*, October 15, 1984.

16. Martyn Chase, "Soviet Nickel Ban Extension Nixed," *American Metal Market*, August 8, 1984, p. 2.

17. Roberta C. Yafie, "AIIS Continues Fight on Pipe, Tube Embargo," *American Metal Market*, December 4, 1984, p. 1; Peter Wilkinson and Roberta C. Yafie, "Steel Embargo Appeal Weighed by Plaintiffs," *American Metal Market*, December 7, 1984, p. 7.

18. "Imported Cutting Tool Marketing Rules Tightened," *American Metal Market*, October 22, 1984, p. 6.

19. Jan Greene, "Steel Industry Fights Customs Staff Cuts," *American Metal Market*, April 9, 1985, p. 6.

20. William G. Ouchi, "The Microeconomic Policy Dialogue: Analysis and Recommendations," *Global Competition: The New Reality, Volume II*, Report of the President's Commission on Industrial Competitiveness (Washington, D.C.: U.S. Government Printing Office, 1985).

21. Interviews with William Rolland, National Electrical Manufacturers Association, and Robert Peabody, American Iron and Steel Institute, Wash-

ington, D.C., Nov. 30, 1984, and with Joe Franklin, NMTBA.

22. Interview with Franklin.

23. Staff for the Speciality Steel Industry of the United States visited negotiations sites in Korea, where talks with South Korea and Japan regarding voluntary export restraints on specialty steel products were under way. Martyn Chase, "U.S. Producers Win Some Import Category Relief," American Metal Market, Metalworking News, February 25, 1985, p. 70.

24. Interview, R. Thomas Wilson, American Iron and Steel Institute, Washington, D.C., January 13, 1985.

25. This occurred in 1970. See NMTBA, The National Machine Tool Builders Association, McLean, Va., 1981, p. 7.

26. "U.S. Show in Shanghai Seen a Success," American Machinist, May 1985, p. 47.

27. "China Industrial Minister Invites NMTA Mission in '85," American Metal Market, November 5, 1984, p. 7.

28. If foreign producers are experiencing capacity utilization problems, particularly in an industry with substantial economies of scale, then any selling price that exceeds marginal cost would be preferable to not selling.

29. James R. Atwood and Kingman Brewster, Antitrust and American Business Abroad, 2nd ed. (Colorado Springs, Colo.: Shepard's/McGraw-Hill, 1981).

30. Ibid., p. 320.

31. Statement of James M. Nicholson, U.S. Chamber of Commerce, "Failure of Webb-Pomerene Act," in International Aspects of Antitrust Laws: Hearings Before the Subcommittee on Antitrust and Monopoly of the Senate Judiciary Committee on the Present Laws, Current Theory and Trends of International Antitrust Laws, 93rd Congress, 1st and 2d sessions, (1973–1947), p. 162.

32. Bureau of National Affairs, U.S. Export Weekly, February 9, 1982, p. 517.

33. Dennis Unkovic et al., International Opportunities and the Export Trading Company Act of 1982 (Washington, D.C.: Bureau of National Affairs, 1984), p. A-6.

34. Federal Trade Commission, Webb-Pomerene Export Trade Associations, 1982.

35. Unkovic et al., International Opportunities, p. A-4.

36. Public Law 97–290, Title III section 306, 96 Stat. 1243; 15 U.S.C.S. 4001 et seq.

37. List of certificates issued by Office of Export Trading Company Affairs, International Trade Administration, Department of Commerce, July 1985.

38. Steve Weiner and Robert Johnson, "Falling Short: Export-Trading Firms in U.S. Are Failing to Fulfill Promise," Wall Street Journal, May 24, 1984, p. 1.

39. Richard L. Barovick, "U.S. Bank Trading Companies: Results Prove Mixed So Far," Journal of Commerce, October 15, 1985, p. 10.

40. Unkovic et al., International Opportunities, pp. A-5, A-6.

41. Nippon Tekko Renmei, Sengo Tekkoshi (Tokyo: Nippon Tekko Renmei, 1959), pp. 608–09.

42. Kozai Club, Kozai Kurabu Sanjugonen Shi (Tokyo: Kozai Club, 1982), pp. 161–62.

43. A generation earlier the first major laws regulating corporate conduct in

modern Japan also concerned exports. These included the Export Society Law and the Important Export Commodities Industrial Society Law, which were both enacted in 1925. These earlier laws allowed exporters to form associations and in some cases delegated governmental powers to them. Most disappeared during the Occupation. See E. B. Schumpeter, ed., *The Industrialization of Japan and Manchukuo, 1930–1940* (New York: Macmillan, 1940).

44. The official history of the Machinery Exporters Association describes this association's rush to organize. Japan Machinery Exporters Association, *Nippon Kikai Yushutsu Kumiai Sanjunenshi* (Tokyo: Japan Machinery Exporters Association, 1982), p. 34

45. Masanao Nakagawa, *Antimonopoly Legislation of Japan* (Tokyo: Kosei Torihiki Kyokai, 1985), pp. 263–64.

46. See Ibid., pp. 270–72 for Article 28 and MITI, *Tsusho Sangyo Roppo, 1977* (Tokyo: MITI, 1977), pp. 145–48 for the implementation ordinance. The list of associations given the authority to enforce ordinances is from Japan External Trade Organization, *A History of Japan's Postwar Export Policy* (Tokyo: JETRO, 1983), p. 52.

47. Japan, Administrative Management Bureau, *Shingikai Soran, 1983* (Tokyo: Ministry of Finance Bureau of Printing, 1983).

48. The Japan Steel Information Center (an office of the Japan Iron and Steel Exporters Association), Press Release, June 22, 1984. Few U.S. associations have offices in Japan that would allow a close monitoring of Japanese legal developments. One recent exception is the American Electronics Association which, with the aid of the U.S. Department of Commerce, opened an office in Tokyo in 1984.

49. Tsukawa Furukawa, "Japan to Restructure Steel Exports, Emphasizing Value-added Products," *American Metal Market*, December 17, 1984, p. 4.

50. Tsukawa Furukawa, "2 Groups Formed to Monitor Japan's Steel Exports to U.S.," *American Metal Market*, May 15, 1985, p. 4; Japan Iron and Steel Exporters Association, "Beikoku-muke Tekko Yushutsu Kumiai Hossoku," *Geppo*, vol. 881 (May 1985), pp. 2–4; and Japan Iron and Steel Exporters Association, "Beikoku-muke Tekko Yushutsu no Yushutsu Torihiki Shoninsei Iko ni Tsuite," *Geppo*, vol. 882 (May 1985), pp. 8–9.

51. Ibid.

52. Since the emphasis of this law was on the development of technology, we give more detail on it in chapter 7.

53. See Ezra Vogel, *Comeback: Case by Case—Building the Resurgence of American Business* (New York: Simon & Schuster, 1985), pp. 74–75; Japan Machine Tool Builders Association, *Haha Naru Kikai "20-nen no Ayumin"* (Tokyo: JMTBA, 1982), pp. 51–52, 70–71. The Japan External Trade Organization (JETRO) is a nonprofit trade promotion organization that was established by the Japanese government in 1958 to help businesses collect foreign trade information. Among its network of offices are four in the United States. The staff of the overseas offices study market conditions and relay their findings back to Japanese business firms. JETRO also organizes trade fairs, publicizes Japanese products, collects design information to allow modification of Japanese products for foreign markets, and "watches for signs of oncoming

import restrictions and strives to develop flexible responses to keep such restrictions from materializing and affecting trade." JETRO, *A History of Japan's Postwar Export Policy*.

54. Garner Ackley and Hiromitsu Ishi, "Fiscal, Monetary and Related Policies," in Hugh Patrick and Henry Rosovsky, *Asia's New Giant* (Washington, D.C.: The Brookings Institution, 1976, pp. 155–247.

7

Trade Associations and Industrial Research

Trade associations in both the United States and Japan have frequently provided their members with important services related to technology: giving them information on new technological developments, conducting research on their behalf, and on occasion receiving government research subsidies for them. These activities have, however, tended to be more constant and more intensive in Japan than in the United States.

It has been widely argued in recent years that Japanese businesses—fairly or unfairly—gain major advantages in international competition because they have fewer legal constraints and more official encouragement to collaborate on research than their American counterparts. James Abegglen and William Ouchi suggest that these Japanese policies carry lessons for the United States.[1] Nor is it just those comparing the United States with Japan who argue that the United States needs more collaborative research. As long ago as 1970 a German machine tool laboratory director argued:

> The American industry has too little research and no joint research at all. Everybody does his own research, meaning that research is limited to the big companies. [The Americans always say] that it is impossible to research jointly and to compete in the marketplace. As long as this view prevails, the industry will be declining. It will be outpaced by the young, fresh industries of Europe and especially Japan.[2]

More recently, a U.S. Department of Commerce study of the machine tool industry argued that it was "too fragmented and disorganized" to compete effectively against foreign producers.[3]

Collaboration, as is often pointed out, can prevent a wasteful duplication of research effort and might allow firms to carry out mutually beneficial activities that would not be done at all by any firm acting alone. An example is surveillance of technological developments in foreign countries. An association of firms may find it worthwhile to carry out basic research on behalf of an industry that

140

individual firms might be unwilling to undertake alone. A traditional concern has been that collaborative research could result in firms conspiring to withhold innovations from markets. The counterargument, heard with increasing frequency, is that the growth in power of foreign competitors makes this unlikely; if a cartel of U.S. firms failed to introduce the innovation they would lose market share to foreign competitors.

There are also critics of the Japanese "research cartels." Some representatives of U.S. industry, notably the Semiconductor Industry Association and Houdaille Industries, have argued that Japanese collaborative research is part of a "conspiracy" to target certain high-tech industries. The critics see collaborative research as an unfair concentration of Japanese economic and technological resources, forcing U.S. firms to compete not against individual Japanese businesses, but against "Japan, Incorporated."[4]

The arguments that collaborative research in Japan (and in some other countries) is effective and must be coped with have already had substantial influence on U.S. policy. One result was the passage of the National Cooperative Research Act of 1984 and the formation of research associations in a number of industries. The Keyworth Initiative and a range of other policy proposals have also surfaced in recent years.

This chapter describes some of the major Japanese trade association activities related to technology and Japanese research associations—organizations that are not themselves trade associations, but that are closely linked to them. We then turn our attention to similar activities of U.S. associations, and finally we discuss the Keyworth Initiative and the initial effects of the National Cooperative Research Act.

Japanese Trade Associations and Technology

Japanese trade associations play a broad and multifaceted role with respect to technology. They routinely collect and disseminate technical information, serve as conduits for government assistance to develop or use new technology, and conduct collaborative research.

The Collection of Information. The Japan Iron and Steel Federation (JISF) and the Iron and Steel Institute of Japan (ISIJ) have long monitored foreign technology on behalf of the Japanese steel industry. A JISF publication, *Seitetsu Gijutsu Soran* (Metallurgical Abstracts), was a major source of information for engineers and others in the steel industry from at least the early 1950s. The scope of this publication a generation ago is suggested by its January 1953 issue, which included abstracts of some 113 foreign articles and sixty-six Japanese-language articles. More recently, the JISF has published the *Tekko Shiryo Indekkusu* (Steel Data Index) and the *Kaigai Tekko Joho Juyo Kiji Sakuin* (Index to Important Foreign Articles on Iron and Steel). These monthly publications list and abstract a large number of recent articles (in the late 1970s they typically covered around 200 articles per month, most of them less than six weeks old). They are now published by the ISIJ, which also provides translations of foreign language articles. In the late 1970s the Japanese associations installed new computer systems in their libraries to enhance research by engineers from their member firms.

These activities stand in stark contrast with those of the major association representing the U.S. steel industry, the American Iron and Steel Institute (AISI). AISI has never scanned or translated foreign literature. It did maintain a library for its members, but at around the time the ISIJ was computerizing its library, the AISI was disbanding its library. In an added irony, many of the AISI library books on the Japanese steel industry were acquired by a consultant working for the Japan Iron and Steel Exporters Association.[5]

The Japanese Machine Tool Builders Association (JMTBA) surveys foreign patents and publishes information about them in its journal, *Kosaku Kikai News*. Associations in the machinery industries, including JMTBA, are supported in their information collecting by the Japan Society for the Promotion of the Machinery Industries (JSPMI), a foundation associated with MITI's Machinery and Information Industries Bureau. JSPMI was set up in its present form in 1964 with funds from the Japan Bicycle Promotion Association. As was mentioned in chapter 4, JSPMI manages an office building that is the headquarters for many trade associations in the machinery sector and that offers a library and computer center for trade associations to use.[6]

One of the earliest JSPMI activities was the collection and dissemination of foreign technical and economic information. This activity goes back to the late 1950s when it was performed by a public foundation that is identified as the predecessor of the JSPMI. The earlier organization set up a data room to provide foreign technical and economic information. The data room, which was taken over by the JSPMI, is widely used not only by people from the machinery industry trade associations, but also by people from individual firms, banks, and government. By the mid-1970s it included nearly 30,000 books.

JSPMI periodicals provide additional data to business and government. The *Kikai Kogyo Kaigai Joho* (Machinery Industry Overseas

Report) which began publication in 1959, offers economic information, digests of articles, and listings of important publications. By the mid-1970s monthly issues of the report came to about 180 pages, covering some 800 to 900 items. In the late 1960s JSPMI also started publishing the *Kigyo Joho Fairu* (Enterprise Information File) to make it easier for the Japanese to collect information on foreign companies.

JSPMI also sponsors overseas trips by researchers and technicians to international conferences and plant visits to facilitate the study of conditions and prospects for technology in other advanced countries. The researchers present their findings at special symposia and in the JSPMI publication, *Kikai Shinko* (Machinery Promotion).

JSPMI and other organizations, including the Japan Machine Tool Builders Association, have also imported high-technology foreign products for examination by Japanese firms. In the 1950s the JMTBA established a special committee for research on foreign-made machine tools and worked with researchers at government and university laboratories to collect and examine them.[7] In 1967 the JSPMI cleared and submitted applications for subsidy funds to the Japan Bicycle Rehabilitation Association and the Japan Motorcycle Rehabilitation Association for the purchase and examination of foreign-made numerically controlled machine tools. A report by the Semiconductor Industry Association claims that one-third to one-half of the money used to promote "research" in the very large scale integrated (VLSI) circuit program was used to purchase state-of-the-art U.S. semiconductor and test equipment. The implication is that this equipment is used for "study" by Japanese firms, allowing them a free ride on U.S. development costs.[8]

Other Japanese trade and technical associations collect similar kinds of information. The Japan Industrial Robotics Association (JIRA), for example, reviews and summarizes patents, articles, and symposia proceedings from around the world, collects catalogs and other materials, translates foreign literature, and sponsors studies and seminars in Japan on foreign technology and markets. JIRA has organized tours of universities and companies in the United States and Europe to study robotics research and invites foreign researchers to give lectures at universities and companies in Japan.

Collaborative Research. In addition to scanning the world for new technologies, Japanese business associations have also long engaged in collaborative research and development. The Iron and Steel Institute of Japan (ISIJ) had five technology committees for this purpose as early as 1925. In 1934 the Japan Society for the Promotion of Science set up a joint research committee on steelmaking and a comparable committee on ironmaking in 1943. Other cooperative research was jointly organized during the war years by the Iron and Steel Industry Control Association's research committee, the ISIJ, and the government. The Joint Iron and Steel Research Association (Tekko Gijutsu Kyodo Kenkyu Kai) was established in 1950 by the Iron and Steel Bureau of the Ministry of Commerce (now MITI), the ISIJ, and the Japan Steel Federation (which later became part of the Japan Iron and Steel Federation). The association carried out several research projects including joint research on oxygen steelmaking, with the participation of engineers from several companies.[9] In 1954 the Japan Iron and Steel Federation and the Japan Institute of Refractories organized collaborative research under the approval of MITI to develop high-quality domestic refractory brick for use in blast furnaces.

After the Joint Iron and Steel Research Association was absorbed by the ISIJ in 1961, its activities continued to expand, as did the scope of the collaborative efforts. In 1965 the association joined with other components of the ISIJ, the Japan Institute of Metals, and other academic associations to form the Iron and Steel Fundamental Research Association. In 1966 an equipment technology committee was set up to promote the "Japanization" of the steel plant equipment industry. The new committee included steelmakers as well as producers of steelmaking equipment.

In recent discussions in the United States, the most widely cited example of collaborative research involving several firms in Japan has been the very large scale integrated circuit project.[10] The Semiconductor Industry Association (SIA) focused on this project in alleging that research cartels form a major part of the Japanese government industrial targeting strategy. The SIA and others argue that the VLSI circuit project substantially speeded up the ability of Japanese firms to become internationally competitive in the semiconductor industry by allowing them to avoid wasteful duplicative research, saving them millions of dollars, and marshalling scarce resources to allow rapid and economical progress. They also argue that the research cartel received government subsidies that encouraged predatory pricing overseas of the products the technology developed. A result, according to SIA, is the recent inability of U.S. firms to compete with the Japanese in certain product lines, most notably 64K RAMs. The SIA argues that the patterns observed in the semiconductor industry also apply to other industries in which Japan has rapidly increased its competitive strength. For these reasons, it is worthwhile to quickly review the VLSI project, and then to give some sense as to how pervasive the relevant policies are. We will then turn to a discussion of the relationship between trade associations and research associations of the sort involved in the VLSI project.

The VLSI project. From 1976 until 1980, a cartel made up of the Japanese government and Japan's five leading semiconductor firms (Toshiba, Hitachi, NEC, Mitsubsihi, and Fujitsu) allocated research assignments to several research laboratories. MITI provided some $130 million in interest-free conditional loans to support the research, and participating firms provided $190 million in "matching funds." Different sources give different indicators of the success of the project, but several mention that it generated more than 1,000 new VLSI patents. It also sometimes noted that by 1982 Japanese firms had some 70 percent of the world market for 64K RAM computer chips.

The VLSI research association conducted its research at several sites and included researchers from all of the participating organizations. At the central research laboratory housed in the Nippon Electric Corporation (NEC) facility, some 100 researchers from MITI's Electronic-Technology Laboratories and association members spent four years developing the basic technological underpinnings for the project. Two other laboratories concentrated on applied research. One was most concerned with developing technologies for IBM-compatible computers, the other with developing technology for IBM-non-compatible computers. The VLSI projects at the two applied labs each included more than 300 researchers from member firms.[11] The SIA quotes a NEC executive as saying that without the program Japanese chip makers would have spent five times as much to develop the electron beam technology that came out of the project. The Japan Economic Institute, which is funded by the Japanese government, sought to rebut this claim:

> Any evidence for the SIA charge that the project resulted in R&D costs that were a fraction of what would have otherwise been the case is almost nonexistent (they rely on one quotation from a Japanese scientist). A bit of countervailing evidence is that one of the 6 Japanese producers of 64K RAMs (the production of technologies for which were the focus of the VLSI project), Oki Electric, was not a participant in the project.[12]

Oki, however, took twice as long to move from the sampling to the production stage with the 64K RAM firms as the VLSI association firms. Further, although Oki Electric was not a member of the project association, it may still have gained technology from it. Oki was involved in another VLSI project coordinated by Nippon Telephone

145

and Telegraph (NTT). Members of the two projects met about once every four months.[13] According to Ezra Vogel: "Oki was by no means discarded, because it continued to concentrate on peripherals, facsimiles, and other office equipment, and NTT later sent management and shared technology with its beloved but weakened child to enable it to produce viable semiconductors."[14]

As can be seen from table 7–1, between the enactment in 1961 and 1983 of legal provisions allowing the formation of research cartels, some sixty-three research cartels were formed. Unlike research associations in the United Kingdom and continental Europe, those in Japan tend to be made up of major firms engaged in specific high-technology research. The Japanese research cartels are dissolved when their research project is completed (some eighteen of those listed in table 7–1 have been dissolved).[15]

Japanese Law, Business Associations, and Technology. In discussing the antitrust environment for trade associations in Japan (chapter 3) we described special provisions that allow business associations exemptions from the Antimonopoly Law. We described some specific exemptions in our account of trade associations and export trade (chapter 6). Similar exemptions, indeed a series of laws, also permit and actively encourage some of the cooperative research efforts we have already described in this chapter.

Research associations (*kenkyu kumiai*) are authorized under the Mining and Manufacturing Technology Research Association Law (Kokogyo Gijutsu Kenkyu Kumiai Ho) of 1961.[16] Research associations can be organized at the initiative of either the government or private groups. Often the research associations, like export associations, are in fact organized and dominated by the trade associations.[17]

Other laws have encouraged associations of firms to collaborate on research, sometimes through the use of subsidies. Of special importance in the machine tool industry was a series of Extraordinary Measures Laws. The first of these, the Extraordinary Measures Law for the Promotion of the Machinery Industry (*kishinho*), was passed in 1956 and remained in effect until 1971. This law helped the machine tool builders in their research on foreign-made machine tools in the 1950s and 1960s. In 1971, the day after the 1956 law expired, the Extraordinary Measures Law for the Promotion of Specific Electronic Industries and Specific Machinery Industries (*kidenho*) was passed. A notification under the law allowed machine tool makers to engage in joint activities related to technology and called for the establishment of a system of joint research. This law, in turn, was replaced by another, the Extraordinary Measures Law for the Promotion of Spe-

TABLE 7-1
Japanese Research Associations, 1961–1983

Association	Date	Members
1. Polymer Materials	1961 (disbanded)	Asahi Glass, Asahi Chemical, Ajinomoto, 20 others
2. Industrialization of High-Grade Alcohol	1961 (disbanded)	Maruzen Oil, Hitachi, Nippon Soda
3. Amachi Research Lab.	1962 (disbanded)	7 companies in wool, etc.
4. Creep Testing	1962 (disbanded)	Yawata Steel and 21 others
5. Optical Industry	1962 (disbanded)	Asahi Optical, Canon, 43 others
6. Priority Refining	1962 (disbanded)	Fuji Steel, 2 others
7. Electronic Computer	1962 (disbanded)	Fujitsu, NEC Corp., Oki Electric Industry
8. Wool Products Solvent Dyeing	1962 (disbanded)	Kataoka Woolen Goods, Asahi Denka Kogyo, 2 others
9. Naniwa Casting	1963 (disbanded)	18 small casters in Osaka area
10. Dampening Material	1964 (disbanded)	6 firms, aviation standard packing firms
11. Aluminum Surface Treatment	1965–	33 firms
12. Heavy Oil Calcination of Coal	1965 (disbanded)	38 lime producers
13. Automotive Pollution and Safety Equipment	1971–	Hitachi, Jidosha Denki Kogyo, 3 others
14. General Automotive Safety and Pollution	1971–	Mitsubishi Electric, Nippon Air Brake, 4 others
15. Light Metal Composite Material	1971 (disbanded)	Nippon Light Metal Co., Sumitomo Chemical, 24 others
16. Super Computer	1972–	Fujitsu, Hitachi, 3 others

(Table continues)

147

Table 7–1 (continued)

Association	Date	Members
17. New Computer Series	1972–	NEC, Toshiba, 5 others
18. Super Computer	1972–	Mitsubishi Electric, Mitsubishi Research Institute
19. Medical Instruments	1973–	Shimadzu, Toshiba, 9 others
20. Nuclear Steelmaking	1973 (disbanded)	Nippon Steel, Nippon Kokan, Kawasaki Steel, Mitsubishi Heavy Industries, Ishikawajima-Harima Heavy Industries, 8 others
21. Steel Industry Nitrogen Oxide Prevention/Removal	1974 (disbanded)	Nippon Steel, Nippon Kokan, Kawasaki Steel, Sumitomo Metals, 5 others
22. Management Software Module	1974–	Nippon Computer System, Kinki Computer Consultants, 3 others
23. Office Software Module	1974–	Nippon Timeshare, 13 others
24. Design/Computation Software Module	1974–	5 companies
25. Operations Research Calculation Module	1974–	Kyoei Keisan Center, 7 others
26. Automatic Control Software Module	1974–	Control Engineering Laboratories, 3 others
27. Automatic Measurements	1974–	Ando Electric, 6 others
28. High Temperature Structural Safety	1974–	Kawasaki Heavy Industries, Toshiba, Hitachi, Mitsubishi Heavy Industries, 15 others

(Table continues)

Table 7–1 (continued)

Association	Date	Members
29. Comprehensive Traffic Control	1974 (disbanded)	NEC, Hitachi, Omron Tateishi Electronics, Toyota
30. Vinylchloride Environmental	1975 (disbanded)	Asahi Glass, Shinetsu Chemical, 17 others
31. Heavy Oil Chemical Raw Materials	1975–	Idemitsu Kosan, Showa Denko, Sumitomo Chemicals, 3 others
32. Aircraft Jet Engine	1976–	Kawasaki Heavy Industries, Mitsubishi Heavy Industries, Ishikawajima-Harima Heavy Industries
33. VLSI	1976–	General Computer Laboratories, NEC, Toshiba Information Systems, 4 others
34. Medical Equipment Research Lab. Laboratory	1976–	Asahi Chemical Industry Co., Toshiba, Hitachi, 2 others
35. New Housing Supply Systems	1977 (disbanded)	Takenaka Construction, Nippon Steel, 9 others
36. Pattern Information Processing System	1977 (disbanded)	Toshiba, NEC, Hitachi, 2 others
37. Electric Automobile	1978–	Daihatsu Motor Co., Toyo Kogyo, Hitachi, 7 others
38. Subsea Oil Production Laboratory	1978–	Arabian Oil, Ishikawajima-Harima Heavy Industries, Nippon Steel, 13 others

(Table continues)

Table 7–1 (continued)

Association	Date	Members
39. Flexible Manufacturing System Complex with Lasers	1978–	Toshiba Machine Co., Aida Engineering, Mitsubishi Electric, 17 others
40. High-Efficiency Gas Turbine	1978–	Central Electric Power Lab., Asahi Glass, Ishikawajima-Harima Heavy Industries, 12 others
41. Heavy Oil Countermeasures	1979–	Asia Oil, Ishikawajima-Harima Heavy Industries, Idemitsu, Kajima Oil, 28 others
42. Basic Computer	1979–	General Computer Lab., Fujitsu, Hitachi, 7 others
43. New Fuel Oil Development Technology Research Association	1980–	Asia Oil, Ajinomoto, Idemitsu, 20 others
44. Polymer Applications	1980–	Asahi Chemical, Asahi Glass, Teijin Ltd., Toray Industries, 5 others
45. Residential Waste Water Treatment Equipment System	1980–	Ebara Corp., Kurita Water Industries, Takenaka Construction, 5 others
46. One-Carbon-Molecule (C1) Chemical Technology Research Association	1980–	Mitsubishi Chemical Industries, Ube Industries, Ltd., Deicel Chemical, Kogyo, 12 others

(Table continues)

Table 7–1 (continued)

Association	Date	Members
47. Optical Application Systems	1981–	Optical Industry Technology Promotion Association, Fujitsu, Mitsubishi Electric, 12 others
48. Small-Scale Gas Cooling Technology	1981–	Tokyo Gas, Osaka Gas, Matsushita, 12 others
49. Synthetic Dye Technology	1981–	Nippon Karaku, Mitsubishi Chemical Industries, Sumitomo Kasei, Hodogaya Kagaku
50. Fine Ceramics	1981–	Toshiba, Kyocera, Asahi Glass, 12 others
51. Biotechnology Development	1981–	Mitsubishi Chemical, Sumitomo Chemical, Kyowa, 11 others
52. Fundamental Polymer	1981–	Toray, Mitsubishi, Asahi Glass, 8 others
53. High-Speed Computing System for Science and Technology	1981–	Fujitsu, Oki Electric, Toshiba, NEC, 2 others
54. Research Laboratory for Manganese Nodule Mining System	1982–	Ishikawajima-Harima Heavy Industries, Osaka S.B./Mitsui S.B., Metals Association
55. Industrial Furnace Research Laboratories	1982–	Ishikawajima-Harima Heavy Industries, Isolite Insulating Products, Chino Works, 4 others

(Table continues)

151

Table 7–1 (continued)

Association	Date	Members
56. New Basic Refining Technology	1982–	Nippon Steel, Nippon Kokan, Kawasaki Steel, Sumitomo Metals, 13 others
57. Oxygen Enriched Membrane Combustion	1982–	Asahi Glass, Teijin, Toyobo Co., Toray, 3 others
58. Paper Production	1982–	Oji, Jujo, Honshu Paper, Mitsubishi Heavy Industries, 22 others
59. Secondary and Tertiary Crude Petroleum Recovery Technology	1982–	Arabian Oil, Teikoku Oil, Nippon Kokan, 7 others
60. Surface Activator for Energy Development	1982–	Daiichi Kogyo, Kao Soap, Lion Corp., 3 others
61. Automated Sewing System	1982–	Aishin Seiki, Asahi Kasei, Ashikkusu, 25 others
62. Open-Pit Coal Mining Equipment	1983–	Kawasaki Heavy Industries, Hitachi Construction, Bridgestone Tire Co., 8 others
63. New Aluminum Refining	1983–	Nippon Light Metal, Showa Light Metal, Mitsui Aluminum, 4 others

SOURCE: MITI Agency for Industrial Science and Technology, *Kenkyu Kaihatsu Josei Seido* (Tokyo: MITI, 1983).

cific Machinery and Information Industries, which was in effect from 1978 through 1985.[18]

Research Subsidies from Government. The research associations listed in table 7–1 enjoy tax and other benefits. Many also receive special government subsidies and loans, often (as was the case with the VLSI research association) as part of the program of Japanese National R&D Projects administered by MITI's Agency for Industrial Science and Technology. Samuels observes that in recent years Japanese companies have seldom bothered to participate in research associations of this sort unless government funds were involved.[19] At this point it is not clear how extensively the Japanese government has subsidized the joint research association. The two major forms of assistance are conditional loans (hojokin) of the sort described by SIA in its descriptions of the VLSI, and consignment payments (itakuhi).[20] The assets used by firms for research association activities can be depreciated in one year, but in 1982 the Japanese Ministry of Finance estimated that only $17 million in tax revenues were lost because of appreciation.[21]

Conditional loans are offered at low and sometimes no interest at all. Repayment depends on the success of the project—if no successful technologies result, there may be no repayment requirement. If the research is successful, a seven-year grace period is allowed before the loan has to be repaid. Vogel argues that in practice the loans have only rarely been repaid, and calls them "matching grants." Materials published by the USITC, however, indicate that more than 40 percent of the loans made from 1974–1978 had been repaid by 1982.[22] Conditional loans finance about half the cost of a research project, with the rest provided by the organizations conducting the research. The companies receiving hojokin are allowed to keep any patents resulting from the research. Allocations of the loans are at MITI's discretion with the usual budgetary and political constraints. Under the Japanese government's system of subsidies for R&D in important technologies, some 52 billion yen in hojokin were allocated between 1950 and 1982, the largest for the VLSI project and for a project developing basic computer technology.[23]

Itakuhi is sometimes translated as "consignment payments," sometimes as "research contracts." In principle, itakuhi are for research that is relatively far removed from producing commercially applicable products. The government grants the money, specifies what is to be done, and retains rights to any patents that are developed. Significant itakuhi between 1976 and 1981 included $15.4 million for the research project on optical measurement and control system technology and $1.4 million for the project on scientific computing system technology (see table 7–1).

Trade associations have often been involved in the establishment and operation of these research cartels. In 1963–1965, for example, the Iron and Steel Technology Joint Research Association (a part of the Iron and Steel Institute of Japan and formerly a joint association with the Japan Iron and Steel Federation) formed a research association with the welding association to test materials used in nuclear furnaces. The government provided a grant of 85 million yen for this work. In its thirtieth anniversary history, the Japan Machine Tool Builders Association lists as one of its major technology-related activities cooperation in establishing the association to study the flexible manufacturing system complex with lasers. The director of the new association was the president of Toshiba Machine, a JMTBA member, and JMTBA members formed the core of the new association.

Trade associations also receive direct research subsidies from the Japanese government. Houdaille Industries documents these subsidies in its charges that a Japanese machine tool cartel, by which they refer collectively to the Japan Machine Tool Builders Association and the Japan Machine Tool Exporters Association, receives grants from the Japan Bicycle Rehabilitation Association and the Japan Motorcycle Rehabilitation Association. These MITI-affiliated organizations distribute funds from bicycle and motorcycle racing. According to Houdaille, in the fiscal year 1978 they distributed 28 billion yen, some 90 million of which went to the "machine tool cartel."

The Japan Industrial Robotics Association has also received subsidies from the Japan Motorcycle Rehabilitation Association. In 1982 JIRA received nearly 40 million yen (around $170,000) in *hojokin* from this source, more than a quarter of which went to sponsor lectures on robotics technology aimed at small and medium-sized firms. Much of the rest was spent on market research or research related to standard setting. JIRA also received about 19 million yen in direct government funds *(itakuhi)*, primarily for research on standard setting. Finally, in 1982 JIRA received about 8 million yen in government general funds. In turn, JIRA relays some money to individual firms for research on robotics. In 1983, for example, it gave around 20 million yen to robot producers such as Sankyo Seiki, Motoda Denshi, Toshiba Seiki, and Orii. In 1973 the JIRA began providing interest-free loans from the Motorcycle Rehabilitation Association to help robot producers develop software and other technology needed by their customers. By September 1982 some 4.3 billion yen had been lent out in 265 loans under this program.[24]

Before closing our discussion of research cartels in Japan, we would like to emphasize that from the standpoint of individual firms the strength of the carrots and sticks wielded by MITI is limited, as is the appeal of collaborative research to eliminate duplication. Firms that lead in a technology, not surprisingly, are reluctant to give up that lead by participating in a research cartel. This was reportedly the reason that Hitachi resisted strong pressure to participate in the design of a high power CO_2 laser in the Flexible Manufacturing System Complex with Laser Project.[25]

U.S. Trade Associations and Technology

The various activities of Japanese associations in research are not without parallel in the United States. The establishment of trade association labs or semiprivate or private nonprofit research institutes in the United States began before World War I; prominent examples of early trade association labs were the National Electric Lamp Association's Nela Park lab established in 1907 in Cleveland, the National Canners Association lab established in 1913, and other labs established by the Portland Cement Association, the Tanning Institute of Scientific Research, the American Textile Research Institute, the Horological Institute, and the American Institute of Baking.[26] As early as 1918 a formal conference on "cooperation in industrial research" was initiated by Dr. John Johnson (at that time secretary of the National Research Council, later director of the research department of U.S. Steel) and held under the auspices of the American Society for Testing Materials at its annual meeting. A Commerce Department report mentions a dozen associations that had established their own research labs by the mid-1920s.[27] At least some Americans were aware of cooperative research efforts in foreign countries and watched them closely.

In the mid-1950s at least sixty-six organizations operated industrial-type research laboratories, which employed about 700 scientists and engineers and accounted for 53 percent of the total cooperative private R&D effort at that time. Not all were trade associations: a Battelle study encompassed over 5,000 professional and technical societies, agricultural cooperatives, research-educational cooperatives, and "other cooperative groups." From this large sample, however, they were able to identify only 173 organizations as performing significant cooperative research.[28]

An alternative open to trade associations that did not operate their own labs was to enter into agreements with nongovernmental, nonprofit research institutes such as the Mellon Institute (established 1913) or the Battelle Memorial Institute (established 1929). By the interwar period the practice of setting up fellowships within educational institutions or research institutes for work on research problems germane to the associations' business activities was well established; such a program existed at the University of Kansas as early as 1907.

An association also might provide cooperative research support by serving as a clearinghouse for individual firms' innovations, as a collector of statistics pertaining to the performance of equipment and plants, and as a publisher of technical literature of use to members. At least some of these activities were becoming common as early as the 1920s. In the ebullient words of the Department of Commerce of that era: "Competitors today interchange experience and information and carry on, as a matter of course, cooperative activities which yesterday they would have looked upon as fantastic."[29]

In Japan several activities related to technology were carried out by the prewar steel industry, whereas little was done by the machine tool associations. In the United States in the same era the situation was similar. The prewar machine tool industry was fragmented. Although we do not have any statistics or details on prewar collective research, a study of U.S. cooperative research from the mid-1950s found that for manufacturing machinery (except electrical) (SIC 35) two cooperative organizations were engaged in research, with total expenditures of only $11,000. The average for all industries in the 1950s was $101,000 per research organization,[30] suggesting an extremely modest level of collective research in machine tools. The odds are good that the level of collective effort was no higher in the interwar period.

According to contemporary estimates by the National Research Council, in 1931 the steel industry spent $50,000 per plant on research; nationally the total budget for research for the industry was estimated at $30 million, divided between basic and applied research in a ratio of 2:1.[31] AISI did not begin financial support for research until 1933, when a group of state governments became interested in the industrial pollution of streams and rivers. As a protective measure, the institute established a modest research program to determine any facts that would be helpful to the companies in avoiding punitive legislation for stream pollution control. A research committee was first organized in AISI in 1940; its initial project involved contracting with a government agency to ascertain the cause of failure of paint films applied to steel. The research agenda broadened during World War II; after the war, the emphasis shifted from defense to basic research for the steel industry through the sponsorship of university research.

Some of the important developments in cooperative research in the industry during the interwar period did not directly involve AISI. A research project at the U.S. Bureau of Mines was undertaken partially at the private expense of some seventy companies. Personnel from the bureau worked with researchers from Carnegie Institute of Technology (CIT) and private industry in the study of the physical chemistry of steel making, refractories, abnormalities in steel, and other studies of value to the iron and steel industry. The project was initiated in 1923 when Dr. Thomas Baker, president of CIT, invited representatives of several industries and the Bureau of Mines to discuss cooperative metallurgical research in Pittsburgh. An advisory board of industry, CIT, and bureau representatives was then established, and each constituent agreed to contribute in cash or in kind to the work. At least one trade association in the steel industry, the Acid Open Hearth Association, which included most of the large equipment manufacturers, conducted similar joint research for twenty-one years in this same era. A team of observers from the British iron and steel industry who toured American facilities in 1951 concluded that

> perhaps the most surprising thing about iron and steel research in America is the extent to which it is carried on or supported by Government agencies. Extensive high-quality work is carried out by the various laboratories of the Bureau of Mines, by the Bureau of Standards, and by laboratories associated with the defense services. Equally if not more important is the work done in a large number of university laboratories and commercial research institutes under Government grants; most of the research in these places on iron and steel and in many other fields is so financed.[32]

Some Recent U.S. Association Activities in R&D. Although there are not as many highly visible institutionalized research centers in the United States as in Japan, it is probable that much joint research and development is simply not publicized by the participants.[33] There is no legal requirement to report cooperative research to the Justice Department or the Federal Trade Commission, and the only advantage to reporting it is that one avoids paying treble damages if one is sued on antitrust grounds and loses. In the steel industry at least fourteen collaborative research projects are under way, but a summary of industry joint ventures that were reported in the *New York Times* and the *Wall Street Journal* between October 1983 and June 1984 did not list any such activities in the steel industry. Caution in assessing the extent of joint research by firms is therefore in order.[34]

AISI staff facilitated the start-up of many of the joint research projects in the steel industry, but AISI itself is not a participant, and no AISI research funds are used.[35] In recent years AISI has allocated around $1.8 million to its own technical budget, compared with an annual research budget for U.S. Steel in 1982 (a terrible year for the steel industry) of $84 million.[36] These funds support a long-standing program of university-based research—AISI currently is sponsoring thirty-one different research programs at various universities. Funds also go to research councils and to such projects as the Arc Stability Improvement Project jointly developed by the Electric Power Research Institute and AISI.[37] AISI at this time is actually opposed to the creation of a government-funded central steel research institute, partly because it believes that the steel industry is more heterogeneous in its technical requirements than industries already served by central institutes (such as electric utilities, natural gas, telephone companies) and that the form of centralized research institute that has worked in those sectors would not work as well in the steel industry.[38] Opposition may also stem from a perception that such institutes have not been particularly effective in Great Britain[39] and from a desire to minimize government involvement in the selection and performance of the research agenda of the industry.

Recently the steel industry has returned to the pattern of collaborative research that existed in the interwar period. The Electric Power Research Institute operates a research center, the Center for Metals Production (CMP) in the Mellon Institute of Carnegie-Mellon University; it is currently working on projects that promise near-term benefits to the steel and aluminum industries.[40] The CMP advisory board consists of representatives of electric utilities, AISI, the Aluminum Association, one steel company and one aluminum company, the Department of Energy, three universities, and two representatives of the Electric Power Research Institute. Although its primary objective is to produce near-term benefits, CMP also supports the National Science Foundation–sponsored University-Industry Cooperative Research Center for Iron and Steelmaking at Carnegie-Mellon, as well as basic research in aluminum production. CMP envisions trade associations as a communication channel between the center and the member firms; AISI and the Aluminum Association are already playing this role. The director of CMP comments that his center could not have existed ten years ago because at that time steel companies were not ready for the idea of joint research.[41] Although the industry "forgot" its interwar experience, it does seem to have reinvented a remarkably similar organization.

In recent years the machine tool industry has become more concerned about its ability to remain ahead of foreign competition in technological competition. "The biggest key to the future survival and success of United States machine tool builders lies in their ability to stay ahead of the rest of the pack in developing new technology. Most of the builders have already realized that," Anthony M. Bratkovitch, engineering director of NMTBA has commented. "Those that didn't aren't alive anymore, or they're hardly alive. You have to keep on running."[42] He further argues that since U.S. builders cannot compete just on sticker price, they have to develop new concepts and new products to maintain their competitive position.

NMTBA is expanding its technical services to members by planning a "technical forum." The work of universities and private research organizations will be screened by NMTBA staff for applicability to machine tool manufacturing technology, and perhaps a dozen groups will be invited to make presentations. Trade association members could then strike individual bargains with those vendors that interest them. NMTBA also plans to upgrade its technical library and add electronic database search capabilities and hopes to take part in curriculum development at engineering schools. Although NMTBA thus seems to be committed in principle to devoting substantial effort to maintaining technological superiority, its current president seems skeptical that substantial cooperative efforts will succeed in a fragmented and highly competitive industry.[43]

Another trade association, the National Electrical Machinery Association, is in the process of establishing an "automation forum" that initially would distribute "success stories" to participants, pool expertise from six trade associations and develop a forecasting model, and form a coalition to promote government action to accelerate the application of automation. Producers, users, consultants, and trade associations are banding together in this effort and will, in addition, cosponsor technology conferences with NEMA. The Automation Forum and NEMA have hosted a workshop on export controls and their impact on high-technology industries.

Research Subsidies from Government. Japan is not unique in passing government subsidies to industry through private business associations. In the United States, federal government assistance to private research dates from at least 1892, when Congress opened government research facilities to scientific investigators and students of institutions of higher education. By 1939 there were eighty-four research associates in the Bureau of Standards from fifty different industries. The Building and Housing Division of the bureau, founded in 1921, became a center of study for cooperating committees and study groups affiliated with the major trade and professional associations in the housing field. This development was no doubt consistent with the desire of Herbert Hoover, then Secretary of Commerce, to turn the Bureau of Standards into a "super-consultant" for American industry, but hardly the culmination of his ambition.[44] Since there were about 1,200 national trade associations at that time, it is obvious that only a small percentage were involved in the Bureau of Standards projects.

The surge of federally financed research occasioned by the outbreak of World War II did not necessarily produce a surge in trade association research activities. One example of the effect of the wartime research programs on American industry is provided by David Noble's *Forces of Production*, a history of the development of numerically controlled (NC) machine tools.[45] The major developers of the numerically controlled technology were the U.S. Air Force and the Department of Defense, Massachusetts Institute of Technology and individual faculty members of MIT, and individual firms and their chief executives. Some machine tool builders at that time were certainly aware of the significance of the NC technology, but the NMTBA itself was not significantly involved in developing it. In contrast, the Aerospace Industries Association established a panel to deal with the standardization of NC technology (punched paper tape, axis nomenclature, and tool holders) for the industry; it developed software for programming NC machines, working with the Department of Defense, machine tool and control-systems builders, and other trade associations. As development of the software progressed and it became obvious that many nonaerospace companies could make use of the technology and products, the Aerospace Industries Association turned over its development effort in 1964 to the Illinois Institute of Technology Research Institute. Development was originally funded primarily by individual aerospace companies but broadened to include major engineering companies, machine tool and control system manufacturers, and computer manufacturers.[46]

Today several government programs assist research and development—Defense Department programs such as TechMod (technical modernization), ManTech (manufacturing technology), and the concluded program in Integrated Computer Aided Manufacturing, which worked with individual companies (generally defense contractors). Because the programs generally are implemented by firms for individual projects, they are not covered here.[47] For the machine tool industry, work performed in government laboratories has been significant to the industry's technological development. Those laboratories are among the few customers for ultra-precise machine tools with an accuracy on the order of one-millionth of an inch, and they thus create demand for this kind of product. Workers in those labs also possess machining skills and techniques that may be of use to civilian producers.

General Patterns of Cooperative Research in the United States. A 1984 estimate of collective private industrial research expenditures is about $1.6 billion, or 3 percent of the total industrial expenditures for that year. About 85 percent of this collective effort is accounted for by just three organizations: the Electric Power Research Institute, the Gas Research Institute, and Bell Communications Research, Inc.[48] In 1982, the distribution of sites for cooperative research was as follows: in-house facilities, 27 percent; universities, 25 percent; independent nonprofit institutes, 13 percent; commercial laboratories, 11 percent; member/sponsor facilities, 10 percent; government facilities, 9 percent; other, 4 percent.

The most recent survey of private research activity identified twenty-eight industrial associations that perform at least some work at government labs. Surveys of government agencies that operate laboratories disclose very modest levels of research association participation in laboratory work.[49] More common is for American trade associations to establish their own research laboratories. At least a dozen such labs were in operation in the 1920s, and a few of them predate World War I.[50]

Early Developments under the New Federal Legislation on R&D. Joint research and development conducted by American manufacturing trade associations seems to have declined significantly since 1980; moreover, the decline over the period 1980–1982 was followed by an even sharper decline in the period 1983–1985, part of which was covered by the new law (see table 4–2). It seems that this legislation has not offered any significant inducements to alter the pattern of declining association involvement in research and development.

The passage of the National Cooperative Research Act was followed by the announced formation of thirty-five research consortia (see table 7–2). Perhaps the increasing rate of decline in joint research and development conducted through trade associations in the period 1982–1985 can be partly explained by the creation of the research consortia. But the predominance of projects in electronics, communications, and computers suggests that this particular institutional form is highly important for only a few industries.

The Keyworth Initiative. The Keyworth Initiative is the proposal by former presidential science adviser Dr. George A. Keyworth to use the personnel and equipment of the national laboratories for research of benefit to the American steel industry. The national labs handle about one-sixth of the total public and private R&D in the United States. A year-long review by the White House Science Council of the activities of the labs completed in 1983 provided a basis for a concerted effort by the Reagan administration to develop a new and closer pattern of lab/industry/university cooperation.

TABLE 7-2

Name	Date	Participants	Research Area
Exxon-Halliburton	1/85[a]	2 firms	oil and gas well cementing
Microelectronics & Computer Technology Corp.	1/85	20 firms	computer architecture; semiconductor packaging; software VLSI/CAD
Software Productivity Consortium	1/85	13 firms	advanced software technology
Computer Aided Manufacturing International	1/85[b]	35 firms, 2 government labs	CAM; robotics, advanced NC
Bell Communications Research	1/85[c]	9 firms	telecommunications; computer science
Bethlehem-U.S. Steel	1/85	2 firms	thin section continuous casting
Semiconductor Research Corp.	1/85	36 firms	semiconductor technology
Center for Advanced Television Studies	1/85	9 firms and Public Broadcasting Service	television transmission systems
Medium Range Truck Transmission Project	2/85[d]	3 firms[e]	truck transmissions
Portland Cement Association	2/85[f]	38 firms	improving quality and uses of concrete, cement
Motor Vehicle Manufacturing Association	2/85[g]	3 associations	air pollution research
Motor Vehicle Manufacturing Association	2/85	3 associations	tractor/trailer braking
Agrigenetics Corp.	2/85[h]	partnership	recombinant DNA

(Table continues)

Table 7–2 (continued)

Name	Date	Participants	Research Area
Empire State Electric Energy Research Corp.	2/85	7 utilities	environmental and power generation
Motor Vehicle Manufacturing Association	2/85	4 associations, 3 firms, 1 university	automobile air pollution
Uninet Research & Development Co.	3/85	2 firms	packet-switching data networks
Bellcore-Honeywell	3/85	2 firms	integrated circuits
International Fuel Cells Corp.	4/85	2 firms[i]	fuel cells
International Partners in Glass Research	4/85	7 firms[j]	glass containers
Oncagen Limited Partnership	4/85	3 firms and individuals	diagnosis, treatment of human cancer
Kaiser Aluminum & Reynolds Metals	5/85	2 firms	aluminum-lithium alloys
Plastics Recycling Foundation	5/85	19 firms, 1 association	plastics recycling
Bellcore-Avantek	5/85	2 firms	integrated circuits in telecommunications
Bellcore-Racal	5/85	2 firms	telecommunications
Bellcore-U.S. Army	5/85	1 firm and 1 government agency	semiconductors
Bellcore-ADC	9/85	2 firms	integrated circuits and telecommunications
Applied Information Technologies	10/85	3 firms, 2 associations	artificial intelligence; telecommunications; microelectronics; computer science
Smart House Project	10/85	27 firms, 3 associations	coordinated home control and energy distribution system
Deet Joint Research Venture	10/85	16 firms[k]	pesticides

(Table continues)

Table 7–2 (continued)

Name	Date	Participants	Research Area
Geothermal Drilling Organization	10/85	16 firms, 1 govt. lab	geothermal well drilling
Pump Research & Development Committee	11/85	4 firms	centrifugal pumps
Battelle project	11/85	6 firms, 1 association	optoelectronics; robotics
Bellcore-Hitachi	12/85	2 firms[k]	telecommunications; optical transmission
IntelXicor	12/85	2 firms	computer memory circuits
Industry Cooperative Research Center	12/85	4 firms, 1 university	fluidization & fluid particles

NOTES: Date refers to date of publication in the *Federal Register.* At least one month elapses between notification of Justice Department and FTC and subsequent publication.
a. Formed in May 1983. Scheduled to terminate December 31, 1985.
b. Incorporated May 1972.
c. Part of reorganization of Bell System. Formed in January 1984.
d. Scheduled to end December 31, 1985.
e. Two are foreign.
f. Began operations in 1916.
g. Began collaboration in 1967.
h. Founded in 1981.
i. One firm is Japanese.
j. Four firms are foreign.
k. One firm is foreign.
SOURCE: *Federal Register.*

The Keyworth Initiative emerged from conversations held in early 1984 between Keyworth and Pete Love, the president of National Steel, both of whom served on the President's Commission on Industrial Competitiveness. After those discussions, Love formed an unofficial steering committee in February 1984, which consisted of the vice-presidents for research of six steel companies; representatives of the Department of Energy, Argonne National Laboratory, and Oak Ridge National Laboratory; and William Dennis, the director of research at AISI.

Keyworth presented the idea of an alliance between the industry and government labs to the American Iron and Steel Institute in a speech at its May 1984 annual meeting. Keyworth argued that, since U.S. industry will always be at a labor cost disadvantage and can at best hope for parity in capital costs and purchasing power of the currency, whatever advantages U.S. industry would gain in the world market would be technological ones. What the United States needs, Keyworth argued, is to do a better job of harnessing its scientific and technical strengths for the benefit of industry through a strong, competitive partnership between government, universities, and industry. Conventional contract research will not work, Keyworth argued, because the lab people do not know enough about the problems of the steel industry, and the industry people do not know enough about the capabilities of the labs. He foresaw little *direct* role for the federal government in such a partnership: "The last thing we need is for some program manager in Washington to get in the way of a developing partnership and muddle the process." Keyworth saw the steel–lab partnership as a "model for American industry and for American science and technology, a model based clearly on our own national strengths and needs, not Japan's or anyone else's."[51]

The Keyworth Initiative steering committee created a working group on technical issues to explore the feasibility of the proposed research and the fit of the research agenda to the capabilities of the labs. By the autumn of 1984 those technical issues had been explored and some possibilities for long-range cooperative research and development were identified. The Department of Energy and the Bureau of Standards requested funds for the start-up of this program (about $10 million) in the FY 1986 budget.[52] The Office of Management and Budget (OMB), however, objected strenuously to the program as a subsidy to industry and as a de facto industrial policy, and deleted funding for it from the executive budget. Congress eventually passed the Keyworth Initiative over OMB's objections.

At this time property rights issues involving work performed under the program have not been resolved. Although the purchase of half of National Steel by NKK, a Japanese steel firm, has not affected the participation of National Steel in the development of the initiative, questions about the ownership of technology developed in government labs and about limitations on access to technology developed with public monies obviously are central and must be resolved. In particular, if Keyworth's goal of restoring a technological edge to American industry is to be realized, it is necessary to confront the question of what exactly constitutes an "American" company in an era when international joint ventures are proliferating, when American manufacturers in many industries are producing products abroad, and when foreign multinationals are establishing branch plants in the

United States and buying partial or complete interest in American firms. (The business press has even reported that an interest in an American machine tool manufacturer was recently purchased by a state enterprise of the People's Republic of China.[53]) Although there may be benefits to humanity at large from learning to make steel more cheaply, Keyworth's narrower objectives imply some ability to restrict access by foreigners to this technology. How this can be done remains to be seen.

Some Observations

Both U.S. and Japanese firms have long been engaged in collective activities related to technology, going back at least to the early years of this century. In both countries trade associations have played a significant role in these activities, though other organizations in both the public and private sector have been involved as well. One difference is that in the United States firms engaging in collaborative research or cooperating in government-sponsored programs often have had little or no relationship with trade associations. In Japan the trade associations often organize and dominate research associations. Moreover, the government agencies involved in promoting research much more often work through trade associations in Japan than in the United States.

U.S. trade associations have shown a diminishing inclination to engage in collaborative research in recent years. The reasons for this are not completely clear, but we doubt it has much to do with U.S. antitrust laws. Frequently association R&D efforts are intended to answer technical questions raised by potential or actual government regulations,[54] and the decline in federal regulatory activity under the Reagan administration may have led associations to reduce such research efforts correspondingly. Some contend that a removal of antitrust barriers would give U.S. industry all the advantages the Japanese are alleged to have received from collaborative research. Much less attention has been given to the fact that collaborative research is so prevalent in Japan not only because the antitrust environment allows this, but also because it is actively encouraged by government subsidies and tax benefits.

Some may believe the U.S. government should go to similar lengths to encourage collaborative research; it is not clear, however, that the benefits the Japanese receive in this area are as pronounced as is sometimes claimed. The successes observers point to in Japan tend to have come from a very few of the dozens of research associations that have operated over the past twenty-five years. Indeed, even these few "successes" have been questioned.[55] Clearly, systematic research on the costs and benefits of the Japanese research associations is essential before drawing the conclusions that whatever benefits the Japanese may receive from subsidized collaborative research could be duplicated in the United States.

Japanese trade associations and related organizations have given more attention than their American counterparts to collecting and providing access to foreign technical information. Japanese trade associations frequently provide Japanese language abstracts of technical articles, organize overseas study trips, and keep files of materials on foreign companies and products. They also seem to have been more apt to consider this activity, along with the purchase of foreign equipment and products, as a legitimate part of their collaborative reasearch effort. American associations generally lag behind their Japanese counterparts in these activities. Closer monitoring of foreign developments might provide U.S. associations with a relatively low cost source of technological information. As the technological sophistication of foreign competitors comes to equal or surpass that of American producers, it is no longer safe to assume that American practices are the most advanced or that the only foreign competitors of importance are Japan and Western Europe. It has been suggested, for example, that the U.S. metalworking industry is missing a chance to obtain high quality research results at little expense by failing to monitor technological publications from the Soviet Union.[56] As foreign competition intensifies, the costs to U.S. firms of ignorance of foreign development can only increase.

Notes

1. James Abegglen and George Stalk, Jr., *Kaisha: The Japanese Corporation* (New York: Basic Books, 1985), pp. 139–40; and William Ouchi, *The M-Form Society* (Reading, Mass.: Addison-Wesley Publishing Co., 1984), pp. 93–123.

2. *American Machinist*, June 1985, p. 107.

3. "Machine-Tool Charges against Japanese Split U.S. Industry, Officials," *Wall Street Journal*, March 29, 1983.

4. Semiconductor Industry Association, *The Effect of Government Targeting on World Semiconductor Competition* (Cupertino, Calif.: Semiconductor Industry Association, 1983); Houdaille Industries, Inc., *Petition to the President of the United States through the Office of the United States Trade Representative for the Exercise of Presidential Discretion Authorized by Section 103 of the Revenue Act of 1971, 26 U.S.C.* (Washington, D.C.: 1982).

5. For additional information on the international information collecting activities of the Japanese steel industry, see Leonard Lynn, *How Japan Innovates: A Comparison with the U.S. in the Case of Oxygen Steelmaking* (Boulder, Colo.: Westview Press, 1982).

6. Most of the information on the Japan Society for the Promotion of the Machinery Industries is taken from JSPMI, *Kikai Shinko Kyokai Ju-nen Shi* (Tokyo: JSPMI, 1976).

7. Japan Machine Tool Builders Association, *The Japan Machine Tool Builders Association*, pp. 70, 80.

8. Semiconductor Industry Association, *The Effect of Government Targeting*, p. 23.

9. Ken'ichi Iida, *Origin and Development of Iron and Steel Technology in Japan* (Tokyo: The United Nations University, 1980). This program helped prepare Japanese steelmakers to introduce the epochal basic oxygen steelmaking process a few years later. See Lynn, *How Japan Innovates*.

10. See, for example, the discussions in Ezra Vogel, *Comeback: Case by Case—Building the Resurgence of American Business* (New York: Simon and Schuster, 1985); Daniel Okimoto, Takuo Sugano, and Franklin Weinstein, *Competitive Edge* (Stanford, Calif.: Stanford University Press, 1984); Michael Borrus, James Millstein, and John Zysmann, *U.S.–Japanese Competition in the Semiconductor Industry* (Berkeley, Calif.: Institute of International Studies, 1982); and Semiconductor Industry Association, *Effect of Government Targeting*.

11. Vogel, *Comeback*, pp. 144–45.

12. Edward J. Lincoln, *Japan's Industrial Policies* (Washington, D.C.: Japan Economic Institute of America, 1984), p. 27.

13. David Methe, "Technology, Transactions Cost, and the Diffusion of Innovation: The Evolution of the U.S. and Japanese DRAM Markets" (Ph.D. diss., University of California, Irvine, 1985) pp. 165, 191.

14. Vogel, *Comeback*, p. 144. Vogel earlier describes Oki as the weakest of the four major Japanese communications companies, but also the most cooperative with NTT.

15. Goto Akira and Wakasugi Ryuhei, "Gijutsu Seisaku," in Komiya Ryutaro, Okuno Masahiro, and Suzumura Kotaro, eds., *Nihon no Sangyo Seisaku* (Tokyo: Tokyo University Press, 1984), pp. 159–80.

16. See MITI, *Tsusan Sangyo Roppo* (Tokyo: MITI, 1977), pp. 409–11.

17. Trade associations form these new organizations because the trade associations themselves are not eligible to receive certain subsidies.

18. Several accounts of these laws are now available in English; see, for example, Vogel, *Comeback*, pp. 71–72, 83, 139. Vogel notes that under the laws trade associations work out plans (say, to "rationalize" an industry) and then have their plans enforced by MITI.

19. Richard J. Samuels, "Research Collaboration in Japan" (Paper presented at the 1987 Annual Meeting of the Association of Asian Studies, Boston, April 11, 1987).

20. These are described in Jimmy Wheeler, et al., *Japanese Industrial Development Policies in the 1980s: Implications for U.S. Trade and Investment* (Croton-on-Hudson, N.Y.: Hudson Institute, 1982), pp. 147–53.

21. U.S. International Trade Commission, *Foreign Industrial Targeting and Its Effects on U.S. Industries, Phase I: Japan* (Washington, D.C.: USITC, 1983), p. 106.

22. Ibid., pp. 104–05.

23. Exchange rates ranged from about 180 to 360 yen to the dollar over this period, giving a dollar equivalent of from $144 million to $288 million.

24. Other government subsidies for research that have been funneled through trade associations have been mentioned in various English-language sources, but unfortunately little detail is generally provided. Magaziner and Hout, for example, say that roughly 1 million dollars in subsidies were awarded to the Automobile Technology Association in the 1950s, but give no further information. See Ira C. Magaziner and Thomas Hout, *Japanese Industrial Policy* (Berkeley, Calif.: Institute of International Studies, 1980), p. 70.

25. Thomas W. Eager, "Technology Transfer and Cooperative Research in Japan," *ONR Scientific Bulletin*, vol. 10 (July to September 1985), pp. 32–41.

26. David F. Noble, *America by Design* (New York: Alfred A. Knopf, 1977), pp. 121–22.

27. U.S. Department of Commerce, *Trade Association Activities* (Washington, D.C.: U.S. Government Printing Office, 1927), pp. 67–70.

28. *Research by Cooperative Organizations: A Survey of Scientific Research by Trade Associations, Professional and Technical Societies, and Other Cooperative Groups, 1953*, prepared for the National Science Foundation by the Battelle Memorial Institute (Washington, D.C.: U.S. Government Printing Office, 1956), p. 1.

29. Commerce Department, *Trade Association Activities*, p. 9.

30. Battelle Memorial Institute, *Research by Cooperative Organizations*, p. 23.

31. F. N. Speller, "Cooperative Research in the Iron and Steel Industry," *Yearbook of the American Iron & Steel Institute, 1931* (New York: AISI, 1932).

32. Anglo-American Council on Productivity, *Iron and Steel: Report of a Productivity Team representing the British Iron and Steel Industry which visited the United States of America in 1951* (London, June 1952), pp. 116–17.

33. Japan is not the only foreign country to have had highly visible on-going, institutionalized research centers for many industries for much longer than the United States. The West German equivalent of the National Science Foundation has supported three such centers for the machine tool industry: the Laboratory for Machine Tools & Production Engineering at Aachen, the Institute for Machine Tools & Production Techniques at the Technical University of Berlin, and the Institute for Machine-Tool Control & Production Systems at the University of Stüttgart. The Aachen facility, the oldest, dates from 1936. *American Machinist*, June 1985, p. 107.

34. Camela S. Haklisch, Herbert I. Fusfeld, and Alan D. Levenson, *Trends in Collective Industrial Research* (New York: New York University Center for Science and Technology Policy, August 1984), pp. 63–66.

35. Interview with Dr. William E. Dennis, AISI, Washington, D.C., Jan. 17, 1985.

36. Haklisch, Fusfeld, and Levenson, *Trends in Collective Industrial Research*, pp. 105–06.

37. American Iron and Steel Institute, *Research 1984–5* (Washington, D.C., no date).

38. Robert P. Peabody, Executive Director, American Iron and Steel Institute, letter to Senator John Heinz, chairman, Subcommittee on Economic

Growth, Employment & Revenue Sharing, November 21, 1983.

39. Interview with William Dennis; see also David C. Mowery, "Firm Structure, Government Policy, and the Organization of Industrial Research: Great Britain and the United States, 1900–1950," *Business History Review* 58 (Winter 1984), pp. 504–27.

40. Mellon Institute, *Center for Metals Production: A Collaborative Research Venture for the Metals Industries* (Pittsburgh, Penn.: Mellon Institute, November 1984.) The motivation for the Electric Power Research Institute to sponsor work on metals production arises from the fact that the aluminum industry purchases 5 percent of the electricity generated in the United States, while the steel industry consumes about 3 percent.

41. J. R. Miller, "The North American Steel Industry's Program for Research and Development," *Iron & Steelmaker* (reprint, n.p., October 1984).

42. Mark Sfiligo, "Technological Advances by Builders Are Key: Emphasis on Providing Complete Systems," *American Metal Market*, IMTS edition, August 27, 1984, p. 6a.

43. Rosanne Brooks, "NMTBA Technology Drive Will Feature Forum," *American Metal Market*, April 29, 1985, p. 8.

44. Ellis Hawley, "Herbert Hoover and Economic Stabilization, 1921–1922," in Hawley, ed., *Herbert Hoover as Secretary of Commerce: Studies in New Era Thought and Practice* (Iowa City: Univ. of Iowa Press, 1981), pp. 43–79; and Robert K. Murray, "Herbert Hoover and the Harding Cabinet," in ibid., pp. 17–40.

45. David F. Noble, *Forces of Production: A Social History of Industrial Automation* (New York: Alfred A. Knopf, 1984).

46. Nils O. Olesten, *Numerical Control* (New York: John Wiley, 1970), pp. 43–44.

47. An illustrative example of the workings of TechMod can be found in Barbara Weiss, "Military Set to Assist U.S. Bearing Producers," *American Metal Market*, June 17, 1985, pp. 1, 29. For a discussion of recent federal efforts to induce U.S. firms to integrate new technologies more quickly into their production processes, see Rosanne Brooks, "Air Force, NASA Each Encourage Integration of New Technologies," *American Metal Market*, February 4, 1985, p. 4.

48. Haklisch, Fusfeld, and Levenson, *Trends in Collective Industrial Research*, p. 16.

49. Ibid., p. 138, pp. 144–46.

50. *Trade Association Activities*, pp. 67–70; and Noble, *America by Design*, pp. 121–22.

51. George A. Keyworth, Speech to the 92nd General Meeting, AISI, New York, May 24, 1984.

52. These agencies became involved because they already possessed research programs into which the early work on the Keyworth Initiative could be comfortably fitted. Interview with Ora Smith, Office of the Presidential Science Adviser, Washington, D.C., April 18, 1985.

53. "Autonumerics Sold to Chinese Interests," *American Machinist*, January 1985, p. 29.

54. Udo H. Staber, "The Organizational Properties of Trade Associations" (Ph.D. diss., Cornell University, 1982), p. 270.

55. For a skeptical look at the value of Japanese research associations, see Gary R. Saxonhouse, "The Micro- and Macro-economics of Foreign Sales to Japan," in William R. Cline, ed., *Trade Policy in the 1980s* (Washington, D.C.: Institute for International Economics, 1983), pp. 259–304.

56. The Soviet Union's large expenditures on R&D and information dissemination are said to generate much information that is easily obtainable by American producers, were they to make the effort to obtain it. See Eugene I. Rivin, "U.S. Engineers Should Mine Soviet Research," *American Metal Market*, May 4, 1984, p. 30.

8
Conclusions and
Policy Implications

Our brief comparison of trade associations in Japan and the United States does not probe important issues in nearly the depth they deserve. Nonetheless, we think it does allow some informed speculation on the issues raised at the beginning of this volume. We begin our reprisal and extension of the conclusions reached in this book by outlining what seem to be the most important differences in the systems of business representation in the two countries.

The network of associations in Japan is denser, somewhat more amply endowed with financial resources, and more intimately connected to the state than the corresponding network in the United States. The Japanese machine tool industry, for example, includes not only associations analogous to the National Machine Tool Builders Association in the United States, but also a federation of associations representing the machinery industries, a special standing committee of machine tool associations, and a government-subsidized "society" for the promotion of the machinery industries. Major steel producers are represented by the Japan Iron and Steel Federation, Kozai Club, Japan Iron and Steel Exporters Association, and various other associations concerned with the production or sale of steel products and the acquisition of raw materials. Firms in the machinery and steel industries (as well as all other major industries) can claim additional influence over policy through Keidanren and other peak associations. While encompassing organizations exist in the United States, they tend to be too weak to be effective in shaping a broad range of public policies. The Japanese peak and semi-peak associations have the resources and support to effectively represent their cross-sectoral constituencies.

The legal status of Japanese associations is far more clearly spelled out and far more stable than that of U.S. associations. Laws specifically allowing the formation of export trade associations, research associations, depression cartels, and the like were put into place within weeks of the end of the Occupation. The laws specify

172

what the associations can do and in some cases provide them with governmental assistance. Beyond this, the Japanese have had little fear of new interpretations of antitrust laws overriding previous understandings.[1]

Action has also been easier for Japanese business associations because of Japan's long governance by one probusiness political party. Japanese trade associations also enjoy generous representation in the system of advisory commissions. Unlike the short-lived and narrowly focused advisory commissions common in the United States, those in Japan are long-standing organizations with broad responsibilities.

One consequence of the difference in the stability of the political and legal environment in the two countries is that in the United States business interests frequently organize ad hoc groups to promote positions as new issues arise, while in Japan business interests are more likely to use existing organizations. Since Japanese businesses need not organize each time they launch collective efforts, they can more easily mobilize and sustain effective collective action.

Trade Associations and the Rise of Japan

Olson's argument in *The Rise and Decline of Nations* suggests that the decline in the vitality of the U.S. economy in recent years can be attributed to increased social and political rigidity. U.S. society, according to Olson, has lost flexibility because more and more groups representing more and more specialized interests have organized. These groups may represent their own memberships quite well, but as each competes with the others to gain a larger share of the economic resources available in the United States, none works toward economic growth and other benefits for the society as a whole. Indeed this competition allegedly results in a kind of gridlock where little can be done at all. In support of this argument, Olson points out that the countries that were defeated in World War II have been far more successful in attaining economic growth than the victors. He suggests that the reason is that the defeated countries were cleansed of special interest groups and thus were able to develop new encompassing groups that successfully sought economic growth.

We believe Olson very much exaggerates the extent to which special interest groups were abolished in Japan under the rule of the militarists during the war and under the Occupation after it. He notes that only 19 percent of the Japanese associations that existed in 1971 had existed in 1939, compared with a much larger percentage in Great Britain and other countries. But, as we saw in chapter 2, much of this seeming lack of continuity might be explained by the widespread rechartering and reorganization of existing associations in Japan. We found, for example, substantial continuity in the steel industry. Although the Japan Iron and Steel Federation, Kozai Club, and Japan Iron and Steel Exporters Association did not exist in precisely their present form in 1939, all have lineages that can be traced back at least that far. Nor should encompassing organizations in Japan be considered a postwar phenomenon; most also had their wartime and prewar ancestors. Much of Olson's concern, moreover, is not just with business groups, but with political and labor groups. In this aspect the Occupation should have had a negative effect on Japanese economic growth, since the Occupation authorities strongly encouraged the proliferation of these groups.[2]

Perhaps the clearing away of the military and the landlords during the Occupation facilitated economic growth. If this was the case, however, we believe our description of what happened to the Japanese steel industry implies that the reforms required to allow the "rise" of a nation are not nearly as sweeping as Olson implies. New work on the consequences of economic reforms under the Occupation of Japan could be extremely valuable in clarifying this issue.[3]

We lean toward a very simple explanation for the differences in the structure of interest group representation in the United States and Japan: the network of associations in Japan arose under a mercantilist, nationalist state; by contrast, the network of associations in the United States developed under a state that seldom resorted to direct intervention in specific economic activities, and which more rigorously enforced a distinction between private and public activity.

Industrial Policy and Trade Associations

Is the Japanese system more flexible in its ability to aggregate interests and thus better able to work toward the good of the society as a whole? The Japanese were able to subordinate many other concerns effectively for rapid economic growth, particularly in the 1950s and 1960s. And the network of trade associations and peak associations played a prominent role in policy making during this period. It is not clear, however, what implications Americans should draw from this.

Some believe the Japanese economy is controlled by MITI and suggest that the United States needs a comparable organ to coordinate U.S. industrial policy. To the extent that such an industrial policy would work through trade associations as some have alleged that it does in Japan, we are skeptical of its value in the United States. It is difficult to attribute the nature of the Japanese association network simply to government actions. Government funding of associations

174

has certainly occurred, but it seems to have been relatively modest and is not sufficient to account for the somewhat higher level of resources held by Japanese associations compared with American associations in the same industries.

Japanese industry has frequently assigned important roles to its trade associations in areas where American industry does not. A prominent example is their activity in the collection of information about foreign technology and foreign markets. These activities were both important to the Japanese and difficult for them, given their relative isolation from the societies that provided the most important markets and sources of technology. MITI may have helped associations to address these problems, but the trade associations have been far more than passive tools in Japanese industrial policy. They have substantial input into policy through the advisory councils and LDP policy affairs research councils. Some of their leaders have been among the most influential shapers of postwar Japanese economic policy. Institutional redesigners in the United States would need, somehow, to introduce simultaneously an American MITI and a new network of more active trade associations.

But even if this could be done, would it be desirable? Even in Japan the situation is changing: although there is evidence of a mercantilist, interventionist, and nationalist Japanese government approach to industrial development and industrial policy, in the past decade or so government intervention has become more consistently "liberal." We saw this in the growing strength of the Japan Fair Trade Commission, for example, and the complementary decline in the ability of the Ministry of International Trade and Industry to carry out its industrial policies. Ironically, U.S. pressures for the establishment of quotas may inhibit the increasing tendency toward independence from MITI supervision in Japan. In part the Japanese trend toward liberalization may be a result of the increasing complexity of the Japanese economy. The political and economic preeminence of the steel industry is likely to be increasingly eroded as new interests compete for a voice in policy making and as less-developed countries gain a comparative advantage in the production of carbon steel. Further, a less cohesive younger generation is finally replacing the relatively small group of men who were central figures in business and behind-the-scenes powers in government for decades after World War II. One lesson we would like to underline here is suggested strongly in the work of Chalmers Johnson: characterizations of Japanese practice that do not distinguish between present policies and those of the recent past can be fundamentally misleading.[4] The evolution away from a central industrial policy in Japan suggests there may

175

be limits to the applicability of a Japanese-style industrial policy in the United States.

Which System Is More Equitable?

It is still an open question whether the Japanese way of aggregating business interests into more encompassing groups provides a model that would lead to faster economic growth in the United States. Independently of this issue, it is important that sight not be lost of a different concern. What would be the implications of a Japanese-style system in the United States for other values, such as equity?

Some of those who believe the United States should borrow from Japanese institutions argue that the Japanese capacity for collective action offers advantages to all firms and all industries. William Ouchi claims that in Japan if policy formulation requires the interests of some of the parties to be subordinated to the interests of others, then "all parties know that their sacrifice today will be remembered and repaid in the future."[5] This sounds very appealing, but how accurate a characterization is it? In the Japanese steel industry, the largest firm has an overwhelming ability to pull the levers to initiate action. Its people dominate most of the important associations, and its affiliates provide a substantial block of votes in the most important trade association. Since World War II, Nippon Steel (or Yawata and Fuji, the two firms that merged to form Nippon) has dominated the steel industry and its access to government. The large firms had preferential access to raw materials, export markets, and governmental assistance. The smaller firms were not repaid for their sacrifices; indeed many were forced to merge into the larger firms or to become their subsidiaries.[6] As for the relationships between the major firms in the industry, note what happened in the Sumitomo "incident" of 1965:

> When Yawata [the larger predecessor of Nippon Steel] tried to exercise its leadership by cutting crude steel production and raising steel prices, Sumitomo Metal Industries resolutely opposed it because of its discontent with the assigned quota. The MITI intervened in the dispute, threatening Sumitomo by hinting at a cut in its coal quota.[7]

Sumitomo was not being offered the carrot of future payoffs, but rather the stick of sanctions. We suspect that the power of the steel industry and of its leaders in Keidanren and the other peak associations has similar implications. It would be remarkable if the leaders of the steel industry were to design impartial and fair payoffs to other industries that may in the past have had their interests sacrificed for the good of the steel industry.[8]

176

We think, consequently, that the equity of the Japanese system has been exaggerated. Does this mean it is less equitable than the U.S. system? It seems to us that the Japanese system is likely to be more discriminatory against firms that are outside the elite. In the United States outsider firms can probably leave associations that favor the elite at lower cost than they could in Japan simply because trade associations command more public resources in Japan than in the United States. Those that want any of the subsidies funneled through the associations have to remain members. Moreover, the same U.S. antitrust laws that are sometimes criticized for hindering collective action also make it quite difficult for associations to deny economically valuable services to industry firms that are nonmembers.

General Policy Implications

Proposals to establish American analogues to MITI and thus improve the U.S. ability to make "industrial policy" are far from being implemented, but some smaller-scale efforts to borrow from Japan have already taken place. Our reaction to this is one of ambivalence. Laws facilitating the organization of export trading companies and research associations have been based in part on the widespread impression that Japanese firms have profited from a weaker antitrust regime than that in the United States, allowing them to engage in collective research and export promotion activities. We find it difficult, however, to explain the nonappearance of some forms of collective action in the United States in terms of legal constraints. And even though U.S. laws pertaining to cooperative research have recently been liberalized, new joint ventures in research and development will not necessarily offset the decline in R&D by established trade associations. Indeed, government subsidies to research associations in Japan may account for their widespread appearance rather than the absence of antitrust barriers. Newly authorized American export trading companies may eventually provide a functional equivalent to the Japanese export trade associations and general trading companies and boost U.S. exports, but the initial performance of these companies has been unspectacular. We suspect that simple legal changes allowing U.S. firms to perform these new activities are not enough to allow them to dislodge well-established foreign competitors.[9]

We have touched on other areas of important policy relevance that we could not comprehensively address in this brief survey. Several times in the past few years, for example, the United States has insisted that Japan and other countries "voluntarily" restrict their exports to the United States. Scholars know little about the effects of these demands on the patterns of collective behavior in other countries. It seems likely, however, that after guiding Japan to strong antitrust policies after World War II, the United States in the past two decades may have pushed it in the opposite direction.

To turn away for a moment from our comparisons of the United States and Japan, we were struck by the rapidly increasing foreign participation in and control of firms in American industries, which may have large effects on the political objectives of U.S. trade associations. American firms in both the machine tool and the steel industries are seeing their interests become increasingly entwined with those of their foreign counterparts. The same is true in Japan. Indeed, in 1984 and 1985 there was substantial pressure by American firms to be allowed increased access to various Japanese policy-setting organs. The outcome of all this may be to affect the viability of nationalistic industrial strategies in both countries. Strategies such as those represented in the Keyworth Initiative, which seemingly are predicated on conferring an advantage to U.S.-owned firms, will face a series of difficult legal, economic, and political choices. What constitutes an "American" firm? Does National Steel (50 percent of which is owned by Nippon Kokan) qualify? What about Wheeling-Pittsburgh Steel (10 percent of which is owned by Nisshin Steel)? The largest "American" producer of industrial robots is GM-Fanuc, a joint venture between General Motors and Fanuc (a Japanese firm). The largest "Japanese" producer of computers until recent years was IBM-Japan. Such firms as Motorola and Texas Instruments, meanwhile, have demanded that their Japanese subsidiaries be treated as equal to other "Japanese" firms by the Japanese government. How should firms with substantial foreign participation and product and technology sharing agreements with foreign firms be treated? It may be that what some observers see as a "merger" of the U.S. and Japanese economies is pushing the Japanese to abandon whatever remains of their mercantilist policies, while making it impractical for the United States to adopt industrial policies patterned on those of Japan. It may be as well that these developments will effectively eliminate any Japanese government efforts at "targeting."

These conclusions may sound skeptical about U.S. efforts to borrow policy ideas from Japan; but the skepticism is with the approaches to borrowing that have so far occurred, not with the idea of borrowing. That the Japanese have continued to do well despite oil shocks and other disruptions that some once believed would be fatal to their economy suggests that Americans should continue to look to Japan (and elsewhere) for good policy ideas. Learning from Japan, however, implies far more than a quick legal restructuring. Successful borrowing from Japan requires knowing more about both countries' policy successes and failures. We have our own history of experiments in this century with joint action by business in research and foreign trade and we would do well to better understand the results of these experiments before undertaking new ones.

Notes

1. As we noted, however, MITI is less free to offer the umbrella protection of "administrative guidance" than it was in the past.

2. As Galenson and Odaka note: "Japan has a long history of trade unionism, but the movement achieved no substantial organization or economic power before World War II." Walter Galenson and Konosuke Odaka, "The Japanese Labor Market," in Hugh Patrick and Henry Rosovsky, eds., *Asia's New Giant* (Washington, D.C.: The Brookings Institution, 1976), pp. 587–671. The Trade Union Law imposed by U.S. military authorities shortly after the beginning of the Occupation established the legal right for workers to organize trade unions for the first time in Japan's history. Within three months of the passage of the law the number of union members increased from 380,000 to 3 million. By the end of 1948 there were 6.7 million union members in Japan. Tatsuro Uchino, *Japan's Postwar Economy* (Tokyo: Kodansha, 1978), p. 21.

3. One important economic effect of the Occupation reforms may well have been the enhancement of competition through both the antitrust laws and the deconcentration of economic power in such industries as steel.

4. Chalmers Johnson, *MITI and the Japanese Miracle: The Growth of Industrial Policy 1925–1975* (Stanford, Calif.: Stanford University Press, 1982).

5. William Ouchi, *The M-Form Society: How American Teamwork Can Recapture the Competitive Edge* (Reading, Mass.: Addison-Wesley, 1984), p. 56.

6. Many of the postwar mergers are listed by Ichikawa Hirokatsu, *Nippon Tekkogyo no Saihensei* (Tokyo: Shinhyoron, 1977), p. 195.

7. Ken'ichi Imai, "Iron and Steel," in Kazuo Sato, ed., *Industry and Business in Japan* (White Plains, N.Y.: M.E. Sharpe, 1980), pp. 191–244.

8. Destler et al. describe how a split between large and small firms in the Japanese textile industry contributed to difficulties in negotiating a trade agreement between the United States and Japan in 1970. See I. M. Destler, Haruhiro Fukui, and Hideo Sato, *The Textile Wrangle* (Ithaca, New York: Cornell University Press, 1979), pp. 169–71.

9. Indeed, the largest U.S. trading firms are subsidiaries of Japanese general trading firms.

Index

rationalization cartels, 42
research efforts, 143–44, 156–58, 161, 164–66
steel quotas, 111, 125, 131–33
trade protection, 121, 124, 125
U.S./Japanese comparisons, x, 31–32, 60–61
U.S. trade associations, 9–10, 61–65
Iron and Steel Institute of Japan (ISIJ), 67, 68, 141, 143, 144
Iron and Steel Materials Conference (Kozai Konwakai), 27
Iron and Steel Materials Sales Co. (Daini Kozai Hanbai Kabushiki Kaisha), 21
Iron and Steel Raw Materials Control Corp., 22
Iron and Steel Sales Corp., 22, 27
Iron and Steel Study Group, 16–17
Iron and Steel Technology Joint Research Association, 153–54
Ishizaka Taizo, 79
Itakuhi (consignment payments), 153, 154
Iwamura, H., 96
Iwata Kazuo, 74
Izumi Shoichi, 97

Japan Automobile Export Association, 131
Japan Bench Machine Tool Builders Association, 75
Japan Bicycle Exporters Association, 131
Japan Bicycle Promotion Association, 73, 142
Japan Bicycle Rehabilitation Association, 143, 154
Japan Chamber of Commerce and Industry (JCCI) (Nippon Shoko Kaigisho), 13, 78, 79
Japan Chemical Industry Association, 131
Japan Cold Finished Steel Bar Industry Trade Association, 69
Japan Committee for Economic Development (Keizai Doyukai), 13–14, 23, 78, 80
Japan Cotton Spinners Association, 11
Japan Economic Federation (Nippon Keizai Renmei), 11–12
Japan Economic Institute, 145
Japan Electric Wire and Cable Exporters Association, 131
Japanese Communist Party, 80
Japanese Fair Trade Commission (JFTC), 14, 28, 92, 129
    AML administration, 39, 41–45
    MITI administrative guidance, conflicts with, 93–94

Japanese Iron and Steel Association (Nippon Tekko Rengokai), 27
Japanese Scrap Industry Association, 69
Japanese Small Business Finance Corp., 80
Japan External Trade Organization, 76, 134
Japan Galvanized Iron Sheet Exporters Association, 68, 69, 132
"Japan, Inc.," 91
Japan Industrial Club (Nippon Kogyo Kurabu), 11
Japan Industrial Robotics Association (JIRA), 73, 75–77, 143, 154
Japan Industrial Standards, 71
Japan Institute of Metals, 144
Japan Institute of Refractories, 144
Japan International Machine Tool Trade Exhibition, 71, 75
Japan Iron and Steel Council (Nippon Tekko Kyogikai), 26
Japan Iron and Steel Exporters Association (JISEA), 67, 68, 84, 130–32, 172, 174
Japan Iron and Steel Exporters Association for the United States of America (Beikoku-muke Tekko Yushutsu Kumiai), 132
Japan Iron and Steel Federation (JISF), 17, 27, 32, 56, 68, 69, 78, 79, 144, 172, 174
    antitrust exemption efforts, 40, 42
    information collection, 141–42
    MITI administrative guidance, 93
    political contributions, 112–13
    staff, governance, and activities, 57, 62–63, 84
Japan Iron and Steel Industry Managers Association (Nippon Tekkogyo Keieisha Renmei), 27
Japan Iron and Steel Materials Federation (Nippon Kozai Rengokai), 21, 22
Japan Iron and Steel Materials Sales Co. (Nippon Kozai Hanbai Kabushiki Kaisha), 21
Japan Iron and Steel Sales Federation (Nippon Kozai Hanbai Rengokai), 20
Japan Iron and Steel Society (Nippon Tekkokai), 27
Japan Iron and Steel Wholesalers Association, 67, 68
Japan Light Industry Products Exporters Association, 131
Japan Machinery Association (Nippon Kikai Kyokai), 30
Japan Machinery Exporters Association (JMEA) (Nippon Kikai Yushutsu

185

Kumiai), 30, 74, 85, 129, 131, 133
Japan Machinery Federation (Nippon Kikai Kogyo Rengokai), 30, 73, 78, 85
Japan Machine Tool Builders Association (JMTBA), 29, 30, 57, 96, 154
  activities, 71–72, 142, 143
  establishment and organization, 30, 57, 73–75, 85
  export promotion, 129, 133–34
Japan Machine Tool Exporters Association, 154
Japan Machine Tool Export Promotion Association (Nippon Kikai Yushutsu Shingikai), 133–34
Japan Machine Tool Production Industry Association (Nippon Kosaku Kikai Seizo Kogyo Kumiai), 29
Japan Machine Tool Trade Association, 85
Japan–Manchuria Iron and Steel Sales, Inc. (Nichi-man Tekko Hanbai Kabushiki Kaisha), 21, 22
Japan Metal Forming Machine Builders Association (JMFMBA) (Nippon Tan'atsu Kikai Kogyokai), 30, 72–73, 85
Japan Motorcycle Rehabilitation Association, 143, 154
Japan Paper Manufacturing Federation, 11
Japan Pearl Exporters Association, 131
Japan Pipe and Tube Sales Co. (Nippon Kokan Hanbai Kabushiki Kaisha), 21
Japan Pottery Exporters Association, 131
Japan Productivity Center, 71
Japan Project Industry Council, 68
Japan Reinforcing Bar Industry Association, 65, 68
Japan Scrap Federation (Nippon Tetsugusa Renmei), 42
Japan Small Car Promotion Subsidy, 76–77
Japan Society for the Promotion of Science, 143
Japan Society for the Promotion of the Machinery Industry (JSPMI), 73–74, 85, 142–43
Japan Stainless Steel Association, 65
Japan Stainless Steel Exporters Association, 68
Japan Steel Federation, 144
Japan Steel-Rib Fabricators Association, 65
Japan Steel Scrap Reserves Association, 67–69
Japan Wire Products Exporters Association, 132
Jersey Standard Co., 81

Jigyosha Dantai Ho (Trade Association Law), 39, 40
Johnson, Chalmers, 18, 24, 25, 28, 29, 93, 175
Johnson, John, 155
Joint Iron and Steel Research Association (Tekko Gijutsu Kyodo Kenkyu Kai), 144
Joint research. See Research and development
Joint ventures, 127–28
Joko Bunya Kyoteikai (Bar Agreement Association), 17
Jones, Jesse, 82
Justice Department, U.S., 39
Juyo Sangyo Dantai Ho (Important Industries Association Ordinance), 22, 29
Juyo Sangyo Kyogikai (Council for Vital Industries), 13
Juyo Sangyo Tosei Ho (Important Industries Control Law), 18

Kaigai Tekko Joho Juyo Kiji Sakuin (Index to Important Foreign Articles on Iron and Steel), 142
Kansas, University of, 155
Kanto Steel Materials Sales Association (Kanto Kozai Hanbai Kumiai), 17–18
Kataoka Naoharu, 17
Kawasaki, 16
Kawasaki Heavy Industries, 26
Kawasaki Steel, 15, 60, 61
Keidanren (Keizai Dantai Rengokai) (Federation of Economic Organizations), 13, 32, 34 n.23, 40, 68, 78–79, 84, 113, 131, 172
Keidanren Building, 68
Keizai Doyukai (Japan Committee for Economic Development), 13–14, 23, 78, 80
Kennedy administration, 107
Keyworth, George A., 161, 164–65
Keyworth Initiative, 141, 161, 164–66, 178
Kigyo Joho Fairu (Enterprise Information File), 143
Kikai Gijutsu Kyokai (Machinery Technology Association), 75
Kikai Kogyo Kaigai Joho (Machinery Industry Overseas Report), 142–43
Kikai Shinko (Machinery Promotion), 143
Kikai Shinkokai (Machinery Promotion Association), 30
Kikai Shinko Kaikan (Machinery Promotion Building), 73
Kikai Shinko Kurabu (Machinery Promotion Club), 73

Kikai Yushutsu Konwakai (Machinery Exporters Association), 30
Kikawada Kazutaka, 14
Kobayashi, S., 96
Kobe Steel, 15, 60, 61, 72
Kokai hanbai seido (public sales system), 28
Kokkai Taisaku Iinkai (Diet Policy Committee), 97
Kokogyo Gijutsu Kenkyu Kumiai Ho (Mining and Manufacturing Technology Research Association Law), 75, 77
Komatsu Yugoro, 39
Korean War, 101
Kosaku Kikai Kanren Dantai Kyogikai (Machine Tool and Related Products Committee), 71, 73, 74
Kosaku Kikai Kyokai (Machine Tool Association), 30
Kosaku Kikai News, 142
Kosaku Kikai Seizo Jigyoho (Machine Tools Production Activity Law), 29
Kozai Club, 17, 27–28, 65–69, 84, 113, 129, 130, 172, 174
Kozai Konwakai (Iron and Steel Materials Conference), 27
Kumagai Yoshifumi, 95, 96
Kurosawa Hiroyasu, 69
Kyoka kaisha (authorized companies), 29

Law on Extraordinary Measures for the Promotion and Development of Specified Machinery and Information Industries, 92
Law Relating to the Prohibition of Private Monopoly and to Methods of Preserving Free Trade. *See* Antimonopoly Law
League of Iron and Steel Products Association, 67, 69
Legal concerns. *See* Antimonopoly Law; Antitrust policy
Lesher, Richard, 81
Liberal-Democratic Party (LDP), 96–99, 112, 175
Lobbyists
lobbying restrictions, 46
trade association employment of, 108
Love, Pete, 164
LTV Steel, 105

McBride, Lloyd, 110
Machinery and Information Industries Bureau, MITI, 142
Machinery Exporters Conference (Kikai Yushutsu Konwakai), 30
Machinery Industry Overseas Report

(Kikai Kogyo Kaigai Joho), 142–43
Machinery Information Bureau, MITI, 76, 92
Machinery Promotion *(Kikai Shinko)*, 143
Machinery Promotion Association (Kikai Shinkokai), 30
Machinery Promotion Building (Kikai Shinko Kaikan), 73
Machinery Promotion Club (Kikai Shinko Kurabu), 73
Machinery Technology Association (Kikai Gijutsu Kyokai), 75
Machine Tool and Related Products Committee (Kosaku Kikai Kanren Dantai Kyogikai), 71, 73, 74
Machine Tool Association (Kosaku Kikai Kyokai), 30
Machine tool industry, 166
AML exemptions, 43
export promotion, 124–25, 133–34
foreign participation and control, 178
government relations, 92, 95, 96, 101
information collection, 142–43
Japan, 4, 69–70, 129
Japanese trade associations, 14–15, 28–30, 70–75, 80, 85, 172
NAM formation, 7–8
policy positions, 56
political action committees, 105
research activities, 140, 146, 152, 154, 156, 158–60
trade protection, 121–22
U.S./Japanese comparisons, x
U.S. trade associations, 10, 70–75
Machine ToolPAC, 105
Machine Tool Production Activity Law (Kosaku Kikai Seizo Jigyoho), 29, 72
Machine Tool Unit Manufacturers Association of Japan, 75
McQuaid, Kim, 107
McRobie, George, 91
Makino Tsunezo, 74
Management and Budget, Office of (OMB), 165
Manchuria, 17, 18, 21, 22, 128
ManTech (manufacturing technology) program, 160
Manufacturing Shares Deliberation Committee, JMTBA, 72
Maple Flooring Manufacturers Association v. U.S., 47
"March Group," 82
Massachusetts Institute of Technology, 160
Matsuo Kinzo, 95
Medium Angles Steel Cooperative Sales

191

A NOTE ON THE BOOK

This book was edited by Janet Schilling
of the Publications Staff of the American Enterprise Institute.
The index was prepared by Patricia Ruggiero.
The text was set in Palatino, a typeface designed by Hermann Zapf.
Coghill Book Typesetting Company, of Richmond, Virginia,
set the type, and Edwards Brothers Incorporated,
of Ann Arbor, Michigan, printed and bound the book,
using permanent acid-free paper.